THE PLACING
OF T. S. ELIOT

Edited by
Jewel Spears Brooker

UNIVERSITY OF MISSOURI PRESS

Columbia and London

133118

5 4 3 2 1   95 94 93 92 91

Library of Congress Cataloging-in-Publication Data
The placing of T.S. Eliot / edited by Jewel Spears Brooker.
        p.   cm.
     Includes bibliographical references and index.
     ISBN 0-8262-0793-6 (alk. paper)
     1. Eliot, T. S. (Thomas Stearns), 1888–1965—Criticism and
interpretation.   I. Brooker, Jewel Spears, 1940–   .
PS3509.L43Z8145   1991
821'.912—dc20   91-12736
                                                           CIP

∞™ This paper meets the minimum requirements of
the American National Standard for Permanence of Paper
for Printed Library Materials, Z39.48, 1984.

Designer: Elizabeth Fett
Typesetter: Connell-Zeko Type & Graphics
Printer: Thomson-Shore, Inc.
Binder: Thomson-Shore, Inc.
Typeface: Trump Mediaeval

For Leslie Konnyu
Founder of the T. S. Eliot Society

Contents

Acknowledgments

All of the essays in this volume originated as invited lectures for the T. S. Eliot Society, and thus the first debt to be noted is to the Society and its members. The Society's annual keynote addresses—the Eliot Memorial Lectures—for the years 1984–1989 make up the first half of this collection. The other papers here were presented as Centennial Lectures at the Eliot Society's celebration in 1988 of the one-hundredth anniversary of the poet's birth in St. Louis.

For permission to quote from Eliot's work, I am indebted to Mrs. Valerie Eliot and to the poet's publishers at Faber and Faber and at Harcourt Brace Jovanovich. I am grateful to Michael Butler Yeats for permission to include quotations from his collection of unpublished letters written by his father, W. B. Yeats. Two of the essays in this collection have been published previously. The article by Jewel Spears Brooker appeared in *The Southern Review* in 1985 and also in *T. S. Eliot: Essays from The Southern Review*. The essay by Ronald Schuchard was included in *The "Southern Review" and Modern Literature, 1935–1985*. I am grateful to *The Southern Review*, Oxford University Press, and Louisiana State University Press for permission to reprint these two articles.

In preparing these essays for publication, I have benefited from the cooperation and advice of all the contributors. Grover Smith, my successor as president of the T. S. Eliot Society, supplied encouragement and useful impatience. My friend Peter Quartermain made a number of thoughtful and helpful suggestions, and Caroline Maun, my research assistant, brought intelligence and diligence that proved to be a major boost in bringing this project to a conclusion. Lloyd Chapin, the Dean of Eckerd College, supported my work with faculty development grants. H. Ralph Brooker provided substantial support for my scholarship and my activities in the T. S. Eliot Society. I am grateful to all these colleagues and friends.

Unless otherwise indicated, all quotations from Eliot's poetry and plays in this volume are from *The Complete Poems and Plays (1909–1950)* (New York: Harcourt Brace, 1952).

THE PLACING OF T. S. ELIOT

Introduction
Jewel Spears Brooker

Between the idea
And the reality
Between the motion
And the act
Falls the Shadow
        —The Hollow Men

In the beginning, according to Derrida's revision of the creation story, was hermeneutics. Not the Logos, not the Word, but interpretation. Derrida, of course, does not believe in "beginnings," most assuredly not in *the* beginning, and he admits (rather, he disarmingly insists) that he is in the situation of one who can only critique beginnings (and other essentialist concepts) by using (and thus privileging) the vocabulary of his adversaries. Derrida's creation myth invites (to his delight) correction, for hermeneutics entered not with creation but with the fall. Did God say, inquires the serpent, that you shall die on the day in which you eat of the tree? And then the cunning creature proceeds to interpretation. Assuming the position of a literalist, he predicts with assurance that Eve will not *surely* die *on the day* that she eats of the tree of knowledge; on the contrary, she who has known only good will know both good and evil and will become a god herself.

With this dialogue, this interpretation, we enter the postlapsarian world, and it is a defining characteristic of this world that its inhabitants are condemned to interpret everything and, at the same time, to reach no conclusion. The word "hermeneutics," as Heidegger pointed out, comes from *"hermeneuein,"* a Greek word deriving from the messenger god Hermes, and thus, again as Heidegger has argued, hermeneutics is about intersubjective but inconclusive dialogue. The interpreter is an exile from Eden, a post-Edenic figure condemned to wander forever between the idea and the reality, between the conception and the creation. The shadow

1

that makes life possible in this desert is hermeneutics, or interpretation.

In *Reading "The Waste Land"* (1990), Joseph Bentley and I examined modernism and a paradigmatic modernist poem in terms of the meaning and limits of interpretation. We described the manner in which major texts at once demand and defeat interpretation, the way in which they push and pull the reader through hermeneutical loops. Good readers know that their activity will end in a special kind of failure, that the end involves a return to the text from which the journey commenced. Every critic is in a special sense one link in a chain that began with the fateful conversation in Eden and will continue until the end of time—or to change the metaphor, one piece in a puzzle that will never be completed. Artists also inhabit the post-Edenic world of Hermes, and no artist has shown a greater awareness of the problematic nature of existence nor of its inextricable link to interpretation than has Eliot. As a poet and as a critic, he was from beginning to end preoccupied with the contingency of language, and like Conrad, Joyce, Pound, and many other modern artists, he was always aware of living in a gap, of existing between places, of playing Hermes between nobody and nobody, of trying to connect nothing with nothing.

Eliot's awareness of the interrelated problems of existence and interpretation began early. In January of 1910, "Spleen," one of his student poems, appeared in *The Harvard Advocate*. The persona of this ode to dejection is aware, on the one hand, of a "satisfied procession / Of definite Sunday faces; / Bonnets, silk hats, and conscious graces / In repetition"; on the other, from the corner of his eye, he sees "Life, a little bald and gray, / Languid, fastidious, and bland" waiting "hat and gloves in hand, / Punctilious of tie and suit . . . On the doorstep of the Absolute."[1] Caught between mindless conformity and a spiritless rendezvous with destiny, the ironic persona finds himself unable to rally against the "dull conspiracy" of having to choose between life and the polite senescence poised on the doorstep of the Absolute.

In this Laforguian exercise, the poet (through his persona) "places" himself, revealing that he resides in the country of in-between. In one way or another, Eliot spent most of his life either perching on a margin or straddling different worlds. This consciousness of being

---

1. *Poems Written in Early Youth* (New York: Farrar, Straus and Giroux, 1967), 26.

everywhere an alien, an essential part of his ironic imagination, has its roots in his family history. When he was growing up in St. Louis, as he himself has explained, he and members of his family were conscious of being displaced Bostonians, and during their summers in Massachusetts, they became displaced midwesterners. His residence in England, in one sense a solution to his homelessness, was in another sense an aggravation of it. In Europe, he was constantly reminded of his Americanness, and on his visits home, of his Englishness. He married an English woman, a straightforward attempt to situate himself and build a home. But this nesting experience exacerbated his loneliness and pulled him into his worst nightmares. The marriage, as is well known, was unfortunate for all concerned, and it confirmed in the poet that sense of alienation that permeates all of his early work. His letters, particularly those to his brother, contain a number of admissions that he was forever butting up against circumstances which humiliated him and made him aware that he was on many levels a displaced person.

Eliot's residence in the in-between land of unending interpretation was also spiritual, and the poems from "Spleen" through *The Hollow Men* explore in one way or another this phenomenon of living in the shadowland. "Between the idea / And the reality / Between the motion / And the act" . . . "Between the conception / And the creation / Between the emotion / And the response" he walked alone (*The Hollow Men*, V). The tension of being between places persisted, but in the middle of his life, with his conversion, it changed its nature. In the early poems, both of the glimpsed realities—the procession of smug Sunday faces and asthenic languid Life—are unattractive. For example, in "Rhapsody on a Windy Night," the persona makes his way home in the spaces of the dark through streets littered with the debris of bad dreams. One would expect that mounting the steps to his room would provide sanctuary from the horror of the street. But his realization that the effect of sleep is to prepare him to reenter the diurnal round is no relief; to sleep, to prepare for "life," becomes "the last twist of the knife" in a city of twisting streets, twisting grins, and twisted souls. In the middle and later period, the poet accepts participation in the material world (whether sordid or not) as the only means of knowing the ideal. "Only in time can the moment in the rose-garden . . . Be remembered . . . Only through time time is conquered" ("Burnt Norton," II). This acceptance of place, of the material as the means to the immaterial, is at the heart of the doctrine of the Incarnation, a doctrine central to the religious position he embraced as he sought his way out of the dark wood.

Eliot's emphasis in the middle of his life on actual moments and places, on moments in rose gardens and drafty churches, is somewhat parallel to his early critical emphasis on individual talent and the necessary relationship between the individual artist and the tradition, on the specific moment of the artist's work and the timeless ideal which both shapes and is shaped by it. Only through individuality individuality is conquered; only through personality is it possible to escape from personality. And for readers and critics, only through appreciation of individual artists can art be apprehended; only through particular poets can poetry be known. On the road to the universal (the timeless moment, the placeless place, the tradition, and so forth), one cannot bypass the particular. The precarious balance between tradition and the individual talent is in part a consequence of Eliot's combination of skepticism and desire. In spite of his longing for transcendence, his attraction toward the ideal, this self-conscious Hermes argued that such concepts as the "mind of Europe" were mere interpretations, necessary abstractions—not timeless fixed categories, but fluid always coming-to-be and never-to-be-complete entities born of and sustained by individual moments, individual actions, and individual minds.

In his early philosophical writings, which complement the critical essays, Eliot argues that interpretation is endless, that the absolute sought by interpreters can be said to exist only at the moment when it is complete and at that moment it and everything else cease to exist. To put this in terms of literature, the "tradition" as a fixed term is conceivable only when the last word has been penned and the last reader has put down the last book, only when it and everything no longer exist. And so it is with our understanding of Eliot the man and the poet. We can only apprehend him in time, in his time and in the moment of our reading, and we can only imagine him in space, the space of his being and his writing and the space of our contemplation. As he says in the final section of "Burnt Norton," "The detail of the pattern is movement."

The present volume consists of a group of interpretations, of hints and guesses that originated as lectures for the T. S. Eliot Society. The Society has its headquarters in St. Louis, the poet's birthplace, and most of the essays reveal a special awareness of the importance of place. Those attending the annual meeting confront a compound ghost, a shadow that includes not only the young Tom

Eliot, but also his powerful mother Charlotte and his formidable grandfather William Greenleaf Eliot, the educator and clergyman Emerson dubbed the saint of the West. Those gathering for the annual Eliot Society meeting usually go for a walk beside or a ride on the Mississippi River, the rhythm of which was felt in Eliot's nursery bedroom, and which in flood time impressed him with "its cargo of dead Negroes, cows and chicken coops" ("The Dry Salvages," II). The house in which the poet was born no longer exists, but the winding streets of the slums in downtown St. Louis still bear witness to the scenes of his childhood, scenes which are recognizable as part of the urban mosaic forming the locale of the poems in *Prufrock and Other Observations.*

Many of the writers included in this volume first visited St. Louis to present their lectures to the members of the Society, and all show sensitivity to the fact that they are standing in a place sanctified by having served as the cradle of a great poet. A. D. Moody, James Olney, and Leonard Unger make Eliot's geographical roots a central part of their presentations. Moody's meditation on place in Eliot leads him to consider the poet as an American whose tradition includes such figures as Whitman and Emerson. Olney's reflections also begin with the importance of place, but develop in a different direction. Primarily interested in the geography of the imagination, which is etched by consciousness on an outline provided by actual places, Olney could have taken "Home is where one starts from" as his epigraph ("East Coker," V). Unger's focus on actual places in Eliot's poetry also shows a sensitivity to the fact that the actual is always mediated through memory and experience. All deal with Eliot's eastward move from the slums of the turn-of-the-century river town in the heart of the American midwest to the more metropolitan river town of Boston, and then to those other river-based urban capitals Paris and London. Each departure, as the poet reveals in *Four Quartets*, was in another sense a return. The return to England was followed by a return to New England and to St. Louis, with a last return taking him to St. Michael's Church in East Coker. "In my beginning is my end . . . In my end is my beginning" ("East Coker," I and V) The man who returned, of course, was not the man who departed, and the man who arrived discovered in his homing that with each return he came to "know the place for the first time" ("Little Gidding," V). Olney shows that Eliot's conversion and his return to America in the early thirties liberated early childhood memories and made them available for poetry, and Moody shows that Eliot's feeling for Dante, admired in different periods of Eliot's life for different reasons, played a role both in the poet's attraction to Europe and also in his return to America.

The fifth section of each of the *Four Quartets* deals in specific terms with interpretation. In that part of "Burnt Norton," Eliot describes his own attempt to place words, words that

> Crack and sometimes break, under the burden,
> Under the tension, slip, slide, perish,
> Decay with imprecision, will not stay in place,
> Will not stay still.

Several of the essays in this volume focus on language. Moody, again, relates Eliot's use of words to that of other American poets, such as William Carlos Williams. George T. Wright and Linda Wyman focus on language—Wright on the many voices in *Four Quartets* and Wyman on language as plot in *The Family Reunion*. In placing words, of course, Eliot places himself, and in a profound way, he places us, his readers.

The modern artist and, as we now acknowledge, the modern critic live in what Heidegger calls the great "Between," the period after Newton's God has departed but before any successor has appeared. The relation of spiritual homelessness to modernism is a facet of the essays by Cleanth Brooks, Armin Paul Frank, and Cleo McNelly Kearns. Brooks is concerned mainly with the problems any serious poet would have in a society increasingly secularized and without moral reference points. Brooks, whose first article on Eliot was published in the mid-thirties and who knew the poet personally, draws on a half century of experience and reflection as he discusses art and culture. Frank's essay, rooted in his studies of translations of poetic texts, discusses the problematic nature of Eliot's cultural identity and also the parallels between the poet's intellectual and spiritual experiences and those of his French and German translators. He shows how attention to translations can open cracks of insight into the poetry and into the common culture shared by the poet and his first translators. Kearns also deals with the complexities of placing Eliot culturally, bringing to bear the poet's early study of Sanskrit and of Indic and Buddhist texts and suggesting the way in which these studies complicated his response to the crisis of Western culture in the late teens and early twenties. Kearns illuminates Eliot's spiritual quest as he moved toward his own point of no return. Several of the essays in this volume clarify Eliot's religious longings, particularly as they relate to, and are reflected in, his poetry. Russell Kirk, in the fifties and sixties a friend of the poet, writes eloquently about Eliot's Christian imagination and about the secular environment in which the poet developed his moral vision. My own essay traces Eliot's migration from one "ism" to another as he searched for moral and aesthetic reference points and relates his frequent discussion of substitutes for religion to his aesthetic and spiritual odyssey.

A number of essays in this volume are historical in nature. Grover Smith offers a detailed account of Eliot's fascination with *Hamlet*, both the character and the play. In so doing, he raises questions about Eliot's own acedia and his incorporation of Hamlet types into his poetry who exhibit inertia. Smith discusses the history of reading Shakespeare and reveals the Hamlets who were available to the poet in the second decade of the century. He thus places Hamlet, and places Eliot in relation to other interpreters, such as Goethe and Coleridge. Michael Butler Yeats also focuses on a historical relationship, that of his father, William Butler Yeats, to Eliot. Drawing on his own collection of Yeats material and on the first volume of Eliot letters, Michael Yeats describes from his own special vantage point the relation between the two greatest poets of the early twentieth century. Eliot had serious reservations about Yeats's religious commitments, specifically his fascination with the occult, but at the same time, he admired Yeats's poetry and considered him a master of the English language. Yeats did not have the same appreciation for Eliot's work, and when he came to edit *The Oxford Book of Modern Verse* in 1936, with all of Eliot's work through "Burnt Norton" before him, he maintained that only in two quatrains from "Sweeney Among the Nightingales" did Eliot in his early work speak in the "great manner."

Ronald Schuchard's complex interpretation of the Sweeney myth in Eliot is also based on historical scholarship and concentrates on the lines from Eliot's poetry that connect his personal disappointments, particularly in his marriage, to the savage comedy emerging in such poems as "Sweeney Erect." Carol Smith and Linda Wyman also deal with Eliot's comedies. Wyman is primarily interested in language, as has been mentioned, and Smith makes the case for the plays as theater and for their centrality in the Eliot oeuvre. Her focus is on *The Elder Statesman*, a play performed at the Eliot centennial celebration in St. Louis in 1988. Smith's lecture, like most of the lectures in this volume, was given on the occasion of the centennial and quite appropriately addressed the question of Eliot's place in the history of literature and drama.

In a fundamental sense, we cannot place Eliot; he places himself, and in so doing, he places us. Placing is interpretation, and all interpretation, as Eliot realized and often said, is for one moment and one place. This does not mean, however, that placing Eliot (or placing any artist) is futile. We begin with the poet's self-placing through his work; in poem after poem, he placed himself on the margin between despair and hope, that shore on which *The Waste Land* ends. Though a major poet and considered by some to be a prophet, he distrusted language and insisted that we have no firm foothold in the slippery world of Hermes. But for us, there is only the trying. Interpretation is endless, a collaborative, creative, and ongoing process. It is part of the larger enterprise of working with an enduring and masterful poet.

I. Eliot Memorial Lectures

Substitutes for Religion in the
Early Poetry of T. S. Eliot
Jewel Spears Brooker

Thou shalt worship no other god, for the Lord,
whose name is Jealous, is a jealous God.
—Exodus 34:14

In late June of 1927, in a small church in Oxfordshire, T. S. Eliot was baptized into the Anglican Church. He had a hard time coming to this death, this birth, and awoke to find himself uneasy in the old dispensation with an alien people clutching their gods. Knowing he had lately clutched the same gods, he was highly conscious of the need to call them up, Baal and his fellows, and formally dismiss them. He was compelled to this housecleaning by the very first commandment of his new God: "Thou shalt have no other gods before me. . . . for I, the Lord thy God, am a jealous God" (Exodus 20:3-5). The seriousness of his commitment to Christianity can be gauged from the fact that, in the year of his conversion and for about five years thereafter, he repeatedly discussed in print the problem of religion and its substitutes. One by one, like an inventory examiner, he inspected Bergsonianism, humanism, aestheticism, and other early twentieth-century "isms," and in the light of Christianity, rejected them as inadequate.

Eliot's interest in religion (literally, a retying or rebinding, an attempt to reconnect fragments into a whole) did not appear suddenly in his thirty-ninth year. His awareness of fragmentation, his dissatisfaction with brokenness, had been evident in his earliest work. The Harvard masterpieces—"Portrait," "Preludes," "Prufrock," "Rhapsody"—all exhibit a consciousness of broken connections. People are cut off from friends, from lovers, from any community, from God. The great human problem behind *The Waste Land* is "I can connect / Nothing with nothing" (ll. 301-2). This inability to connect, in fact, is precisely what guarantees the bar-

11

renness of the wasteland. Without connection, there can be no birth; without reconnection, no rebirth.

Eliot's early references to religion, found principally in book reviews, indicate that he thought of religion not in terms of a god, or even a primary allegiance, but in terms of a scheme, a system of ideas, whose object is first, to enable one to make sense out of experience, and second, to enable one to live and to act. In an early review, Eliot argued that "both religion and science [are] pragmatic" and must be evaluated on the extent to which they do or do not work.[1] This pragmatic bias is important. In seriously entertaining the Buddhist option, for example, Eliot was attracted not by a god, but by a scheme. In becoming a Christian, he accepted primarily a scheme, a scheme that includes a god, but first of all, a scheme. In a 1931 discussion of Pascal's religious experience, Eliot underscored his belief in the pragmatic nature of commitment by pointing to the process through which a rational person progresses toward Christianity: "[One] finds the world to be so and so; he finds its character inexplicable by any non-religious theory; among religions he finds Christianity . . . to account most satisfactorily for the world and especially for the moral world within; and thus he finds himself inexorably committed."[2]

A year later, Eliot explained his own conversion in similar terms: "the Christian scheme seemed to me the only one which would work . . . the only possible scheme which found a place for values which I must maintain or perish."[3] Religion is seen, again, as a scheme, a system of ideas, an abstraction, which allows one to make sense of the universe and to maintain values.

The need for religion, then, is universal and timeless. The need for religious substitutes, however, is related to special circumstances, usually to paradigmatic epistemological shifts which disorient people about matters ordinarily taken for granted. The early twentieth century was a period of such disorientation. José Ortega y Gasset discusses this period as a time in which the epistemological skeleton of the culture collapsed, a time with no broadly shared or shareable religion, no common philosophy, no framework

1. Review of *Group Theories of Religion and the Religion of the Individual*, by Clement C. J. Webb, *International Journal of Ethics* 27 (October 1916): 117.
2. Introduction to *Pascal's Pensées*, trans. W. F. Trotter (New York: E. P. Dutton, 1931), xii.
3. "Christianity and Communism," *Listener* 7 (16 March 1932): 382–83.

for thought.[4] "When there is distress of nations and perplexity," Eliot says in part V of the "The Dry Salvages," people without religion usually fashion substitutes.

> To communicate with Mars, converse with spirits,
> To report the behaviour of the sea monster,
> Describe the horoscope, haruspicate or scry,
> Observe disease in signatures, evoke
> Biography from the wrinkles of the palm
> And tragedy from fingers; release omens
> By sortilege, or tea leaves, riddle the inevitable
> With playing cards, fiddle with pentagrams
> Or barbituric acids, or dissect
> The recurrent image into pre-conscious terrors—
> To explore the womb, or tomb, or dreams.

W. H. Auden once described the problem of religion and its substitutes as *the* modern problem:

> Yeats, like us, was faced with the modern problem, *i.e.*, of living in a society in which men are no longer supported by tradition without being aware of it, and in which, therefore, every individual who wishes to bring order and coherence into the stream of sensations, emotions, and ideas entering his consciousness . . . is forced to do deliberately for himself what in previous ages had been done for him by family, custom, church, and state, namely [to choose] the principles and presuppositions in terms of which he can make sense of his experience.[5]

For millions of people, the mythic vacuum was filled by political theories, especially when a prophet or savior figure like Mussolini, Stalin, or Hitler did the preaching. In one of several discussions of this phenomenon, Eliot says that "many political beliefs are substitutes for religious beliefs."[6] In most discussions of such matters, however, he focuses on the relation of the decay of religion to modernist imperatives in art: "The ideal condition" is that under which a *"framework* is provided . . . as the condition of [one's] time." The modern artist's position "may seriously [be] call[ed] Promethean. He has to supply his own framework, his own myth."[7] In 1932, Eliot wrote that I. A. Richards's admiration of *The Waste*

---

4. *Man and Crisis*, trans. Mildred Adams (New York: Norton, 1958), 85–89.
5. "Yeats as an Example," *Kenyon Review* 10 (1948): 191–92.
6. "The Literature of Fascism," *Criterion* 8 (December 1928): 282.
7. "The Poetic Drama," review of *Cinnamon and Angelica: A Play*, by John Middleton Murry, *Athenaeum* 4698 (14 May 1920): 635.

Land seems to be based on an acknowledgment that "the present situation is radically different from any in which poetry has been produced in the past: namely, that now there is nothing in which to believe, that Belief itself is dead; and that therefore my poem is the first to respond properly to the modern situation and not call upon Make-Believe."[8] "Make-Believe" is surely a pun, indicating the obvious option when no Belief is given. The master of "Make-Believe," of course, was Yeats, who boldly formulated his own personal religion, and then presented it to his readers in a handbook.

For many years, Eliot thought he was above "Make-Believe," that he was simply doing without. "My own view," he insists in one of his 1932 Harvard lectures, is that "nothing in this world or the next is a substitute for anything else; and if you find that you must do without something, such as religious faith or philosophic belief, then you must just do without it."[9] Eliot had come to this straightforward, no-nonsense, no substitutes view as part of accepting traditional Anglo-Catholic Christianity. But actually, in the twenty years before his conversion, the years during which he had struggled to do without religion, he had been moving from one substitute to another. And although his substitutes are more respectable than Yeats's, they are "Make-Believe" just the same.

Eliot's substitutes for religion can be roughly classified as erotic, religious, aesthetic, and philosophical. In a 1918 review, Eliot noted the important "role which the sexual instinct plays in the religion and mythology of primitive peoples [and] (indeed in all religion)."[10] He early associated his own experience of fragmentation and his longing for the Absolute, both of which are by definition religious, with sexual transcendence. From "The Love Song of J. Alfred Prufrock" through "Sweeney Erect," sexuality, whether desired or dreaded, hovers, full of possibility. An interrelated failure of sex and religion, moreover, is of the essence in *The Waste Land*.

Some critics have claimed that the quality of Eliot's concern with sex makes him especially representative of his generation. I. A. Richards, for example, suggests that Eliot's fascination with

8. "The Modern Mind," in *The Use of Poetry and the Use of Criticism: Studies in the Relation of Criticism to Poetry in England* (London: Faber, 1933), 130.

9. "Matthew Arnold," in *The Use of Poetry,* 113.

10. Review of *Elements of Folk Psychology: Outlines of a Psychological History of the Development of Mankind,* by Wilhelm Wundt, *Monist* 28 (1918): 160.

Canto XXVI of the *Purgatorio* illustrates his "persistent concern with sex, the problem of our generation, as religion was the problem of the last."[11] This striking insight provoked Eliot to retort that "in his contrast of sex and religion [Richards] makes a distinction which is too subtle for me to grasp. One might think that sex and religion were 'problems' like Free Trade and Imperial Preference."[12] The clever evasiveness of Eliot's response suggests that Richards had struck home.

Sexual love has been associated since antiquity with religious rituals, and it includes by definition at least temporary transcendence of physical separateness; it promises, moreover, more complex unities. Sex is one way of overcoming brokenness, of retying or rebinding fragments into a whole. Eliot is not unique in seeing sex as a substitute for religion. At times, even Matthew Arnold presents sexual love as the only option left in a world no longer supported by the bright girdle of Christianity, a world he describes in "Dover Beach" as a darkling plain on which lovers are surrounded by ignorant armies clashing by night.

Eliot's sexual needs as a young man and his sensitivity to the symbolism of love as a binder or a rebinder explain in part his quick and disastrous marriage. This marriage precipitated a reevaluation of eros, and indeed, of all human satisfactions. In a 1919 review, Eliot praised the great French and Russian novelists for having understood "the awful separation between potential passion and any actualization possible in life" and also for "indicat[ing] . . . the indestructible barriers between one human being and another."[13] Such awful knowledge, coming just a few years after his marriage, may represent the death of hope, but unfortunately, not the death of desire. About a decade later, with his wife incurably ill, his marriage irreparably broken, Eliot confided to close friends in the church that he was struggling with the problem of celibacy.[14] In prospect, then, eros is kind, promising to heal the brokenness of the human heart; in retrospect, though, eros is cruel, promising what no human lover can do. Eliot's marital bond came to reinforce rather than

11. *Principles of Literary Criticism* (New York: Harcourt Brace, 1925), 292.
12. "The Modern Mind," in *The Use of Poetry*, 127.
13. "Beyle and Balzac," review of *A History of the French Novel to the Close of the Nineteenth Century*, vol. 2, by George Saintsbury, *Athenaeum* 4648 (30 May 1919): 393.
14. Letter to William Force Stead, 2 December 1930, Osborn Collection, Beinecke Library, Yale University.

alleviate his isolation, to reinforce rather than alleviate his need for transcendence.

Eros, then, offers a scheme which does not work. But is an institutional religion any better? In an essay written the year after his baptism, Eliot quipped, "Our literature is a substitute for religion, and so is our religion."[15] The religion he had come to consider as a substitute for religion was Unitarianism. As a child, Eliot was baptized into the Unitarian Church, and as he grew, he remained aware of the faith of his fathers. And yet, after his conversion when William Force Stead remarked in a magazine that Eliot had returned to the church, the poet wrote in the margin "Return? I was never there!"[16] His response is inseparable from his conviction that Unitarianism leads to skepticism rather than faith. Years before his conversion, in a discussion of the mind of his cousin Henry Adams, Eliot had associated Unitarianism with a quality he called the "Boston Doubt": a "skepticism which is difficult to explain to those who are not born to it. This skepticism is a product, or a cause, or a concomitant, of Unitarianism; it is not destructive, but it is dissolvent. . . . [Adams] could believe in nothing."[17] Eliot, like Adams, was born to the Boston Doubt, but he concluded early on that liberal Protestant theology could not provide a scheme for organizing life and a framework for writing poetry.

The inadequacy of liberal Protestant theology led Eliot away from the institutional church. As artists have done before in times of religious crisis, he and others of his generation turned to art itself as a means of structuring their lives and their work. In the five years after his conversion, Eliot wrote repeatedly about art as a substitute for religion. His aestheticism may be divided into two stages. From 1909 to 1911, he was influenced primarily by Matthew Arnold, Walter Pater, and the French symbolists, especially Mallarmé. In this stage, he used Christian ritual as a framework to support his poetry, somewhat in the way that Mallarmé used it. After the great poems of 1909–1911, he more or less dropped poetry for five or six years and applied himself seriously to the study of philosophy. From 1917 though 1922 he returned to aestheticism, but having

15. "A Dialogue on Dramatic Poetry," in *Selected Essays* (New York: Harcourt Brace, 1950), 32.

16. "Mr. Stead Presents an Old Friend," *Alumnae Magazine of Trinity College* 38 (Winter 1965): 66.

17. "A Sceptical Patrician," review of *The Education of Henry Adams: An Autobiography, Athenaeum* 4647 (23 May 1919): 361.

assimilated much modern science and philosophy, he had transformed the earlier variety. In this stage, he used the mythical method to force art to generate its own framework.

Eliot focuses, in his post-conversion diagnosis of art as a failed
religion, on a central figure in his own heritage, Matthew Arnold.
In "Cousin Nancy," Eliot's early satire on Boston and family, Arnold
the Humanist joins Emerson the Unitarian on respectable book-
shelves, and these guardians of the faith keep watch over Boston.
Arnold had argued, in the nineteenth-century reassessment of Christianity, that religion was at once unbelievable and indispensable. In
order to maintain religion without belief, he set up culture, or literature, in its place. Eliot claims that Arnold was too intelligent and
too temperate "to maintain . . . that religious instruction is best
conveyed by poetry, . . . but he discovered a new formula: poetry is
not religion, but it is a capital substitute for religion—not invalid
port, . . . but coffee without caffeine."[18] In the world of art, Arnold's "Culture" led directly to Pater's aestheticism. "The gospel of
Pater follow[ed] naturally upon the prophecy of Arnold." As quoted
by Eliot, Pater's doctrine is "the love of art for art's sake . . . ; for art
comes to you professing frankly to give nothing but the highest
quality to your moments as they pass, and simply for those moments' sake." This creed, Eliot claims, was a "hopeless admission
of irresponsibility."[19] But to the Eliot of 1908, art for art's sake was
not an admission of irresponsibility, but a means of self-realization
as an artist. Pater's creed, preached by Arthur Symons, gave Eliot
the recipe he needed to make an entirely new liquor from Emerson's watered port and Arnold's decaffeinated coffee. For Symons
led Eliot to the symbolists, particularly to the high priest of aestheticism, Mallarmé. The symbolist merger of art and religion
proved invaluable in writing the great poems of 1909–1911.

Mallarmé's aesthetic consists of a reformulation in which the
forms and rituals of Catholicism are emptied of Christian content
and then appropriated for a new religion of art. Underlying his
work is an analogy between art and Catholicism in which the creative act by an artist is analogous to the Passion of Christ and the
re-creative act by a reader is analogous to the Christian Mass.[20]

18. Introduction to *The Use of Poetry*, 26.
19. "Arnold and Pater," in *Selected Essays*, 390.
20. For a fuller discussion of Mallarmé's religious aesthetic, see my "Dispensations of Art: Mallarmé and the Fallen Reader," *Southern Review* 19 (January 1983): 17–38.

Following Mallarmé, Eliot used Christian ritual as an underlying structural metaphor in "The Love Song of J. Alfred Prufrock" and other early poems. But in his post- conversion reevaluation of aestheticism, he argues that one has no business to use Christian ritual unless one is a Christian. In 1928, just after his conversion, Eliot published a fictional debate on the relation between religion and art. Two of the characters in this discussion, dubbed E and B, closely resemble Eliot himself in two stages of his religious and aesthetic development. E sounds like Tom Eliot, twenty-two years old, an American graduate student spending a year in Paris, a Bergsonian, in the process of writing "The Love Song of J. Alfred Prufrock" and a few other poems. B sounds like T. S. Eliot, thirty-nine years old, in the second decade of his marriage, a British businessman, a literary critic, author of "Gerontion" and *The Waste Land*, a new convert to the Anglican Church.

Eliot number one, E in the debate, argues: "the consummation of the drama, the perfect and ideal drama, is to be found in the ceremony of the Mass. . . . drama springs from religious liturgy, and . . . cannot afford to depart far from religious liturgy. . . . the only dramatic satisfaction that I find now is in a High Mass well performed."[21]

This is a perfect setup for Eliot number two, B in the fictional debate, to comment on aestheticism in his own work. He does this by saying he once knew someone who held such a view, attributing to this friend of long ago his own earlier opinions. Are we to

> say that our cravings for drama are fulfilled by the Mass? . . . No. For I once knew a man who held the same views that you appear to hold, E. He went to High Mass every Sunday, and was particular to find a church where he considered the Mass efficiently performed. . . . The Mass gave him extreme . . . satisfaction. It was almost orgiastic. But when I came to consider his conduct, I realised he was guilty of a *confusion des genres*. His attention was not on the meaning of the Mass, for he was not a believer but a Bergsonian; it was on the Art of the Mass. His dramatic desires were satisfied by the Mass, precisely because he was not interested in the Mass, but in the drama of it. Now what I maintain is, that you have no business to care about the Mass unless you are a believer. . . . Literature can be no substitute for religion, not merely because we need religion, but because we need literature as well. . . . religion is no more a substitute for drama than drama is a substitute for religion. . . . For there is a difference in attention. If we are religious,

21. "A Dialogue on Dramatic Poetry," in *Selected Essays*, 35.

then we will only be aware of the Mass as art, in so far as it is badly done and interferes with our devotion.[22]

Like B, the Eliot of 1927 rejected aestheticism and insisted on a "no substitutes" view. Like E, and also like B's old friend, the Eliot of 1910 was a Bergsonian, living in Paris, using the ritualistic aesthetics of Mallarmé in his poetry. The extent to which Eliot, in his 1928 dialogue, is cleaning his own house, can easily be seen by focusing on "The Love Song of J. Alfred Prufrock." On one level, "Prufrock" is an unanswerable judgment on Arnold's religion of Culture. The poem describes a Mass in Arnold's post-Christian sanctuary, the drawing room of the intelligentsia in Cambridge, Massachusetts, in the shadow of Harvard Square. Mr. Prufrock, in whose mind the drawing room exists, tries to talk himself into going to a communion service in which he and some ladies will share toast and tea and Culture with a capital *C*. A central problem in Prufrock's vision is that Culture can only be shared by using language. He will be forced to use words with these Arnoldian priestesses, and he knows that in a world where belief is impossible, a world without common ground, language will fail as a connector or binder. By mixing gustatory and rhetorical images, Eliot manipulates a parallel between eating together and talking together. In this communion service, the Word is replaced by words; in this social sanctuary, questions, after macaroons, are lifted and dropped onto plates; and here, in this modern eucharist, the table scraps include not only crumbs, but also words.

In Eliot's communion service, as in Mallarmé's, words are substituted for bread and wine; in Eliot's, as in Mallarmé's, a poet or singer stands in for the priest. But though Eliot may have begun with Mallarmé's service, he ends by transforming it. Mallarmé had predicted that artists would liberate ritual from the bloody and barbarous meal celebrated in the church by replacing it with a far more civilized celebration of the death and rebirth of nature.[23] But cleaning up the communion ritual was one thing for Mallarmé and quite another for Eliot. "Prufrock" is in part a poem about the disease of solipsism. This is a poem in which the landscape has been emptied of all objects beyond the self, a world where every object is an extension of some thinking subject, where everything finally is an extension of the speaker or thinker. A true brother of Henry Adams,

22. Ibid., 35–36.
23. See my "The Dispensations of Art," 25–26.

Prufrock can believe in nothing. And believing in nothing, radical skepticism, leads inevitably to solipsism. Mallarmé had predicted that removing Christ from the altar, the body and blood from the table, would purge Christian ritual and enable it to survive as a framework for a higher religion based on art. But in a solipsistic world, an attempt to dispose of Christian dogma while retaining Christian ritual ends by placing the self, the only sure reality, at the center of the ritual. In the modern Mass described in "The Love Song of J. Alfred Prufrock," the god to be divided, to be eaten, to be drunk among whispers, the material substance on the platter, is none other than Prufrock himself. This is the horror at the core of the poem, and it can be seen by looking at any one of several passages. For example:

> Should I, after tea and cakes and ices,
> Have the strength to force the moment to its crisis?
> But though I have wept and fasted, wept and prayed,
> Though I have seen my head (grown slightly bald)
>   brought in upon a platter,
> I am no prophet—and here's no great matter.

Prufrock sees himself here as Christ in Gethsemane ("though I have wept and fasted, wept and prayed") preparing for the sacrifice of his own body, and as John the Baptist, a prophet slain, decapitated, and served on a platter. No wonder Prufrock approaches the drawing room with terror. No wonder he shudders in imagining his own head, grown slightly bald, served up on a platter by these priestesses of Arnold. No wonder he moans in reflecting that his life—the life is in the blood—has been measured out in coffee spoons.

But the greatest shudder comes not from seeing what is upon the platter, but from biting it. In language suggesting both the asking of questions and eating, Prufrock asks himself:

> Would it have been worth while,
> To have bitten off the matter with a smile,
> To have squeezed the universe into a ball
> To roll it toward some overwhelming question . . .

"Matter" here is a troublesome topic, an overwhelming question, and biting it off is bringing it up. But matter is also any physical substance which occupies space and can be served on a platter, something like toast or a communion wafer or the head of John the Baptist—or the head of Prufrock. And matter is "mater" or mother, the great Ur-Womb, the original that both generated and is the universe. When one remembers that the central problem of the poem is that the persona's subjectivity has swallowed up the universe, these and other meanings come together to confirm that Prufrock himself is the universe that must be squeezed and shaped into a ball and dropped onto the plate. He himself is the "mater" and the matter—the universe, the problem, the question, the physical substance to be distributed among the ladies in the drawing room. In this service devoted to culture, watched over by Emerson and Arnold, Prufrock plays all parts. He is the bread, he is the priest, and he is the communicant who must partake of himself, must swallow these vitiated elements. Confused and nauseated, he wonders, "how should I begin / To spit out all the butt-ends of my days and ways?" The repeated association of matter with both the universe and Prufrock's head (his physical head, his mind, and perhaps his genitals) emphasizes the fact that, through his subjectivity, he has become the universe. This brings us back to one meaning of the famous conceit that opens the poem. Prufrock, not the evening, is etherized upon a table. Like everything else in the poem, the tired, sleepy evening is an aspect of Prufrock's mind. The table upon which he projects his etherized head turns out on careful reading to be not only a surgery table, but also a tea table. And the tea table with crumbs of mind beneath is Arnold's communion table.

Eliot's experiments with religious ritual in "Prufrock" and the other poems of 1909–1911 led him to reflect on the drastic situation in which a poet is forced to separate belief in a scheme from use of that scheme. In using Christian ritual without taking seriously the beliefs which had generated it, he came face to face with a special horror, the horror of lifting the veil and finding nothing behind it, or perhaps of finding only a mirror behind it. In going beyond the surface, Laforgue and Mallarmé had discovered the Absolute, but Eliot found an emptiness that sent him scampering back to the surface. As poems, these early works are extremely successful in that they lead to frontiers of consciousness where words fail but meanings persist. As raids on the Absolute, they are failures. Like Mallarmé and the Romantics, Eliot organizes the campaign and makes the trip, but unlike them, he finds the Absolute to be either an image of himself or an absence.

The early experiments with aestheticism sent Eliot back to philosophy in search of some scheme that would enable him to bind up his fragments and unify his life and art. For the next few years, he applied himself diligently to studies preparatory to a career in philosophy. Between 1911 and 1915, at Harvard and at Oxford, he completed all of the course work for a Ph.D., and in 1916, he completed a dissertation on the epistemology of F. H. Bradley.

Eliot found in Bradley a doctrine which, at least on the intellectual level, explains away the fragmentation and chaos that seem to characterize contemporary culture. The relevant Bradleyan principle, common to all absolute idealists and endorsed in Eliot's thesis, is that reality consists of parts that are all interconnected in a single system. Everything that exists, simply by virtue of existing, is included in the Absolute, which is an over-arching, all-inclusive whole. From the fact that the Absolute is all-inclusive, it follows that every perception, every object, everything in the universe, is a part rather than a whole. Any fragment, no matter how isolated it may appear, is connected to other fragments; every fragment is self-transcendent, that is, it reaches beyond itself and participates in successively greater fragments until it reaches the all-inclusive whole. More simply, every fragment has a context, which also has a context, which in turn has a context, which eventually is the Absolute. Because these fragments are all part of one single thing, they are necessarily and systematically related. No fragment has its meaning alone; it exists as part of a unitary and timeless system.[24] This Bradleyan doctrine, with its primary emphasis on rebinding fragments into a whole, is radically religious. Most of Eliot's criticism, including the famous notion of tradition, is rooted in it, and many of his poems, conspicuously "Gerontion," take it as a structural principle.[25]

In the opinion of many critics, "Gerontion" is Eliot's most difficult poem. The difficulty derives not so much from content as from form, or as some would have it, from absence of form. What appears at first to be a Prufrockian interior monologue turns out to be totally lacking in psychological coherence. In "Prufrock," all fragments exist and find their unity in one man's mind, and the fragments are arranged to reflect the flow of his consciousness. In "Gerontion," the fragments exist and find their unity in Bradley's

24. See F. H. Bradley, *Appearance and Reality* (1893; reprint, Oxford: Clarendon Press, 1897), 519–20.

25. For a more detailed version of the following explication of "Gerontion," see my "The Structure of Eliot's 'Gerontion': An Interpretation Based on Bradley's Doctrine of the Systematic Nature of Truth." *ELH* 46 (Summer 1979): 314–40.

Absolute, and are arranged to reflect the systematic relation of all fragments in an overarching system. Eliot arranges the poem into an almost endless number of superimposed contexts by using the image of a house. The idea that every fragment is part of a context, which itself is part of a larger context, is shown by placing houses within houses within houses. The objects contained within the houses become less inclusive houses, which in turn contain other houses; at the same time, all of the houses are included in more inclusive houses.

The house in which Gerontion lives, clearly on the edge of doom, is old, decayed, brittle, windowless, draughty; it is located in a neglected yard composed of rocks, moss, excreta. The tenants—Gerontion and a woman—are old and sick, and they are transients in a rented house. The owner, a Jew squatting on the window sill, clearly represents another important house in this poem. All of these brittle old houses are in trouble, for the dry season has come, and wind is battering the walls. From Gerontion's house, there is a proliferation of houses in many directions, and all of them are replicas of the first one. All of the houses are, from a larger point of view, tenants; all of the tenants, from a smaller point of view, are houses. In the first stanza alone, there is a series of houses (tenants): Gerontion's thoughts, his brain, his body, his house, the yard, the field, and Europe. All of these tenants are dying transients in rented houses. To these doomed houses are added in subsequent stanzas the houses of history and of hell; the houses of Israel and of the Christian Church; and many more, all precisely modeled on the first one. The cause of ruin in all is related to a decay of faith and an expansion of knowledge. The coda of the poem returns the reader to the house which, though small, includes all of the others; that is, it returns to the arid brain of the withered intellectual whose memories and thoughts, visions and revisions, furnished Eliot with a perfect metaphor for his vision of a godless and dying civilization.

On a purely intellectual level, Bradley's idealism is a scheme that works, a scheme that in fundamental ways is consistent with the religious scheme Eliot accepted in 1927. The religious impulse, as I have said, is the impulse to rebind, to transcend fragments, to reunify. To be religious is first to be aware of fragmentation, of brokenness; second, since rebinding suggests previous unity, to be religious is to be aware on some level that we live in a postlapsarian world, that the condition of brokenness and loneliness is not part of our first world. To be religious, finally, is to be discontented with brokenness and to imagine that it can be transcended. The *re* in religion is crucial, for in postulating previous unity, it promises future unity, or at least, establishes the possibility of transcendence. Bradley, in his doctrine of the Absolute, assumes previous unity, acknowledges a falling away into fragments, and posits an intellectual scheme for transcendence. Still, in 1927, when Eliot came to reevaluate his old mentor, he found his philosophy less than adequate. In "Gerontion," all fragments are unified by reference to a larger context. But in the end, Gerontion's ruined houses, even if seen as included in a larger unity, are still ruined. That all the fragments may be unified in some heaven of the mind may be great comfort for the philosopher, but it is little comfort for the individual who must live and work among the ruins.

By the time Eliot finished "Gerontion," he had become disillusioned with most religious substitutes. He had discovered that Unitarianism dissolved the ability to believe in anything, that eros whispered promises it could not keep, that symbolism led him to an abyss beneath surface forms, that idealism failed to take account of his feelings. In the years between 1918 and 1922, partially under the influence of Ezra Pound, whose Penelope was Flaubert, Eliot made a last ditch effort to accept art as a substitute for religion. In a 1919 review, he sounds more like an apostle for art than a literary critic. The romantic, claims Eliot, tends to relate everything to himself. This devotion to one's self and one's caste "will not do in literature. The Arts insist that a man shall dispose of all that he has, even of his family tree, and follow art alone."[26] By alluding to some of the most difficult words Christ ever spoke, Eliot indicates that the cost of discipleship in the arts is high indeed. His words ring true, for unlike the rich young ruler, Eliot at this stage had left father and mother, country and profession, in order to devote himself to his new master and "follow art alone."

Eliot's devotion to literature is evident enough in the essays collected in 1920 in *The Sacred Wood*. That book became a textbook for those who insisted on the autonomy of art, on the self-referential nature of texts, on the irrelevance of belief, or even of life, to art. In 1928, just after his conversion, Eliot issued the second edition of *The Sacred Wood*. The preface to this edition indicates that he was uneasy with the implications of these early essays, especially as they were developed by his friend, I. A. Richards. Poetry,

26. "A Romantic Patrician," review of *Essays in Romantic Literature*, by George Wyndham, *Athenaeum*, 4644 (2 May 1919): 266–67.

Eliot claimed, had been greatly overrated. It is not, as Arnold claimed, a "criticism of life." "And certainly poetry is not the inculcation of morals, or . . . of politics; and no more is it religion or an equivalent of religion, except by some monstrous abuse of words." What is poetry? In a striking about-face, Eliot announced that "poetry is a superior amusement." And he tried to reconnect this amusement with belief. Poetry "has something to do with morals, and with religion, and even with politics perhaps, though we cannot say what."[27]

Eliot made several other attempts to dissociate himself from the implications of his early work, especially as developed by Richards. In the 1929 essay on Dante, for example, he describes as incomprehensible Richards's statement that in *The Waste Land*, poetry is completely severed from belief. A few years later, he takes on Richards for asserting that "poetry is capable of saving us." He ends by placing Richards with Arnold: "salvation by poetry is not quite the same thing for Mr. Richards as it was for Arnold; but so far as I am concerned these are merely different shades of blue."[28]

Eliot's uneasiness with the rise of the New Criticism, especially with Richards's *Principles of Literary Criticism* and *Science and Poetry*, stems from the fact that Richards took *The Sacred Wood* and *The Waste Land* as primary texts. To some extent, Eliot's post-conversion rebukes of Richards are an attempt to clarify his own life. He had been sincerely trying, in the years leading up to *The Waste Land*, to make poetry his Penelope, to make art the still point of his turning world. For years, he had been working on some method which would enable him to construct a great poem without using a framework borrowed from religion or philosophy. In "Prufrock" he had tried using Christian ritual, and in "Gerontion," Bradleyan philosophy. Both seemed in special ways inadequate. In *The Waste Land*, instead of borrowing a framework, Eliot borrows a method. Using the comparative method of modern science, particularly of anthropology, he tries to force the reader to construct the abstraction that will serve as the framework of the poem.[29] It is perhaps his greatest attempt to create a work of art in which an

27. *The Sacred Wood: Essays on Poetry and Criticism*, 2d ed. 1928. Reprint. London: Methuen, 1960. viii, x.
28. "Dante," in *Selected Essays*, 230; "The Modern Mind," in *The Use of Poetry*, 131.
29. For a fuller discussion of the method by which Eliot forces the reader to construct the abstraction, see my "The Case of the Missing Abstraction: Eliot, Frazer, and Modernism," *Massachusetts Review* 25 (Winter 1984): 539–52.

aesthetic order is collaboratively constructed by the poet and his reader.

Within a short time of finishing *The Waste Land*, Eliot had initiated the dialogue that led to his entry into the Anglican Church. He had begun with the Arnoldian position that belief was impossible, but religion or some substitute was essential. He had tried Bergsonianism, eros, aestheticism, humanism, idealism, and had seriously considered Buddhism. But in the end, Christianity was the only scheme satisfying both his intellectual and his emotional needs, the only scheme permitting him to unify his life and his art; or, as he came to say, the Christian scheme was the only one which *worked.* Of poetry, his most serious substitute for religion, he wrote that it "does not matter" ("East Coker," II). From a position of "art for art's sake" in 1910, Eliot in 1951 came to say: "For it is ultimately the function of art, in imposing a credible order upon ordinary reality, and thereby eliciting some perception of an order *in* reality, to bring us to a condition of serenity, stillness, and reconciliation; and then leave us, as Virgil left Dante, to proceed toward a region where that guide can avail us no farther."[30]

Eliot's quest for truth was complicated, as complicated as his mind and his personality. He did not try one scheme at a time, neatly and in sequence—his schemes overlapped both in substance and in sequence. Moreover, in taking seriously one substitute and then rejecting it, he did not obliterate it from his mind. His mind was like the mind he describes in "Tradition and the Individual Talent," "a mind which changes, and . . . this change is a development which abandons nothing *en route,*"[31] which does not superannuate either humanism or aestheticism or Buddhism, but includes them, at least residually, in an ever increasing complexity of intelligence and feeling. The pattern of his inclusive and cultivated imagination is rich and strange, and finally, elusive. His Christianity, certainly, cannot be equated with any handbook definition, but it is Christianity just the same. His substitutes for religion cannot be treated simply as stations on the way to the church; they did lead to the church, however, and to know them is to become aware of the complexity and richness of his Christian assent.

30. "Poetry and Drama," in *On Poetry and Poets* (London: Faber, 1957), 94.
31. "Tradition and the Individual Talent," in *Selected Essays*, 6.

T. S. Eliot: The Savage Comedian and the Sweeney Myth
Ronald Schuchard

T. S. Eliot has never enjoyed a public reputation as a comic poet or as an obscene poet, but his new friends in London in 1915 were well acquainted with the lusty characters who peopled his bawdy ballads and limericks. Eliot playfully interspersed the narrative of his letters to Conrad Aiken with stanzas on the escapades of King Bolo and his Big Black Kween, "that airy fairy hairy-'un, who led the dance on Golder's Green with Cardinal Bessarion." He sent poems entitled "Bullshit" and "Ballad for Big Louise" to Wyndham Lewis, and wrote to Pound from Merton College, Oxford, that Lewis's "Puritanical Principles seem to bar my way to Publicity. . . . I understand that Priapism, Narcissism etc are not approved of, and even so innocent a rhyme as '. . . pulled her stockings off / With a frightful cry of "Hauptbahnhof!"' is considered decadent." Lewis, who saw the poems as "excellent bits of scholarly ribaldry," jokingly told Pound that he was trying to print them in his periodical, *Blast*, but stuck to his "naif determination to have no 'Words Ending in -Uck, -Unt, and -Ugger!'"[1]

There is much in Eliot's juvenile graffiti that is vulgar and coarsely humorous. That said, it is of interest that the impulse to sexual caricature was accompanied by an equally strong impulse to poems of spiritual martyrdom. It is of even greater interest that the bawdy element not only survived his twenty-fifth year but, with the appearance of Sweeney in 1918, became one of the most "serious" and "personal" elements of his art. Between 1915 and 1925, as he read deeply in comedy, myth, and ritual, Eliot created around Sweeney a

---

1. Aiken, "King Bolo and Others," in *T. S. Eliot: A Symposium*, compiled by Tambimuttu and Richard March (Chicago: Regnery, 1949), 22; *Pound/Lewis: The Letters of Ezra Pound and Wyndham Lewis*, ed. Timothy Materer (New York: New Directions, 1985), 8; *The Letters of T. S. Eliot* (1898–1922), ed. Valerie Eliot (San Diego: Harcourt Brace Jovanovich, 1988), 1:86.

comically sordid poetic landscape of brothels, lowlifes, and exotic types: Doris, Mrs. Turner, Mrs. Porter, Fresca, Grishkin, Rachel, and others. Collectively, they inhabit the phantasmagoria through which Eliot expresses his moral convictions about the world of vanity, fear and lust.

Eliot wrote most of his bawdy poems prior to his precipitous marriage in June 1915 to Vivien Haigh-Wood.[2] But the marriage quickly placed them in a rather humorless financial plight, somewhat relieved by the generosity of Bertrand Russell, who took the couple into his London flat for several months and assumed an avuncular role in the struggling marriage. Two years of marital difficulty and poetic dryness were to elapse before Sweeney appeared among Eliot's new quatrain poems of 1918. Where did he come from, this apeneck brothel browser? What prompted Eliot to make a sort of generic slide from martyr to whoremonger, to slip from the tragic and spiritual to the comic and carnal? What is the relationship of the Sweeney poems of 1918 and 1919 to *The Waste Land*, where Sweeney makes a cameo appearance in "The Fire Sermon," and to *Sweeney Agonistes*, where Eliot's mythic figure reenacts an ancient ritual of death and resurrection? These are some of the questions that I want to address in discussing a group of modernist poems that have troubled critics for almost seventy years.

Pound and Lewis knew the witty practical joker in Eliot, but they did not know in 1915 that he was already a serious student of the comic spirit. He had studied Aristophanes at Harvard, and he kept Bekker's five-volume edition close at hand.[3] During his year

---

2. A cache of Eliot's early (c. 1909–1917) Bolo poems is among the Pound archives in the Beinecke Library, Yale University. Eliot continued to write about Bolo for years, circulating the poems among trusted friends. In the midst of their correspondence about revisions for *The Waste Land* in January 1922, Pound replied to Eliot: "You can forward the 'Bolo' to Joyce if you think it won't unhinge his sabbatarian mind. On the hole he might be saved the shock, shaved the sock" (*The Letters of Ezra Pound*, ed. D. D. Paige [New York: Harcourt Brace, 1950], 171). In 1927, he sent Bonamy Dobrée "portions of a Bolovian Epic (not always decorous)" (See *T. S. Eliot: The Man and His Work*, ed. Allen Tate [New York: Dell, 1966], 73). In a 1959 interview, when asked by Donald Hall if he still wrote in the Bolo vein, Eliot replied: "Oh yes, one wants to keep one's hand in, you know, in every type of poem, serious and frivolous and proper and improper. One doesn't want to lose one's skill" (*Paris Review* 21 [Spring/Summer 1959]: 59).

3. Immanuel Bekker's edition, *Aristophanis Comoediae: cum scholiis et varietate lectionis* (5 vols.; London: Whittaker, Treacher, and Arnot, 1829), was among the books in an inventory of Eliot's library in 1936 that was slipped into a private album of Vivien Eliot (Bodleian Library, Oxford University).

abroad in Paris in 1910–1911, where he says he underwent a "temporary conversion" to Bergsonism, Eliot read *Laughter: An Essay on the Meaning of the Comic* (1903), a book-length study in which Bergson develops his belief in the moral function of comedy. "Any incident is comic," Bergson argues, "that calls our attention to the physical in a person, when it is the moral side that is concerned."[4]

Bergson's analysis of the comic pervades the quatrain poems, but Eliot subsequently encountered a more arresting discussion of the comic poet in Baudelaire's essay "On the Essence of Laughter," originally published in 1855. Baudelaire argues that laughter, which is satanic and based on pride and the individual's feeling of superiority over other beings, is the experience of contradictory feelings—of infinite greatness in relation to beasts and of infinite wretchedness in relation to absolute being. Baudelaire distinguishes what he calls the "absolute comic," whose work "has a mysterious, a durable, an eternal element," even as the work is "destined to show men their own moral and physical ugliness."[5] The absolute comic is the superior artist, one who is receptive to absolute ideas and who brings those ideas to bear on the moral degradation of fallen humanity. In playing with the ideas of pride and superiority in his audience, the absolute comic works with laughter that is provoked by the grotesque, which carries the audience beyond its feelings of superiority over other people to its feelings of superiority over nature. In depicting the human slide toward the bestial, the absolute comic reveals not only the guttering moral consciousness that separates men from beasts but the horror of man's separation from absolute being.

Eliot seized upon Baudelaire's definition of the absolute comic, and with it he was directed by Baudelaire to its most ferocious practitioners in England. "To find the ferocious and ultra-ferocious comic," wrote Baudelaire, in a passage quoted by Eliot, "we must cross the Channel and pay a visit to the misty kingdoms of the spleen," where the distinguishing mark of the comic is violence.[6] As he began to write the Sweeney poems in 1918, Eliot immersed himself in the savage and violent tradition of English comedy, from Christopher Marlowe and Ben Jonson to Charles Dickens, thence

4. Henri Bergson, *Laughter: An Essay on the Meaning of the Comic*, trans. Cloudesley Brereton and Fred Rothwell (New York: Macmillan, 1911), 51.

5. "On the Essence of Laughter, and Generally of the Comic," in *Baudelaire: Selected Writings on Art and Artists*, trans. P. E. Charvet (Harmondsworth: Penguin, 1972), 141–42.

6. "London Letter," *Dial* 70 (June 1921): 688–89.

to the most contemporary manifestation of the ferocious comic in England—his bawdy friend Wyndham Lewis.

In his essays on Marlowe and Jonson in 1918 and 1919, Eliot identifies in his masters the techniques of caricature that inform his own work. He focuses on *The Jew of Malta* to characterize Marlowe's genius for achieving serious moral thought through caricature, seeing him in effect as an absolute comic. Arguing that in Elizabethan drama "the more farcical comedy was the more serious," Eliot holds that the play should be read as a farce. "I say farce," he writes, drawing directly upon Baudelaire, "but with the enfeebled humour of our times the word is a misnomer; it is the farce of the old English humour, the terribly serious, even savage comic humour, the humour which spent its last breath in the decadent genius of Dickens." Marlowe's style, Eliot continues, "secures its emphasis by always hesitating on the edge of caricature at the right moment"[7]—a technique that Eliot employs repeatedly in the Sweeney poems, as when Rachel Rabinovitch "Tears at the grapes with murderous paws."

Eliot continued to explore the comic techniques of *The Jew of Malta* by comparing it with Jonson's *Volpone*, where the vice-ridden characters are all linked to the appropriate animal (Volpone the Fox, etc.). Jonson's "type of personality," Eliot observes, "found its relief in something falling under the category of burlesque or farce." In examining Jonson's comic methods of achieving moral seriousness, Eliot praises his mastery of grotesque caricature. Jonson was also an absolute comic for Eliot, and he wrote admiringly in a valuable essay on the "Comic Spirit" that Jonson's drama is therefore "a criticism of humanity far more serious than its conscious moral judgments. 'Volpone' does not merely show that wickedness is punished; it criticizes humanity by intensifying wickedness."[8]

This lost art of serious English caricature, Eliot had discovered, could now be found anew in the fiction of Wyndham Lewis, particularly in his novel *Tarr*, published in 1918, which Eliot reviewed on several occasions. "Mr. Lewis's humour is near to Dickens," he wrote, "but on the right side, for it is not too remote from Ben Jonson." Eliot identified in Lewis those aspects of savage humor

7. "Christopher Marlowe," in *Selected Essays* (New York: Harcourt Brace, 1950), 105.

8. "Ben Jonson," in *Selected Essays*, 137; "The Romantic Englishman, the Comic Spirit, and the Function of Criticism—The Lesson of Baudelaire," *Tyro* (London) 1 (Spring 1921): 4.

that were most important to his own work, singling out, for example, Lewis's mastery of humiliation, which Eliot described as "one of the most important elements in human life, and one little exploited."[9] He subsequently praised *Tarr* for possessing "an element of that British humour, so serious and savage, to which Baudelaire once devoted a short study."[10] Lewis was Eliot's single visible ally; and in connecting himself and Lewis to Baudelaire on the one hand, and to Dickens, Jonson, and Marlowe on the other, Eliot felt that they had revived the absolute comic in England. Each was, to use Lewis's title "A Soldier of Humour."

Thus, in his criticism leading up to *The Waste Land*, Eliot clearly sought to prepare a favorable climate for the ferocious English humor of which he had become both proponent and practitioner. Indeed, we should begin to see that the early thrust of Eliot's literary modernism was in the revival of this comic mode. Ironically, as Eliot began his experiments against an enfeebled humor, his modern audience misread his comic signs. But now the questions press again: what happened in Eliot's personal life to turn the bawdy balladeer into a savage comedian in 1918? What emotional relief, as he described it in Jonson, did his type of personality seek in turning to the comic quatrains? The intellectual, almost evangelical interest in comic theory did not in itself lead him to the new mode; rather, the poems grew out of an urgent need to find an artistic form for the preoccupations of a deeply wounded sensibility. A distinctive feature of humor, Eliot wrote in discussing *Tarr*, is "the instinctive attempt of a sensitive mind to protect beauty against ugliness; and to protect itself against stupidity."[11] What ugliness and stupidity, we want to know, motivates these difficult, stripped-down poems of sexual grotesques involved in adulterous and other illicit encounters, with constant allusions to lechery, cuckoldry, and betrayal? Perhaps we shall never know the full story, but in a recent study, Robert H. Bell lays out the bitter truth of a long-rumored situation, Bertrand Russell's sexual affair with Vivien Eliot. Russell, who had sworn himself to a platonic relationship, had re-

9. Review of *Tarr*, by Wyndham Lewis, *Egoist* 5 (September 1918): 105. On 22 March 1921 Virginia Woolf recorded a conversation with Eliot after missing their train. " 'Missing trains is awful,' I said. 'Yes. But humiliation is the worst thing in life' he replied." *The Diary of Virginia Woolf*, vol. 2, ed. Anne Olivier Bell (New York: Harcourt Brace Jovanovich, 1978), 103.
10. "Contemporary English Prose," *Vanity Fair* (New York) 20 (July 1923): 51.
11. Review of "Tarr," 105.

strained himself for two years, but he wrote to another mistress, Lady Constance Malleson, that he began having sexual relations with Vivien in the autumn of 1917. The evidence at hand makes it all but certain that Eliot knew or had strong intimations of the affair by the summer of 1918, when Russell provided the Eliots with his summer cottage. Eliot later wrote to Ottoline Morrell that the spectacle of Bertie had been a significant factor in his eventual conversion.[12] There is no doubt that in 1918 Eliot's vision of sexual humanity was terribly darkened, little doubt that Russell's lustful betrayal and Vivien's adulterous desire were the cause. To cope with the humiliation, to protect himself from the moral ugliness and stupidity, Eliot turned savagely to the sexual caricature of Sweeney and his friends. In so doing, he gradually created a personal myth of sexual betrayal, psychological retribution, and moral regeneration. We begin with "Sweeney Erect" and its epigraph from Beaumont and Fletcher.

In assigning *The Maid's Tragedy* to his night class of adult students in 1918, Eliot told them that the gifts of Beaumont and Fletcher as dramatists were "on the whole better exhibited in the scene than in the complete play."[13] Little did those students know how much one scene meant to him—the scene that provides the epigraph for "Sweeney Erect," the betrayed Aspatia's bitter lament of her desertion by her lover for the king's mistress. "But man— / Oh, that beast, man!" she cries (act 2, scene 2, ll. 26–27), asking her waiting women to be sad with her as she recounts stories of lost heroines. She asks to see one woman's needlework of Ariadne and Theseus, who abandoned Ariadne on the waste shores of Naxos. Complaining bitterly that the scene does not show the depths of Ariadne's misery, she commands the woman to rework the mythic portrayal. "Do it by me," she exclaims. "Do it again by me, the lost Aspatia" (act 2, scene 2, ll. 65–66). Eliot thus prefaces "Sweeney Erect" with a reference to Aspatia at the height of her hysterical state, deeply upsetting her waiting women ("Dear madam!" one exclaims [act 2, scene 2, l. 79]). His epigraph is taken from the conclusion of Aspatia's frantic identification with Ariadne:

12. See Robert H. Bell, "Bertrand Russell and the Eliots," *American Scholar* 52 (Summer 1983): 309–25; Letter to Lady Ottoline Morrell, 14 March 1933, Ransom Humanities Research Center, University of Texas at Austin.

13. See my "T. S. Eliot as an Extension Lecturer, 1916–1919," *Review of English Studies* 25 (August 1974): 301. Quotations from Francis Beaumont and John Fletcher's *The Maid's Tragedy* are taken from Howard B. Norland's edition (Lincoln: University of Nebraska Press, 1968).

And the trees about me,
Let them be dry and leafless; let the rocks
Groan with continual surges; and behind me
Make all a desolation. Look, look, wenches!
                    (act 2, scene 2, ll. 74–77)

"Sweeney Erect" begins with the poet's recasting of Aspatia's hysterical imperatives in the first two stanzas ("paint me Ariadne; display me the 'perjured sails' of Theseus") as though the poet would, like Aspatia, harshly rework the betrayal. But the summoning of Ariadne's pathos is suddenly, in a jarring shift of myth and style, deflated and displaced by sheet-covered lovers, with only their feet and hands protruding for dawn's searching light. It is as though the poet, in his abrupt redirection of the poem, cannot continue the pathetic mode and is forced to shift to burlesque, dissolving his original impulse in lowlife comedy. The descent of the mythic dimension is swift: if not Ariadne and Theseus, then perhaps Nausicaa and Polypheme? No, all the way down to Sweeney and Doris. Sweeney's prehensile arm, arched over Doris, erupts from the sheets in a "Gesture of orang-outang" as he rises in steam from their torrid undercover rendezvous. Torpid, tousled, and detumescent, he becomes a great gaping yawn, an "oval O cropped out with teeth," and immediately begins his posterectile performance, his aubade, as it were. A violent scissor kick jackknifes him from the supine to the prone in so ungainly a manner, in such exaggerated clumsiness, that he desperately pushes the bedstead for support and, with Eliot's Marlovian touch, "claws" at the pillow slip to regain his balance. Newly and safely erect, our brothel comedian continues the morning entertainment with his madcap ablutions, in the pink. Sweeney, who "Knows the female temperament," prepares to shave, lathering not just his cheeks but his whole face, setting the comic mood for Doris's arousal. Her laughter, we may imagine, is spontaneous and delighted, recalling her later reminiscence in *Sweeney Agonistes:* "He's like a fellow once I knew. / *He* could make you laugh." Even the narrator, as absolute comic, joins the fun; so grotesque is the silhouette of broadbottomed Sweeney at his toilet that the pedantic intruder cannot resist a double-edged gibe at Emerson's noble depiction of man as the shaper of history. Eliot's own unequivocal attitude toward Emerson surfaced in a review that preceded the poem: "Neither Emerson nor any of the others was a real observer of the moral life."[14]

14. "American Literature," review of *A History of American Literature*, vol. 2, ed. William P. Trent et al. *Athenaeum* 4643 (25 April 1919): 237.

For his *pièce de résistance* Sweeney begins toying with his razor, testing its sharpness on the hairs of his leg, an acrobatic gyration that elicits a shriek of animal laughter; indeed, Sweeney's Chaplinesque, music-hall pantomime throws Doris into a paroxysm of uncontrollable laughter, making her clutch breathlessly at her aching, bursting sides.[15] In her seizurelike extremity, Doris is appropriately caricatured as "The epileptic on the bed." The riotous laughter brings the house down, however, and Doris's room is quickly crowded upon by the alarmed "ladies of the corridor." When they discover that they have mistaken hilarity for violence, their solicitude turns sharply to indignation and high-minded propriety. And if Madam Turner is personally perturbed and professionally concerned, Doris is nonchalant and wholly unrepentant in dismissing them. She soon returns, happily spent, washed and toweled, to her sometime fancy man Sweeney, "padding" like a lioness, bountifully toting those old restoratives, those creature comforts, "sal volatile / And a glass of brandy neat." The poet's caricatures of their movements—Sweeney's orangutan gesture and his "clawing," Doris's hyenalike shrieks and her "padding"—are individually comical, but collectively they viciously imprint the bestial on Sweeney's and Doris's actions, implying at poem's end that they will now curl up in their lair with no moral disturbance, with no disquieting metaphysic to trouble their animal coupling, however illicit.

This brothel burlesque is, however, so skillfully amusing on the surface that we forget its tragic origins—forget to recall Aspatia at the crucial moment of misunderstanding in the corridor. In the awkward uncertainty about Doris's hysteria the tragic and the burlesque intersect, and it is here that we sense the poet's comic debasement of Aspatia's grief in a personal myth. Whereas Aspatia, decrying the bestiality of man, rises to hysteria in her grief, Doris, laughing violently at the grotesque antics of Sweeney, rises merely to hysterics. The figures of Aspatia and Doris come together as their separate cries reach a similar pitch, and the parallels force the reader to recognize the sexual bestiality and moral blindness common to both the tragic and the comic action. Eliot's comic creations seem blissfully unaware of their moral natures in this poem,

---

15. She recalls the canceled passage on Fresca's entertainment in *The Waste Land:* "The Russians thrilled her to hysteric fits." (*The Waste Land: A Facsimile and Transcript of the Original Drafts Including the Annotations of Ezra Pound*, ed. Valerie Eliot [New York: Harcourt Brace Jovanovich, 1971], 26).

but the absolute comic is aware of them, just as he is painfully unforgetful of Aspatia, whose betrayal was brought about by a lust that drove the king and his mistress to facilitate a convenient sexual arrangement at Aspatia's expense. Eliot himself is not amused by Sweeney and Doris. His personal voice is unmistakable; this is Aspatia's poem, written for her with great empathy.[16]

After Eliot had collected his quatrain poems for a limited edition entitled *Ara Vos Prec*, he wrote to his brother about them on 15 February 1920: "Some of the new poems, the Sweeney ones, especially 'Among the Nightingales' and 'Burbank' are intensely serious, and I think these two are among the best that I have ever done. But even here I am considered by the ordinary Newspaper critic as a Wit or satirist, and in America I suppose I shall be thought merely disgusting."[17] This rare volume contained a unique printing of "Sweeney Among the Nightingales," which included a second epigraph from an anonymous Elizabethan play, *The Raigne of King Edward the Third*. In the play, King Edward becomes infatuated with the virtuous Countess of Salisbury while her husband is away at war. In contemplating her beautiful features, he compares her voice to the music of the nightingale. His second thought about the comparison provides the epigraph: "And why should I speake of the nightingale? / The nightingale sings of adulterate wrong."[18] The amorous king thinks it too self-satirical to conceive of his desire as adulterous, and he rationalizes semantically that to be virtuous with such a lady would be sinful, and to be sinful with her would be virtuous.

The epigraph was printed in bold block capitals, typographically disproportional to the title and text. However appropriate for the poem, it seems to be deliberately, intemperately emblazoned on the page, as if to catch a guilty eye. Eliot inexplicably stripped the epigraph before the poem reappeared the next year in the first American edition of his work, but in the textual history of the poem, it remains a telling emblem of mind during composition. The succeeding action of the play, which traces the countess's un-

---

16. Eliot was to write again of "The wrong'd Aspatia" in "Elegy," a canceled fragment of *The Waste Land*. See *The Waste Land: A Facsimile*, 117.

17. *The Letters of T. S. Eliot*, (1898–1922), ed. Valerie Eliot (San Diego: Harcourt Brace Jovanovich, 1988), 1:363.

18. Fred Lapides, ed., *The Raigne of King Edward the Third* (New York: Garland 1980), act 2, scene 1, ll. 109–10. Subsequent citations are made parenthetically in the text.

yielding constancy before the lecherous king, illuminates Eliot's ironic personal attraction to the play. When the king begs her to lend her body to him "to sport with all," she eloquently refuses to relinquish the bower of her "intellectual soule": "If I should leave her house, my Lord, to thee, / I kill my poore soule and my poore soule me" (act 2, scene 1, ll. 250–51). When she learns of his further plots to seduce her, she takes up a knife, swearing to kill the husband sleeping in her bosom. Only then does the king awaken from his lust and bow to her fidelity and moral integrity. "Arise," he commands her, "and be my fault thy honors fame, / Which after ages shall enrich thee with. / I am awakened from this idle dream" (act 2, scene 2, ll. 197–99). For Eliot, however, the sexual nightmare continued.

The other, retained epigraph comes from the *Agamemnon* of Aeschylus—the moment when, shortly after his return to Argos from Troy with his unwilling concubine, Cassandra, Agamemnon is brutally slain by his wife, Clytemnestra, who acts in adulterous league with her lover, Aegisthus. Entrapping him in the folds of his robe while he bathes, she slays the king with an axe as he cries out, "Alas, I am struck a mortal blow!" This epigraph and the allusions to Agamemnon's death in the final stanza provide a crucial tragic frame for Eliot's low comedy.

We find Sweeney in a brothel again, on a stormy, threatening night, presumably the object of ribald teasing by the nightingales. Laughing in compound caricature, his simian gestures and the changing coloration of his face make him a figure of protean animal shapes—ape, zebra, giraffe. The narrator, an absolute comic contemplating the epigraph's tragedy, tries to envelop his own comic scene in portent. But the ominous atmosphere, in which Death and the Raven seem to await entry, is laughably deflated by the image of Sweeney guarding the hornèd gates of pleasure—a debunked image from the *Aeneid* by way of Dryden that Eliot reworked in a fragment of *The Waste Land:* "the human engine waits . . . To spring to pleasure through the horn or ivory gates."[19] But the sexual engines in this brothel are run down, and though Sweeney is the object of sexual solicitation by the two conspiring ladies, he is curiously indifferent to their automatic advances. When the mechanical approach of the woman in the Spanish cape results in a clumsy, boisterous pratfall, the seduction becomes a farce. So apa-

19. See *The Waste Land: A Facsimile*, 43.

thetic are the bodily appetites of this "silent vertebrate" that he comically contracts into a concentrated ball of refusal when the waiter offers fruit. And when the ravenous Russian, Rachel *née* Rabinovich, tears at the hothouse grapes in a bestial exaggeration of her adulterous appetite, Sweeney declines her histrionic advance with a gesture of fatigue and removes himself from the sexual game of chess. He feigns good humor, but what, we wonder, has happened to his libidinous ways? He may be spent, but he also seems preoccupied, even disturbed, his weariness as much mental as physical, his golden grin forced. Does Sweeney have that "sense of foreboding" that Eliot claimed, according to Matthiessen, the poem was written to show?[20] We leave him looking in as his host, presumably Mr. Porter, admits another customer and the nightingales resume their seductive song of adulterate wrong.

The portentous voice that earlier acquiesced to the more insistent description of sexual intrigue now resumes authority over the banal scene. Adopting again a constellational perspective, the absolute comic narrator makes the ironic observation that the siren songs of the nightingales are near another human community, the convent of the Sacred Heart, where the chaste brides of Christ sublimate desire in devotion. The observation itself charts the moral distance between brothel and convent, nightingale and nun; and the narrator continues to elevate the perspective with a more distant, more mythical association of Sweeney's nightingales with the nightingales of the "bloody wood." In 1958, Eliot explained that "The wood I had in mind was the grove of the Furies at Colonus; I called it 'bloody' because of the blood of Agamemnon in Argos."[21] This striking revelation almost forty years after the fact explains why the allusions of the final stanza have been so unyielding. In perhaps the clearest example of the modernist technique of dislocating and conflating myths, Eliot purposefully fused scenes from Sophocles' *Oedipus at Colonus* and Aeschylus's *Agamemnon*, borrowing the nightingales from Sophocles for Agamemnon's death scene. "It was a simple matter," Eliot continued, "to bring the dead Agamemnon into the open air, and to transfer the nightingales from one place to another."[22] Singing above the dead Agamemnon,

20. F. O. Matthiessen, *The Achievement of T. S. Eliot*, 3d ed. (London: Oxford University Press, 1958), 129.
21. "The Silver Bough," letter in *Sunday Times* (London) (6 April 1958): 4.
22. Ibid.

wrapped in his blood-stained robe/shroud, the nightingales in this very personal, seemingly vindictive poem, defecate on the sinful king, their "liquid siftings" staining the shroud already dishonored by Clytemnestra's adultery. But their song also awakens the Furies, the All-Seeing Ones, and *that* is the borrowed association that bears upon the poem. Indeed, the sense of foreboding that weighs upon Sweeney's libido, unconsciously felt by Sweeney but strongly perceived by the absolute comic, is a sense that the Furies, the inflexible agents of retribution who pursue men into atonement, are now at hand. The nightingales follow Sweeney into *The Waste Land*, where the song that cries " 'Jug Jug' to dirty ears" again signals the arousal of the Furies, whose pursuit, we shall see, has wreaked a terrible metamorphosis upon the protagonist of *Sweeney Agonistes.*

At the time he wrote "Sweeney Among the Nightingales," Eliot was absorbed by what he called "the phantom-psychology" of Aeschylus, Sophocles, and Shakespeare;[23] and in the Sweeney poems he begins to trace the psychological transformation of promiscuous characters possessed by moral agents. Human beings may tend, comically and tragically, toward the mechanical and bestial, but to Eliot human beings cannot escape the horrible consequences of sensual abandonment. He knew that sexual tragedy brings the greatest spiritual horror, unleashes the Furies, the Dark Angel, the hoo-ha-ha's of the nightmare chorus in *Sweeney Agonistes.* So pursued, Sweeney becomes a study in the phantom-psychology of sexuality, in sensual-spiritual transformation.

Eliot develops this agon between the physical and the spiritual in his seventy-line portrait of Fresca, an excised passage that served as a prelude to Sweeney's brief appearance in "The Fire Sermon." Fresca, languidly dreaming of "pleasant rapes" in her boudoir, has not yet undergone her inevitable transformation into a Mary Magdalene, is herself unaware of the Dark Angel latent in the sexual urge, but the absolute comic narrator identifies the treacherous chemistry of her desire: "The same eternal and consuming itch / Can make a martyr, or plain simple bitch."[24] In contemplating Fresca's sexual reveries, the narrator hears at his back, or at her

23. "The Noh and the Image," review of *Noh, or Accomplishment, a Study of the Classical Stage of Japan,* by Ernest Fenollosa and Ezra Pound, *Egoist* 4 (August 1917): 103.
24. *The Waste Land: A Facsimile,* 26.

back, not time's wingèd chariot, as does Marvell's artful seducer, but the haunting "chuckle" of death. This chuckle, he knows, brings more than a carpe diem awareness of mortality; it brings a horrific awareness of the void that underlies illicit sexuality. Implicitly, the All-Seeing Ones have found her out.

The Waste Land quester, musing on the rat-infested, infertile land, then hears behind his back the blaring horns and motors that herald Sweeney's annual return to Mrs. Porter in the spring. Since the earlier poems, Sweeney and Mrs. Porter have become such personal mythic figures in Eliot's imagination that they can make their appearance in the poem without introduction, casually displacing Acteon and Diana in a mythic parade of passion. Heard in the fanfare are lines from a bawdy ballad.

> O the moon shone bright on Mrs. Porter
> And on her daughter
> They wash their feet in soda water
> (*The Waste Land*, ll. 199–201)

Yet Sweeney and Mrs. Porter are but fleeting figures in the phantasmagoria of this section, this "cauldron of unholy loves,"[25] where the montage of images and allusions will not hold in the quester's mind, flooded as it is with associative fragments of high and low passion, constancy, and betrayal. As Sweeney and Mrs. Porter fade out of the disturbed procession, the wail of the ravished nightingale marks their departure and awakens the Furies, who will drive them toward their ritual deaths.

Even in this brief scene in "The Fire Sermon," we can see that Eliot had already discovered a ritual frame for the moral regeneration of Sweeney and his wayward friends. Since 1916 he had been reading the Cambridge anthropologists, all of whom were making the case that comedy and tragedy had their origins in ancient fertility rituals. As an absolute comic, Eliot had become particularly interested in F. M. Cornford's *The Origins of Attic Comedy*, published in 1914, which argues that a phallic fertility ritual of death and resurrection underlies the development of comedy and that elements of this ritual provide the framework for the plays of Aristophanes. Meticulously following Cornford's reconstruction of the Aristophanic plot formula, with its strong sexual element, Eliot

---

25. Saint Augustine, *Confessions*, 3.1, quoted in *The Waste Land*, note to line 307.

turned immediately from *The Waste Land* to fully ritualize Sweeney's annual visit to Mrs. Porter, making them adversaries in an agon of life and death, making her murder, resurrection, and marriage to Sweeney the modern equivalent of an ancient drama.

Beginning in 1923, *Sweeney Agonistes* went through a succession of titles, subtitles, epigraphs, and scenarios. The earliest title, "Pereira; or, The Marriage of Life and Death, a Dream," not only defines the agon of the play, it points to the dreamlike state of being which Doris has entered in the prologue and which Sweeney tries to describe in the agon. Doris has come home with "a terrible chill." "I *think* it's only a chill," Dusty tells Pereira on the telephone, but we discover that she suffers from a vague apprehension and fear not unlike Sweeney's in "Sweeney Among the Nightingales." Superstitiously cutting a deck of cards, she turns up the two of spades—the coffin, a ritual symbol of death. "I'm sure it's mine," she says frantically. "I dreamt of weddings all last night." She thereby forecasts the ritual death, resurrection, and marriage that she must soon undergo. As the epigraph from Aeschylus's *Choephoroi* (*The Libation Bearers*) now implies, the Furies are aswarm in her consciousness.

When the agon begins, we discover that Sweeney's purgation and metamorphosis have already taken place, and in the ritual drama he appears symbolically as a risen god or king to deliver Doris and Mrs. Porter from their death-in-life. He engages in flirtatious but threatening banter with Doris about the manner of her death—her ritual cooking—preparatory to the sacramental eating of her flesh on a "cannibal isle," where her rebirth will take place. "You wouldn't eat me!" exclaims Doris. "Yes I'd eat you!" Sweeney savagely replies, "In a nice little . . . missionary stew." Sweeney then begins to instruct—no, remind Doris of the transformation of consciousness that takes place on that isle of regeneration, a recognition that there is nothing at all in life but "Birth, and copulation, and death." Sweeney, who has evidently slain her before, gives her a hint of his own horrific transformation.

> I've been born, and once is enough.
> You dont remember, but I remember,
> Once is enough.

His subsequent story of a man who once did a girl in, and of the innate desire of any man to do a girl in, is told by way of analogy to reveal a dispossessed state of mind. "I've gotta use words when I talk to you," he says in frustration, knowing how horribly inexpressible is a mind that is neither dead nor alive, that no longer has any "joint" with the ordinary plane of reality. The chorus, chanting "The Terrors of the Night," chuckle the phantom laugh that signals sexual death: "You've had a cream of a nightmare dream and you've got the hoo-ha's coming to you."

The "Fragment of an Agon" stops abruptly with the insistent "Knock Knock Knock" of death, but we now know from Eliot's synopsis and extant scenarios that the play would follow the Aristophanic formula.[26] In the scene to follow, Mrs. Porter makes her riotous entrance, singing a bawdy refrain from the ballad of Casey Jones: "And the neighbors knew by the shrieks and the groans / That the man at the throttle was Casey Jones." Sweeney, a reborn Casey Jones who, as a canceled epigraph relates, "In the red light district . . . found his fame," then murders Mrs. Porter. Her subsequent resurrection is followed by a marriage and feast, with Sweeney the Cook scrambling the eggs for the wedding breakfast of life and death. "It may not be too fanciful," one critic has recently observed, "to see in the fictional severance and reunion an image of the spiritual condition and the spiritual destiny of Eliot and his wife, as Eliot perceived them."[27]

The Aristophanic ritual thus became Eliot's experimental model for comic purgation, for the dramatization of what we can now see as the Sweeney myth. From the outset there is a thin line between horror and laughter in this myth, but "in the end," says Eliot, "horror and laughter may be one—only when horror and laughter have become as horrible and laughable as they can be . . . then only do you perceive that the aim of the comic and the tragic dramatist is the same: they are equally serious."[28] Eliot tinkered with *Sweeney Agonistes* for productions in the 1930s, but he finally abandoned it—perhaps because the human drama that motivated it had ended

26. Eliot's two-page holograph outline of the play was reproduced in *The Stage Sixty Theatre Club Presents Homage to T. S. Eliot: A Programme of Poetry, Drama and Music* (Globe Theatre, London, 13 June 1965), 4–5. The manuscripts and typescripts related to *Sweeney Agonistes*, including the scenario of an early draft entitled *The Superior Landlord*, are in the Hayward Collection, King's College, Cambridge University.
27. Michael J. Sidnell, *Dances of Death: The Group Theatre of London in the Thirties* (London: Faber, 1984), 264.
28. "Shakespearian Criticism I: From Dryden to Coleridge," in *A Companion to Shakespeare Studies*, ed. Harley Granville-Barker and G. B. Harrison (Cambridge: Cambridge University Press, 1934), 295.

and the comedian had lost his ferocity, perhaps because his marriage itself had died, not to be reborn. The fragments of *Ash-Wednesday* had turned his poetry back to the spiritual quest, and with the announcement of his Russell-inspired conversion in 1928, he was ironically cast into the role of public martyr.

But the bawdy side of Eliot had not died, as was evidenced in 1939 by his contribution to a pamphlet of verse, twenty-five copies of which were printed strictly for private circulation. Entitled *Noctes Binanianae*, it contains, the subtitle says, "Certain Voluntary and Satyrical Verses and Compliments as were lately Exchang'd between some of the Choicest Wits of the Age . . . now printed without castration after the most correct copies." The pretentious Latin title, according to my colleague William Arrowsmith, translates, appropriately, "Buggery Nights."[29] This late collection of doggerel reminds us that Eliot was not, by temperament, a savage comedian. In his bawdy, lighthearted moods, his more natural moods perhaps, he would beg us, as "Possum," as Tom, not always to take him so seriously.

29. The Latinate construction originated from the gathering place of the authors: John Hayward's London flat, 22 Bina Gardens.

T. S. Eliot and the Fascination of *Hamlet*
Grover Smith

Whether T. S. Eliot really was fascinated by *Hamlet* I do not know and cannot precisely know. If he was, the fascination exercised his mind for critical individuality. *Hamlet* fascinates most of us, and its fascination, being a universal and shared affair, constitutes a topic in itself apart from Eliot. And the disparate interest shown by writers who stimulated Eliot's interest in *Hamlet* makes the shared fascination part of Eliot's universe of understanding for the play. Their interest, and not his alone, enters expressly into my topic. It has to be recognized alongside of Eliot's, whether his ever became obsessive or not. Neither *Hamlet* nor anything else in Eliot's intellectual and poetic synthesis controlled his mind: an Eliot dominated by his material is a fictitious Eliot. But evidently *Hamlet* had a very special, possibly intimate, significance for him.

Now, to psychologize Eliot entangles one all too soon in the making of a fiction, and such activity carries grave risks of bathos. Yet psychologize I must—while illustrating my sense of the acceptable bounds of psychological criticism. Beyond the limits of Eliot's rare acknowledgments, quite obliquely, of personal traits that may be reminiscent, for us, of Hamlet, I am not prepared to venture— that is, in the direction of undocumented depth psychology. As I do not claim for *Hamlet* a preponderant influence on Eliot, so I would not superfluously accord to it the role of archetype for a reductionist treatment of his poetry. The affinity between his work and the play need not be sought on unconscious grounds; it is in plain sight. It results from some affinity felt consciously by Eliot, not for the play nor greatly for Hamlet the man, but for a certain viewpoint presented in the play, concerning action and passion. In Eliot's writings over a period of years the figure of Hamlet, under various guises, makes its presence felt. It is always associated with the motif of action.

A theme of hesitation and inertia, of action thwarted or inhibited, runs through Eliot's poetry; and in his poetic ménage such figures as Prufrock, Gerontion, and the Hollow Men seem to be caught between incompatible inner and outer worlds of dream and actuality. Later in Eliot's poetry there comes a stage at which action and inaction are indifferent. They merge through an ethic of right action—equally in *Four Quartets* and in the plays. To what extent a personal history of psychological conflict underlies all of this remains indistinct. As a theme, such conflict is many times referred to: for example, in "Burnt Norton," which envisions transcendence of action and suffering; in *Murder in the Cathedral*, which defines the freedom of the saint in his abdication of the will to act and suffer; and in *The Family Reunion*, which returns to *Hamlet* for its model of action and suffering and resolves the conflict far differently from the tragic hero.

Eliot, in a letter of November 1921 quoted in *The Waste Land: A Facsimile*, wrote that all through his life he had been afflicted with "an aboulie and emotional derangement." Aboulie, or aboulia, is the term applied by the psychoanalyst Ernest Jones to the disorder supposed of Hamlet: paralysis of the will.[1] May it not be assumed that Eliot's repeated portrayals of an impediment to action represented a poetic extension of private psychological conflict? As far as the problems of Hamlet were concerned, aboulia did not exhaust the reasons for Eliot's interest, and however visibly paramount this affliction, Hamlet—whether in Shakespeare or in derivative forms—provided an archetype for further psychological states in Eliot's work. In particular Hamlet (for example in Dostoevsky and Laforgue) has undergone literary transformations that accentuate his conflicts with women, and the psychoanalysts stress such a conflict in the Hamlet of Shakespeare. In the writings of Eliot the conflict is handled at times with the help of these secondary points of view.

Hamlet first enters Eliot's poetry in 1910 in an early draft of "The Love Song of J. Alfred Prufrock." Prufrock, a highly self-conscious personage, may recall to us Eliot's remark about "the self-consciousness and self-dramatization of the Shakespearean hero, of

---

1. *The Waste Land: A Facsimile and Transcript of the Original Drafts Including the Annotations of Ezra Pound*, ed. Valerie Eliot (New York: Harcourt Brace Jovanovich, 1971), xxii; Jones, "The Oedipus-Complex as an Explanation of Hamlet's Mystery: A Study in Motive," *American Journal of Psychology* 21 (January 1910): 77, 86. See also Ernest Jones, *Essays in Applied Psychoanalysis* (London: International Psycho-Analytical Press, 1923).

whom Hamlet is only one."[2] "No! I am not Prince Hamlet, nor was meant to be," declaims Prufrock, belying his words in the delivery of them. But who precisely is this Hamlet, to whom he assimilates himself by denying an identification that we know instinctively is appropriate? Prufrock is translating Eliot's own notion of Hamlet, at that epoch, into a poetic objectification. Prufrock derives "Hamlet stuff" from a variety of traditions—stuff that he may be expected to know, stuff that Eliot alone knows, and stuff that no doubt neither knows—and thus he is padded out for us into a neo-Hamlet. The negative, "I am not Prince Hamlet," proves to no avail: Prufrock, having conceived himself to be no Hamlet, becomes one or many. And thereby adding himself to the sum total of all Hamlets, he imperceptibly alters that composite Hamlet pre-Prufrock into a composite Hamlet post-Prufrock. It is equally true that if Eliot's poem appeals to the image of a Hamlet surpassing in dignity the mere hapless Prufrock, it also appeals to competing images which, in the critical tradition, undercut the heroic Hamlet. At the date of "Prufrock" some of these were very conspicuous, and allowance must be made for them in considering the poem and Eliot's use of the Hamlet figure there and in later contexts.

In the nineteenth century Hamlet underwent critical vicissitudes that produced the image of a man with something gravely amiss either in his constitution or in his response to immediate events. This image, this view of Hamlet, developed on the assumption that the main critical problem of Shakespeare's play was rooted in Hamlet's character. Later critics have tried to escape classical "character" by modernizing it into "behavior" and "psychology." These terms merely disguise his character, so that the main critical problem is unchanged. Nor, once established as the critical focus at center stage, can Hamlet be displaced by topics such as the origins and structure of the play. A twentieth-century scholar, J. M. Robertson, in *The Problem of "Hamlet"* attempted in 1919 to turn emphasis away from Hamlet's character to historical and textual matters. Robertson's work comes within my scope because it evoked Eliot's review article "Hamlet and His Problems," the title of which snubbed Robertson's thesis. Eliot ingeniously demonstrated how the problem of the text and of its evolution before and

2. "Shakespeare and the Stoicism of Seneca," in *Selected Essays* (New York: Harcourt Brace, 1950), 119.

through Shakespeare brought one back to the problem of Hamlet's behavior. Character had been addressed in 1780 by Henry Mackenzie, who considered that Shakespeare had assigned to Hamlet "feelings so delicate as to border on weakness, with sensibility too exquisite to allow of determined action."[3] Goethe, fifteen years later, ventriloquized through the hero of *Wilhelm Meister's Apprenticeship* a similar judgment.

> Shakespeare meant . . . to represent the effects of a great action laid upon a soul unfit for the performance of it . . . A lovely, pure, noble, and most moral nature, without the strength of nerve which forms a hero, sinks beneath a burden it cannot bear and must not cast away. All duties are holy for him: the present is too hard. Impossibilities have been required of him,—not in themselves impossibilities, but such for him.[4]

Almost a century later Hermann Türck would assume that the view taken by Goethe simply projected the character of his own weak-spirited Werther.[5]

Long after Goethe's critique went out of fashion, the more explanatory hypothesis of S. T. Coleridge in his *Hamlet* lecture of 1808 was still commanding respect. Coleridge held that in Hamlet the "equilibrium between the real and the imaginary worlds" is disturbed; Hamlet imagines too much and cannot come to terms with his perceptions. "A great, an almost enormous, intellectual activity" causes "a proportionate aversion to real action." Unable to make up his mind, he spends himself in cravings for "the indefinite," until exhausted by his "disproportionate mental exertion." "Where there is a just coincidence of external and internal action," Coleridge concluded, "pleasure is always the result; but where the former is deficient, and the mind's appetency of the ideal is unchecked, realities will seem cold and unmoving. In such cases, passion combines itself with the indefinite alone."[6]

Though we may find this description curiously applicable to Eliot's Prufrock, A. C. Bradley rejected it as a portrait of Hamlet, declaring in his third lecture on Shakespearean tragedy that the "theory describes . . . a man in certain respects like Coleridge him-

---

3. See J. M. Robertson, *The Problem of "Hamlet"* (London: George Allen and Unwin, 1919), 12.

4. *Wilhelm Meister*, trans. Thomas Carlyle (London: Dent, 1912), 4:13.

5. See Robertson, *The Problem of "Hamlet,"* 12n.

6. Quoted in *Shakespeare Criticism: A Selection*, ed. D. Nichol Smith (London: Oxford University Press, 1946), 256, 257, 262.

self, on one side a man of genius, on the other side, the side of will, deplorably weak, always procrastinating and avoiding unpleasant duties, and often reproaching himself in vain: a man, observe, who at *any* time and in *any* circumstances would be unequal to the task assigned to Hamlet."[7] Bradley found in Hamlet not a constitutional weakness or an inability to act but rather a temporary emotional disability induced by a state of profound melancholy over his mother's adultery and his father's murder. For this reason only, according to Bradley's reading, Hamlet's "native hue of resolution" for revenge "Is sicklied o'er with the pale cast of thought." Bradley thus amended Coleridge's analysis to allow for Hamlet's swift action in other circumstances, but his revision was still partly Coleridgean in postulating a psychological interference with action—that specific action of revenge sought by the Ghost. Bradley's psychological analysis of Hamlet has far less to do with Prufrock, who has no murder to avenge and also no mother; but like Eliot's poem it concerns itself with character and more important with emotion. It also reveals, as the furthest academic advance made in the century following Mackenzie, Goethe, and Coleridge, the range of the critical models available to Eliot in 1909–1910.

Coleridge's Hamlet, he of wool-gathering ineptitude, furnished either in the foreground or in the background a chief model for Prufrock. Like Coleridge's Hamlet, Prufrock temperamentally substitutes mental activity for *all* significant action. Unlike Bradley's Hamlet, he has no dramatically motivated reason (such as "melancholy" resulting from his family's misconduct) for his inaction. He characterizes himself as "afraid" but does not show the genesis of his fears. Nevertheless, unlike Coleridge's Hamlet and rather like Bradley's, he has an emotional basis for vacillation. In him we see Eliot's synthesizing power at an original pitch. And in an aspect that distances Prufrock from Hamlet, a certain sexual hesitancy (better witnessed in the suppressed section of the poem, "Prufrock's Pervigilium," with its aversions from repellent fantasies), Eliot hinted at a moral posture that is possibly implicit in the unexplained fearfulness of "an overwhelming question." Prufrock in his un-Hamletlike difficulty—for his failure to act pertains to a "love song"—resembles Coleridge's Hamlet in perhaps *rationalizing* a moral reluctance. Yet, as Robert M. Seiler has pointed out, Prufrock does not formulate an intellectual argument and does not even utter his

7. *Shakespearean Tragedy* (London: Macmillan, 1904), 107.

"question" to himself like Hamlet; rather, he presents himself in emotional terms.[8] Evidently, however, Prufrock's reticence is appropriate to the intimacy of his dramatic monologue, and above all to Eliot's poetic technique of transforming thought into feeling. Even so, the effect differs greatly from the one outlined by Coleridge, and also the overtones of self-disgust recall details of Hamlet's behavior that Coleridge neglected.

Eliot had probably not read Ernest Jones before writing "Prufrock." Jones's original article, "The Oedipus-Complex as an Explanation of Hamlet's Mystery: A Study in Motive," appeared in January 1910, and so was contemporaneous with the poem; but it dealt with Hamlet and Gertrude and not with aboulia on the order of Prufrock's. Although the Oedipal hypothesis was initiated by Freud, not Jones, it is unlikely that Eliot with his undergraduate stock of German had read the pertinent pages in Freud's then untranslated *The Interpretation of Dreams*, dating from 1900. It is true that he could have known of Freud's speculations about Hamlet. If so, he did not use them. Like Bradley, and unlike Goethe and Coleridge, both Freud and Jones insist on a Hamlet who is *instinctively* active. Freud, writing before Bradley, and Jones, writing after him, continued the emphasis on the character of Hamlet because they saw him as shaped by conditions prior to the incidents of the play. Freud began his account of Hamlet's troubles by citing Coleridge's hypothesis and attributing it in error to Goethe, and then by citing Goethe's hypothesis, very adversely, and attributing it to nobody, not even Coleridge.[9] In his original essay Jones made the same Freudian slip but silently amended it on better acquaintance with Shakespearean scholarship. Of Freud and Jones, more anon.

Eliot, in his 1919 review of Robertson's *The Problem of "Hamlet,"* echoed Türck's remark about Goethe, which he had read in Robertson, and Bradley's remark about Coleridge, which he had got somewhere else. Speaking of minds that "often find in Hamlet a vicarious existence for their own artistic realization," Eliot snapped: "Such a mind had Goethe, who made of Hamlet a Werther; and such had Coleridge, who made of Hamlet a Coleridge." He stuck by his animadversions against Goethe and Coleridge and in 1923 would

---

8. "Prufrock and Hamlet," *English* 21 (Summer 1972): 41–43.
9. *The Basic Writings of Sigmund Freud*, trans. and ed. A. A. Brill (New York: Modern Library, 1938), 309–11.

paraphrase the 1919 comment in "The Function of Criticism."[10] But in 1910 he himself had made of Hamlet a Prufrock, not without Coleridge's conception of Hamlet as a man incapable of action.

The mischief done by Coleridge had diffused itself throughout nineteenth-century *Hamlet* criticism, becoming thereby injurious. His view of Hamlet established itself not merely in criticism but in the theater, and extended also to literary adaptations of the Hamlet figure in the novel. Just as the Werther of Goethe models for Wilhelm Meister's sensitive, *fainéant* Hamlet, so a species of brooding irreconcilables, self-doubting but inwardly challenged to daring, ruminates the peculiar difficulties of practical action in the pages of novelists as different as Dostoevsky, James, and Conrad.

In Coleridgean terms, the Raskolnikov of Dostoevsky's *Crime and Punishment* is an anti-Hamlet, resolving his interior debate by purposive violence. Not by this fact does he deviate truly from the Hamlet forgotten by Coleridge, the Hamlet who runs Polonius through and sends Rosencrantz and Guildenstern to their deaths— but then he has descended in the line of the Byronic hero, himself more faithful to an active Shakespearean archetype. Like both the Byronic hero and the Coleridgean intellectual, Raskolnikov is self-absorbed. His thinking, moreover, is burdened with the suspicion, which he acts upon to prove it a certainty, that no legitimate moral restraints exist. Unlike Hamlet in this, he performs the moral experiment of committing murder on principle. Though consumed with self-loathing, like Hamlet, he embraces the opportunism of the age he lives in and reasons that if necessity rules and right does not prevail, anything is permitted at least to the superior man without moral prejudice. Raskolnikov furnished to the characterization of Prufrock, as we know from the scholarship of John C. Pope, hints for the implication of a moral quandary in Prufrock's meditated visit to a woman—though almost nothing of Raskolnikov's urge towards violence which recalls Hamlet.[11]

Obviously Hamlet, Raskolnikov, and Prufrock each come from a different matrix of philosophical motivation; in their self-con-

10. "Hamlet and His Problems," in *Selected Essays*, 121; "The Function of Criticism" in *Selected Essays*, 21–22.

11. "Prufrock and Raskolnikov," *American Literature* 17 (November 1945): 213–30. See also Pope's "Prufrock and Raskolnikov Again: A Letter from Eliot," *American Literature* 18 (January 1947): 319–21.

scious debates within themselves they conform to the common example. Just as the seventeenth-century audience for *Hamlet* had a topical understanding of human nature and the decayed moral universe, so Dostoevsky's mid-nineteenth-century audience could relate topically to Raskolnikov's fatal adventure in the climate of modern thought. Prufrock no more draws from Raskolnikov than from Hamlet an outdated philosophical perplexity. His world—or rather Eliot's world of 1910–1911—was one of scientific doubt and moral skepticism, post-Darwinian, post-Spencerian, tentatively Bergsonian but too pessimistic to be wholeheartedly so. It was not altogether unlike Raskolnikov's world of moral despair, partly because it was shadowed by the somewhat similar, though almost wholly irreligious, world of the French poet Jules Laforgue.

The philosophical postulates of "The Love Song of J. Alfred Prufrock," such as they may have been, remain muted because Eliot made the poem an expression of character through feelings. For this reason, the example of Laforgue as much as that of Dostoevsky is evidenced in the shape of Prufrock's personal life of the emotions, not in a struggle of ideas. Laforgue had set forth the inward debate of his protagonist in the early prose sketch "Hamlet" (*Moralités légendaires*, 1887) as a mere confrontation with the absurdity of all action. This Hamlet, insofar as active at all, finds everything pointless. Having thought too much about the impotence of his will, he believes that his every judgment on existence escapes his control. Laforgue's Hamlet has fallen consciously, as he admits, under the influence of the philosopher Eduard von Hartmann, inventor of the panpsychic Unconscious. Unlike Raskolnikov's philosophers of self-interest, Hartmann snatches away from the individual all power of choice. To the positivists' repudiation of cause and purpose he presents the complementary image of a universe managed by the Unconscious, whose cosmic purposes are unfathomable. Under the blind eye of the Unconscious—what Thomas Hardy called the "immanent will"—every human act is meaningless automatism. But the Hamlet of the *Moralités légendaires* is tormented by a double vision—of this biological automatism and of a sentimental aspiration toward beauty and decency (Baudelaire's double vision of spleen and ideal). No more than Prufrock does he act constructively, but he does act, committing petty acts of atrocious cruelty in a spirit of "it's of no consequence." He somewhat recalls Raskolnikov in his experimental amorality; but more exquisitely divided in his feelings, he suffers agonies repeatedly for his clinical daring. This Hamlet, less than a generation after Dostoevsky's novel, takes refuge in the maxim "everything is allowed" but finds no solace.[12] Perhaps something of the double vision, in a paradoxical form of resignation and yearning, passes to Prufrock from this Hamlet, who confesses love for his Ophelia but cannot trust her. Yet, though Prufrock's heritage of self-doubling, self-doubting, self-preening is Laforguian in general, the hesitancy in paying court to a woman partakes more of timidity and sloth than of Laforguian cynicism.

The manner in which the Hamlet of Shakespeare as variously interpreted was combined with Hamletlike traits in Dostoevsky, with the tragical burlesque of Laforgue, and with compatible materials from Henry James, to make Prufrock into a new Hamlet, is not remarkable in Eliot's poetry. Composite transformation of sources occurs as a usual technique; it was deliberate, but the poetic act must have required from Eliot much unconscious synthesis. Those who have troubled to follow the zigzag of my demonstration will have noted that the theme of frustrated action, similar to Eliot's personal inhibition, shapes Prufrock to the model of a Hamlet regarded in one critical tradition (Coleridge) as incapable of acting, in another (Bradley) as balked by his emotional state. The theme of suppressed violence, intrinsic to the Hamlet story and elaborated into barbarity in other sources used by Eliot (Dostoevsky and Laforgue), receives different treatment in the poem. Though Prufrock refers once to murder as something he might do, any death theme is self-directed. As a creature pierced by a pin or drowned in sea caves, or as a fantasized self in transformation as Lazarus or a victim for some Salome, he himself suffers. In Laforgue's "Hamlet" the protagonist is killed by Laertes with a dagger; none of the obvious sources show violence inflicted on a Hamlet by a woman. But all of Prufrock's imagined perils involve the female, and even Lazarus resurrected would be restored to the ministrations of his sisters! Prufrock runs no risk of killing a woman, like Raskolnikov. He is throughout a Jamesian submissive male. Such was Eliot's primary addition to the Hamlet image, a Hamlet strained through the fine gauze of a Jamesian sensibility.

The theme of inaction in Eliot's poems is overshadowed by the situation in which it generally occurs: the confrontation with a

12. *Selected Writings of Jules Laforgue*, trans. and ed. William Jay Smith (Westport, Conn.: Greenwood, 1972), 116.

woman. This takes us back to Shakespeare and again also to Robertson. Robertson argued that Shakespeare's play exhibited the textual evolution of its hero from occupation with revenge into obsession with disgust. *Hamlet,* for purely textual reasons, mingles the characteristics of Kyd's Ur-*Hamlet* with others introduced by Shakespeare himself. Robertson, dismissing the perennial problem of Hamlet's character, quoted Poe's comment: "It is not . . . the inconsistencies of [Hamlet] which we have as a subject of discussion . . . but the whims and vacillations, the conflicting energies and indolences of the poet." The question suggested by Poe is different from the one addressed by Robertson. Poe is stimulating our curiosity as to *why* Shakespeare made the character of Hamlet inconsistent, and as to *what* "whims and vacillations . . . conflicting energies and indolences" prevented Shakespeare from solving his technical "problem of adaptation," as Robertson repeatedly termed it.[13]

Eliot in "Hamlet and His Problems" responds not to Robertson but to Poe. Challenged to enlarge on Poe's discernment, Eliot grants to Robertson that *Hamlet* "is a play dealing with the effect of a mother's guilt upon her son, and that Shakespeare was unable to impose this motive successfully upon the 'intractable' material of the old play." So his play is "an artistic failure." And why is it so? Because, Eliot says,

> *Hamlet,* like the sonnets, is full of some stuff that the writer could not drag to light, contemplate, or manipulate into art. . . . Hamlet (the man) is dominated by an emotion which is inexpressible, because it is in *excess* of the facts as they appear. And the supposed identity of Hamlet with his author is genuine to this point: that Hamlet's bafflement at the absence of objective equivalent to his feelings is a prolongation of the bafflement of his creator in the face of his artistic problem. Hamlet is up against the difficulty that his disgust is occasioned by his mother, but that his mother is not an adequate equivalent for it; his disgust envelops and exceeds her. . . . None of the possible actions can satisfy it; and nothing that Shakespeare can do with the plot can express Hamlet for him. . . . The intense feeling, ecstatic or terrible, without an object or exceeding its object, is something which every person of sensibility has known; it is doubtless a subject of study for pathologists. It often occurs in adolescence: the ordinary person puts these feelings to sleep, or trims down his feelings to fit the business world; the artist keeps them alive by his ability to intensify the world to his emotions. The Hamlet of Laforgue is an

13. Robertson, *The Problem of "Hamlet,"* 25.

adolescent; the Hamlet of Shakespeare is not, he has not that explanation and excuse. We must simply admit that here Shakespeare tackled a problem which proved too much for him . . . . [U]nder compulsion of what experience he attempted to express the inexpressibly horrible, we cannot ever know . . . . We should have to understand things which Shakespeare did not understand himself.[14]

The presence in the play of an indistinct but violent emotion, one not objectified—this, according to Eliot, implies an anterior emotion, conceived through some personal experience, that Shakespeare could not objectify. In this advance beyond Robertson and Poe into a dimension of psychology where the motives of what Poe terms "conflicting energies and indolences" have their origin, but which remains mysterious to the conscious artist, Eliot has ventured to invade the domain of Freud and Ernest Jones. But he has not subscribed to the Freudian interpretation of Hamlet. Instead he has silently ratified its assumption that Hamlet is blocked by feelings he cannot define, and that Shakespeare suffers from a like powerlessness. He does not say, "blocked by an Oedipus complex."

This is well, for Ernest Jones's demonstration of Hamlet's Oedipal dilemma analyzes, logically but absurdly, a fictional personage about whom a good deal is known psychologically but who possesses no psyche. In order to do this it has to attribute, according to its reductive principle, an Oedipus complex to Shakespeare, a real person with a psyche but about whom little is known psychologically. That Shakespeare had an Oedipus complex before Freud invented it was impossible to document, and neither Freud nor Jones attempted to do so. Eliot, though by 1919 he must have read or heard of Jones's Hamlet article of 1910 or the German enlarged version of 1911, was clearly not prepared to embrace the Oedipal interpretation. In form, however, his appeal to a kind of universal that he imputes to Shakespeare (an "intense feeling, ecstatic or terrible, without an object or exceeding its object") and his hypothesis of parallelism between Shakespeare and Hamlet are consonant with the Freudian doctrine that the disease of the writer can be diagnosed in his creation. In "Hamlet and His Problems," Eliot is psychologizing, and with some fidelity to the Freudian method, though not the theory. He always psychologized, as *The Waste Land* broadly exemplifies, and he was to toy with Freudian methods once again in *The Family Reunion.*

14. "Hamlet" (1932 text), in *Selected Essays*, 123, 124–26.

The review of Robertson in effect reaffirms the centrality of Hamlet the character, but against Robertson it confirms Poe's and the Freudians' involvement of the personal Shakespeare in the criticism. Eliot in 1919 was concerned to involve also the personal Eliot. I make no question that, to his later mention of aboulia or paralysis of will, we should now add this account of "intense feeling . . . without an object" as another self-analysis. I have discussed in a recent monograph the opinion I hold of the poem "Gerontion" (written in the spring before the Hamlet essay), namely that the poem demonstrates an effort to objectify, through an intense self-dramatization on the part of its protagonist, exactly such intense feeling without the failure alleged of Shakespeare's Hamlet.[15] "Gerontion," like "Prufrock," depicts a confrontation with a woman. As in "Prufrock," she is not a mother-figure; at the same time she is less visible but more immediate than the remote lady of Prufrock's imagined solicitations, for she is the unspeaking auditor of Gerontion's dramatic monologue. "Gerontion" constitutes a new transformation of the Hamlet type and situation enriched by Eliot's mature observations on Shakespeare, with conscious attention to Hamlet's disgust with women, particularly his mother, and to Shakespeare's supposed writer's block—something familiar to Eliot himself. A more complex and elaborate rendering of the Hamlet archetype than "Prufrock," it contains more diverse associated source materials and is more maturely personal. It joins to its passage reminiscent of Hamlet's confrontations the hint of an analogous moment in Tourneur's *The Revenger's Tragedy*, a play that Eliot, as he wrote a decade later, considered to be like *Hamlet* in expressing "the poet's inner world of nightmare, some horror beyond words."[16] The theme of arrested or inhibited action from "Prufrock" passes over into "Gerontion" as the speaker's history of inaction.

The paralysis and bafflement supposed of Hamlet recur in Eliot's poetic work, but it is otiose to identify them further; *The Hollow Men* explores them with a new music and paradoxically a fresh artistic vigor—their practical defeat through art. The theme of transcendence of inaction through an ethic of right action, artistic and otherwise, merits my notice here because of its advanced in-

15. See my *The Waste Land* (London: George Allen and Unwin, 1983), 29–34.
16. "Cyril Tourneur," in *Selected Essays*, 166.

volvement of *Hamlet* as a model for *The Family Reunion*, Eliot's play of 1939. This is a drama more complicated in its sources and allusiveness than its philosophical content. It seems to me now a sound play, with philosophic premises easily within the reach of the educated, and perplexing only in the obscurity of its mythological vaudeville; it is a play that at first teases curiosity without appeasing it. The connection with *Hamlet* begins with the protagonist but extends to the plot. The Hamletlike hero, Harry Lord Monchensey, brings mental activity into a cast and setting that are strangely static, but he also soon displays a kind of social paralysis. The reason is that activity is not action. The quest for vocation, something to occupy a life with right action, needs to attain definition and acceptance. This I think is the dominant theme of *The Family Reunion*.

Harry comes home, like Hamlet, from foreign travel. He is distraught and is bearing the delusion that he has murdered his wife by drowning her. He is persecuted by specters, three family ghosts, apparently—styled the Eumenides in the list of characters. They replace the Ghost of Hamlet's father and have a comparable function, inciting Harry to come to terms with his moral responsibilities through self-knowledge and right action. They project the past of his family: his father as he was in life, his mother and aunt as they were in his childhood. But Harry must learn from the living the truth about the past and his relation to it. By his aunt, Agatha, he is told of the family curse that eclipsed his childhood with portents of his present unhappiness. A murder had been planned while Harry was yet unborn: Harry's father and Agatha herself, linked adulterously, had meditated killing her sister Amy, Harry's mother.[17] The murder never occurred; but Amy, rejected by her husband, became fixated on her son Harry and determined his future psychological ills by her destructive mother-will.

The liberation of Harry from the burden of his past unhappy marriage and from the other consequences of his mother's domination—especially from his powerlessness to revitalize his emotional forces (his ignorance of the family past grips him in something analogous to aboulia)—is achieved with the help of Agatha. With her

17. Eliot's substitution in the murder plot of the aunt for Hamlet's uncle as murderer, of the father for Hamlet's mother as accomplice, and of the mother for Hamlet's father as victim has apparently kept critics from seeing the resemblance to *Hamlet*.

he rediscovers his power to live; sharing her emotional history and that of his parents, he can separate himself from the evil consequences of their sins. The doubleness of Agatha's function as an agent both of past ills and of present good derives not from *Hamlet*, of course, but from Eliot's adapting the role of Athena from the *Oresteia* of Aeschylus, a parallel source for the play and the main source along with Ibsen's *Ghosts* for the motif of a family curse. This curse can destroy or redeem its heir. The Eumenides, no goddesses, represent both aspects of Agatha, and so Harry is seen fleeing them at the start of the play, following them at the end. Putting behind him his aunt (no longer needed as a foster-mother), his own mother (who indeed dies in the final minutes of the play), and his already rejected cousin, Mary (who offers nothing sustaining in her Ophelia role), Harry departs like a Shavian realist to his liberation and spiritual cleansing. He will devote himself to action unspecified, but in a selfless and un-self-regarding spirit.

That Eliot had in mind the Freud-Jones hypothesis about Hamlet's "bafflement," as he himself had called it, is strongly indicated by the juxtaposition of Hamlet to an Oedipal situation in *The Family Reunion*. That the play uses Freud to a religious purpose shows Eliot's ingenuity and talent for strategic surprise. The ethic of the play, less Christian than Buddhist, draws upon the doctrine of karma, right action with the acceptance of consequences, which forms the dominant ethical principle of Eliot's dramas as a group, as well as *Four Quartets.* The mythology of the Eumenides comes from the Greek theater with the backing of Gilbert Murray's celebrated treatise *Hamlet and Orestes*, in which Eliot may have found inspiration for the ritualistic portrayal of Harry as a scapegoat or expiatory figure.[18] Murray provides various anthropological sidelights on both Orestes and Hamlet in this respect. All in all, however, the most significant artistic transformation achieved in *The Family Reunion* is the reversal of Hamlet's traditional inaction in Harry's conversion to right action.

Eliot's poetry contains many ghosts; and the most remarkable, if artificial, one appears in part II of the final *Quartet*, "Little Gidding." I do not propose to enumerate the literary and historical components, some unfamiliar, of this "familiar compound ghost." I will only mention two: first the Ghost of Hamlet's father, who, in the

18. See Gilbert Murray, *Hamlet and Orestes: A Study in Traditional Types* (New York: Oxford University Press, 1914).

line spoken by Marcellus, "faded on the crowing of the cock," and in the person of the poet-ghost of "Little Gidding" "faded on the blowing of the horn"—the battlements of Elsinore having been transformed into a bombarded London street, and the dawn after the fire-raid being heralded by a modern signal of relief and recommitment to purgation.

The other is the ghost of Hamlet himself. In act 4, scene 4, Hamlet soliloquizes before the army of Fortinbras, arrayed to take a mere "patch of ground" in Poland, and muses on the triviality of the war and on the reproach it implies to his delays. In this small enterprise a vast number of men must fall in death simply for a point of honor, while he, for reasons scarcely clear to himself, is not roused in a cause far greater. With a fine Stoic reasoning he exclaims:

> What is a man,
> If his chief good and market of his time
> Be but to sleep and feed? a beast, no more.
> Sure, he that made us with such large discourse,
> Looking before and after, gave us not
> That capability and god-like reason
> To fust in us unused.[19]

The compound ghost in "Little Gidding" employs some of the same expressions to turn upside down Hamlet's whole argument for dedicated action. The life of fame, the life of the hero or poet, yields a temporary fruit—the fruit of action in the Indic framework of the *Quartets*—that satisfies but the passing appetite of the animal man: "Last season's fruit is eaten / And the fullfed beast shall kick the empty pail." The superior man hungry for fame inherits at best the "bitter tastelessness of shadow fruit / As body and soul begin to fall asunder," with ever greater repugnance both toward the world without and toward the self of the personal world with its mounting conviction of unworthiness and failure. In the mouth of the ghost in "Little Gidding," the gift (in Shakespeare's words) of "large discourse, / Looking before and after" executes no longer the task of the living poet (in Eliot's words) to "urge the mind to aftersight and foresight"; instead it is employed by the dead poet intent upon counseling the living one, from an eternal perspective, on his moral reality. The ghost testifies to a doctrine of eternal consequences, the law of karma which implies that every action leads to

19. *The Complete Works of Shakespeare*, ed. Hardin Craig (Chicago: Scott, Foresman, 1961), act 4, scene 4, lines 33–39.

another in an unending sequence of responsibilities. Like the Ghost of Hamlet's father, this ghost, at break of day, goes again to his purgation; his message has transformed the rhetoric of Hamlet the son, here the Eliot figure in the duologue, into that of Hamlet the father, here the multiplex dead generations of Eliot's poet predecessors.

I should like to establish a further Hamlet link between this scene of the battlefield of wartime London and the moment in the third *Quartet*, "The Dry Salvages," when Eliot invokes the Hindu god Krishna. Hamlet, at the end of the soliloquy from which I have quoted, summons up the contrast between the soon dead of Fortinbras's army and himself in his inaction:

> How stand I then,
> That have a father kill'd, a mother stain'd,
> Excitements of my reason and my blood,
> And let all sleep? while, to my shame, I see
> The imminent death of twenty thousand men,
> That, for a fantasy and trick of fame,
> Go to their graves like beds, fight for a plot
> Whereon the numbers cannot try the cause,
> Which is not tomb enough and continent
> To hide the slain?[20]

The warrior prince Arjuna, in the *Bhagavad-Gita*, stands like Hamlet contemplating impending battle and questions the god Krishna, incarnate as his charioteer, concerning the morality of the violent action into which his army, following his lead, is about to be plunged. What, he asks, can justify so terrible an action? Krishna tells him that the action, the karma, does not matter, if only he enters into it selflessly, if only he does not seek the fruits of action. In "The Dry Salvages" the situation of Hamlet, consciously or unconsciously for Eliot, becomes a type of the hesitation that lays hold of Arjuna. The moral self-doubt of Hamlet, too, is now rebuked by the voice of the god: so long as his duty is done, no man need fear the moral consequences, but his duty is to confer good upon others and seek nothing for himself. And so in "The Dry Salvages" Eliot writes:

> At the moment which is not of action or inaction
> You can receive this: 'on whatever sphere of being
> The mind of a man may be intent

20. Ibid., act 4, scene 4, lines 56–65.

At the time of death'—that is the one action
(And the time of death is every moment)
Which shall fructify in the lives of others:
And do not think of the fruit of action.
Fare forward.

In Eliot the figure of Hamlet, at the period of *Four Quartets* in the 1940s, no longer represented the spirit of inaction. It had transcended its own form to participate in a poetic reconciliation of the paralyzed will with its elusive active function. Hamlet at last was fully sane. Eliot's work shows no finer example of the gradual and at length perfected assimilation of a literary model to a developing art.

Mixing Memory and Imagination
James Olney

My title is a conflation of two phrases from T. S. Eliot: the first and more famous is from the first lines of *The Waste Land*, in which April, "the cruellest month," comes "mixing/ Memory and desire"; the second, less well-known phrase occurs in *The Use of Poetry and the Use of Criticism* when, after an extraordinarily interesting discussion of the place of memory in the imaginative life of the poet (in this case, Coleridge), Eliot remarks, "There is so much memory in imagination. . . ."[1] My essential subject, then, is memory, and because of that, I want to begin with a memory of a memory of a memory and I want to end in a similar fashion with a memory of a memory of a memory. In this way I wish, first, to point up something of the *layeredness* of memory—we are forever adding to the sum of ourselves not only memories of experience but also memories of memories. Second, I wish to suggest that we can never possess consciousness of experience in the moment of experience but only in memory of it.

Up to this point I have been referring to memories of memories that in large part constitute the conscious life of any individual and that, I believe, play an extremely important part in producing the material of poetry. But the memories that I will begin and end with are not of this individual nature; they are memories shared around or passed on from one person to another, and this kind of remembering activity has much to do, I think, with the way we respond to poetry and in some fashion take it into ourselves. The first layered series of memories is made up of my memory of Valerie Eliot's memory of T. S. Eliot's memory of his childhood years in St. Louis. In the number of *The Southern Review* devoted to Eliot, I quoted these relevant sentences from one of Mrs. Eliot's letters about their visit to St. Louis in 1958: "I shall never forget [that is, she shall

---

1. *The Use of Poetry and the Use of Criticism: Studies in the Relation of Criticism to Poetry in England* (London: Faber, 1933), 79.

always remember] being taken there for my first and only time by Tom. He almost became a schoolboy as the train approached the station."[2] Surely it was recalled experiences of sixty and more years before that caused Eliot's excitement and that transformed him into the schoolboy he had been in St. Louis long ago. With this memoried experience—as recalled from Valerie Eliot's memory of T. S. Eliot's memory of boyhood—I want to reflect for a moment on the nature of memories of very early experience, especially as those memories return in age, and then I want to go on to consider what I think to be a pattern of change in the exercise of memory in Eliot's poetry.

Sir Herbert Read, who was a friend of Eliot's for nearly fifty years, has said some pertinent things about early memory in a beautiful little book called *The Innocent Eye*, and as I am going to base much of what I want to say about the progress of memory in Eliot's poetry on Read's rather Wordsworthian notions of memory, I want to quote two or three extended passages from *The Innocent Eye*. The beauty of the passages, even if they were not so intensely relevant to my subject, would go a long way toward justifying their quotation here. In the first passage Read describes the night sounds he heard as a child growing up on an isolated farm in Yorkshire:

> The night-sound that still echoes in my mind, however, is not of this kind [i.e., "the abysmal cry of some hellish beast"]: it is gentler and more musical—the distant sound of horse-hooves on the highroad, at first dim and uncertain, but growing louder until they more suddenly cease. To that distant sound I realized later, I must have come into the world, for the doctor arrived on horseback at four o'clock one December morning to find me uttering my first shriek.
>
> I think I heard those hooves again the night my father died, but of this I am not certain; perhaps I shall remember when I come to relate that event, for now the memory of those years, which end shortly after my tenth birthday, comes fitfully, when the proper associations are aroused. If only I can recover the sense and uncertainty of those innocent years, years in which we seemed not so much to live as to be lived by forces outside us, by the wind and trees and moving clouds and all the mobile engines of our expanding world—then I am convinced I shall possess a key to much that has happened to me in this other world of conscious living. The echoes of my life which I find in my early childhood are too many to be dismissed as vain coincidences; but it is perhaps my conscious life which is the echo, the only real experi-

2. Valerie Eliot, "A Photographic Memoir, with a Note by James Olney," *Southern Review* 21 (October 1985): 988.

ences in life being those lived with a virgin sensibility—so that we only hear a tone once, only see a colour once, see, hear, touch, taste, and smell everything but once, the first time. All life is an echo of our first sensations, and we build up our consciousness, our whole mental life, by variations and combinations of these elementary sensations. But it is more complicated than that, for the senses apprehend not only colours and tones and shapes, but also patterns and atmospheres, and our first discovery of these determines the larger patterns and subtler atmospheres of all our subsequent existence.[3]

That we hear a tone and see a color only once, with all subsequent sensory encounters being but echoes and memories of these pristine experiences, is an immensely suggestive idea and one that hints at the profound depths at which such experiences remain with us—far beneath the reach and scrutiny of consciousness—and it hints also at the perdurability and the tenacity of such experiences.

In a second passage in *The Innocent Eye*, Read describes in expanded terms the intimate relationship of memory and imagination hinted at in the previous passage.

The kitchen was the scene of many events which afterwards flowed into my mind from the pages of books. Whenever in a tale a belated traveller saw a light and came through the darkness to ask for shelter, it was to this kitchen door. I can no longer identify the particular stories, but they do not belong to this period of childhood so much as to my later boyhood and youth, long after I had left the Farm; and even today my first memories easily usurp the function of the imagination, and clothe in familiar dimensions and patterns, exact and objective, the scenes which the romancer has purposely left vague. Perhaps the effect of all romance depends on this faculty we have of giving our own definition to the fancies of others. A mind without memories means a body without sensibility; our memories make our imaginative life, and it is only as we increase our memories, widening the imbricated shutters which divide our mind from the light, that we find with quick recognition those images of truth which the world is pleased to attribute to our creative gift.[4]

"There is," as Eliot says, "so much memory in imagination" that any reader of poetry or romance who would offer to say where one begins and the other leaves off is rushing in where the poet him-

3. *The Innocent Eye* (New York: Henry Holt, 1947), 7–8. Read is mixing memory and imagination very thoroughly indeed in his idea of what might be produced as memories when he comes to put into words the experience that is imagined as much as remembered, remembered as much as imagined.
4. Ibid., 11.

self fears to tread.[5] Not only can we not separate the two, but as Read claims, "our memories *make* our imaginative life," shaping our creative sensibilities in ways of which we can never be conscious.

My final passage from *The Innocent Eye* comes in the last chapter called "Death"; it describes the end of Read's early childhood on the Yorkshire farm. After his father's death, Read writes:

> the elder of my two brothers and I left for a boarding school, far away from these scenes; my childhood, the first phase of my life, was isolated: it grew detached in my memory and floated away like a leaf on a stream. But it never finally disappeared, as these pages witness. Instead, as this body of mine passes through the rays of experience, it meets bright points of ecstasy which come from the heart of this lost realm. But the realm is never wholly lost: it is reconstructed stage by stage whenever the sensibility recovers its first innocence, whenever eye and ear and touch and tongue and quivering nostril revive sensation in all its child-godly passivity.
>
> Today I found a withered stem of honesty, and shelled the pods between my thumb and finger; silver pennies, which grew between the fragrant currant-bushes. Their glistening surfaces, seeded, the very faint rustle they make in the wind—these sensations come direct to me from a moment thirty years ago. As they expand in my mind, they carry everything in their widening circle—the low crisp box-hedge which would be at my feet, the pear-trees on the wall behind me, the potato-flowers on the patch beyond the bushes, the ivy-clad privy at the end of the path, the cow pasture, the fairy rings—everything shimmers for a second on the expanding rim of my memory. The farthest tremor of this perturbation is lost only at the finest edge where sensation passes beyond the confines of experience; for memory is a flower which only opens fully in the kingdom of heaven, where the eye is eternally innocent.[6]

Now, Read himself maintains, rather peculiarly and I believe quite incorrectly, that Eliot ceased to write what Read calls "*pure* poetry" (in favor of what he terms "moralistic poetry") after *The Hollow Men* of 1925; there is, I believe, a rather dramatic change in the play of memory in the post–1925 poetry, but Read's separation of the oeuvre into "pure poetry" and "moralistic poetry" is not critically helpful nor is it particularly accurate.[7] It seems to me that what Eliot really does—and precisely in the poetry that comes after *The*

5. *The Use of Poetry*, 67.
6. *The Innocent Eye*, 57–58.
7. Herbert Read, "T. S. E.: A Memoir," in *T. S. Eliot: The Man and His Work*, ed. Allen Tate (New York: Dell Publishing, 1966), 34–37.

Hollow Men—is to begin to inform his poetry, in a very Read-like manner, with those earliest memories of his childhood when the eye was still innocent and *The Waste Land* and *The Hollow Men* were still unimagined.

Before considering the nature of the change that occurs in the poetry after *The Hollow Men*, I would like to look briefly at what memories are like in the earlier poems. I am almost tempted to say that there are no memories in the early poems. This, however, while not far off the mark, would not be quite true, so I will not yield to the temptation but will rather say that many of the memories of the early poetry are demonstrably not Eliot's own and that the imagery in which other memories find expression is so abstract, so generalized, so stylized that, as memories, they seem to have no location in a specific individual sensibility. Of the former kind—memories that are clearly not Eliot's—one might cite from *The Waste Land* the recollections of the three Thames-daughters of the occasions on which they separately lost their virginity.

> "Trams and dusty trees.
> Highbury bore me. Richmond and Kew
> Undid me. By Richmond I raised my knees
> Supine on the floor of a narrow canoe."
>   (ll. 292–95)

Thus the first of the three. This is a memory, but in the poem it is presented as what the speaker hears or overhears and what he offers to us as a representative experience in the modern wasteland world. It is wrapped in quotation marks to suggest that this is the song of one of the Thames-daughters, but otherwise it is quite like the following passage, shorn of quotation marks, from "The Burial of the Dead":

> And when we were children, staying at the archduke's,
> My cousin's, he took me out on a sled,
> And I was frightened. He said, Marie,
> Marie, hold on tight. And down we went.
> In the mountains, there you feel free.
> I read, much of the night, and go south in the winter.
>   (ll. 13–18)

In an often cited note on a later passage in *The Waste Land*, Eliot tells us that "Tiresias, although a mere spectator and not indeed a 'character,' is yet the most important personage in the poem, uniting all the rest" and further writes that "What Tiresias *sees*, in fact, is the substance of the poem" (note to l. 218). I suppose that one might say that *The Waste Land* is composed of Tiresias's memories of what he has seen and heard in his experience, which spans centuries and embraces both genders, and part of what he has seen and heard is the memories of others, but this hardly brings the matter any closer to Eliot himself or to Eliot's memories. The characteristic psychic activity of the early poems is not a recollection, willed or unwilled, of past experience, but is instead observation— observation of the doings of others. The speaker of the early poems typically wanders the streets at evening or midnight, looking on, observing, recording. Prufrock, for example, begins with "Let us go then, you and I, / When the evening is spread out against the sky/ Like a patient etherised upon a table. . . ."

When I said earlier that other putative memories of the early poetry are expressed in imagery that is so abstract, so generalized, and so stylized that they cannot be located in any particular sensibility, I had in mind passages like the following, again from *The Waste Land*:

> Who are those hooded hordes swarming
> Over endless plains, stumbling in cracked earth
> Ringed by the flat horizon only
> What is the city over the mountains
> Cracks and reforms and bursts in the violet air
> Falling towers
> Jerusalem Athens Alexandria
> Vienna London
> Unreal
>
> (ll. 369–77)

Again, this might be said to be Tiresias's multi-various memory in operation, but the generic landscape of "cracked earth," "flat horizon," and "mountains" is altogether without those sensory specifics that might relate the recollections to the particular sensibility of the poet. Indeed if one thinks about it, the early poetry is lacking in any sense of landscape at all; the locus of the early poetry is almost entirely urban and there is little, if any, reference to natural scenes. Does this mean that Eliot had no memories attached to landscape? I think we will discover that this is not at all what it means, but it is a relevant fact that if he had such memories they are seldom evident in the poems through *The Hollow Men*.

Having mentioned the absence of memories attached to landscape in the early poems, let me cite an example that might seem to confute this. The passage is again from *The Waste Land*:

> The boat responded
> Gaily, to the hand expert with sail and oar
> The sea was calm, your heart would have responded
> Gaily, when invited, beating obedient
> To controlling hands
>
> (ll. 419–23)

Eliot, as is well known, loved the sea and sailing, and something of this feeling from past experience infuses these lines; nevertheless the scene remains a generalized one and it is important to recognize that the experience associated with the scene is one of irretrievable failure—failure to invite response (the same kind of failure found in the earlier passage about the "hyacinth girl")—and this association of failure with memories realized in images from nature or natural landscape is something we find in early poems but not in the later poems.

I will suggest in a moment that certain passages from "Rhapsody on a Windy Night" make in the most effective way many of the points that I have been at pains to make about memory in the early poems. Before I do that, however, I would remark that what Trevor Nunn and Andrew Lloyd Webber have done in *Cats* with "Rhapsody on a Windy Night" and phrases from other early poems is about as far removed as one could imagine from the reality of those poems.

> Memory. All alone in the moonlight
> I can smile at the old days.
> I was beautiful then.
> I remember the time I knew what happiness was,
> Let the memory live again.
> . . . .
> Daylight. I must wait for the sunrise
> I must think of a new life
> And I mustn't give in.
> . . . .
> Touch me. It's so easy to leave me
> All alone with the memory
> Of my days in the sun.
> If you touch me you'll understand what happiness is.
> Look, a new day has begun.[8]

These are not lines written by T. S. Eliot nor could they ever have been. The note to "Memory" in the program for *Cats* says the lyric "Memory" by Trevor Nunn incorporates lines from Eliot's "Rhapsody on a Windy Night" and other Prufrock poems, but it does so

8. *Cats: The Book of the Musical* (London: Faber, 1981), 98.

in a context so utterly different that if anyone should imagine it possible to go to "Memory" for a sense of what that faculty represents in Eliot's early poetry, he or she would be sadly misguided and disappointed. I insist on this because "Rhapsody on a Windy Night" (in contrast to Trevor Nunn's lyric) gives a particularly clear and grim indication of the nature of memory—or, rather, of the *failures* of memory—in the early poetry. Here is the authentic vision of "Rhapsody on a Windy Night":

> Twelve o'clock.
> Along the reaches of the street
> Held in a lunar synthesis,
> Whispering lunar incantations
> Dissolve the floors of memory
> And all its clear relations
> Its divisions and precisions,
> Every street lamp that I pass
> Beats like a fatalistic drum,
> And through the spaces of the dark
> Midnight shakes the memory
> As a madman shakes a dead geranium.
> . . . .
> The memory throws up high and dry
> A crowd of twisted things,
> A twisted branch . . .
> A broken spring in a factory yard. . . .
> . . . .
> "The moon has lost her memory.
> A washed-out smallpox cracks her face . . . ,
> She is alone
> With all the old nocturnal smells
> That cross and cross across her brain."
> The reminiscence comes
> Of sunless dry geraniums
> And dust in crevices,
> Smells of chestnuts in the streets,
> And female smells in shuttered rooms,
> And cigarettes in corridors
> And cocktail smells in bars.

As the "lunar incantations / Dissolve the floors of memory" and "Midnight shakes the memory / As a madman shakes a dead geranium," the images of reminiscence are all urban, surrealistic, hallucinatory, diseased, to a certain degree terrifying, and almost entirely repugnant and repulsive.

Here I want to turn for a moment to the meditation on memory that occupies the tenth book of St. Augustine's *Confessions*, and I do so the more readily because I believe that Eliot was intensely aware of Augustine and profoundly influenced by his thought throughout his career and especially in the poetry that came after his conversion in 1927. "It is I myself who remember, I, the mind," Augustine writes. "Yet this force of my memory is incomprehensible to me, even though, without it, I should not be able to call myself myself."[9] It is an absolute equivalence between memory and selfhood that Augustine argues for, and he maintains, as do modern researchers like Oliver Sacks and A. R. Luria, not to mention a Wordsworthian poet like Herbert Read, that an achieved identity is impossible without memory. In some real sense we *are* our memories. "Great indeed is the power of memory!" Augustine exclaims. "It is something terrifying, my God, a profound and infinite multiplicity; and this thing is the mind and this thing is I myself."[10] Thus, to return to "Rhapsody on a Windy Night," the midnight dissolution of "the floors of memory" signifies something like the disintegration of ego, the loss of an integrated identity or selfhood—hence the surrealistic and hallucinatory images that assault the consciousness of that poem.

I have already suggested that memory figures in a radically new way in the poetry Eliot wrote after his conversion, and I should now like to locate the change more specifically in *Ash-Wednesday* (published in parts from 1927 to 1930), in "Marina" (which was the Ariel poem for 1930), in "Landscapes" (some of which were written during the year 1932–1933 when Eliot was in America to deliver the Charles Eliot Norton lectures in poetry at Harvard University), and in the Norton lectures themselves, which Eliot published in 1933 under the title *The Use of Poetry and the Use of Criticism*. I will take a single passage from *Ash-Wednesday* as an example because, while I believe the change is quite evident in this passage, there are other things going on in that poem that make the transition less than complete or less than unqualified. The passage I choose is from the third section of the poem:

> At the first turning of the third stair
> Was a slotted window bellied like the fig's fruit
> And beyond the hawthorn blossom and the pasture scene

9. *The Confessions of Saint Augustine*, trans. Rex Warner (New York: New American Library, 1963), 226.
    10. Ibid., 227.

The broadbacked figure drest in blue and green
Enchanted the maytime with an antique flute.
Blown hair is sweet, brown hair over the mouth blown,
Lilac and brown hair;
Distraction, music of the flute, stops and steps of the mind
    over the third stair,
Fading, fading; strength beyond hope and despair
Climbing the third stair.

The sense and the feel of this passage are very different from what might be thought comparable passages in earlier poems, yet I would not say that this represents fully the change that will come to complete fruition in *Four Quartets* because the memories of "a slotted window bellied like the fig's fruit," of "hawthorn blossom and a pasture scene," of "brown hair over the mouth blown, / Lilac and brown hair" are all of them, like the "music of the flute," felt at this stage of memorial progression to be "Distraction . . . stops and steps of the mind over the third stair, / Fading, fading." I do believe, however, that although such memories are said to be distractions, they are powerfully effective and appealing (therefore, at this point, perhaps the "fittest for renunciation" ["The Dry Salvages," II]), and they provide convincing evidence that they and similar recollections existed at some level of Eliot's memory even in those years when he chose not to bring them to consciousness and into the poems—or perhaps one should say in those years when he *could* not bring them to consciousness and into the poems. Such a conversion as Eliot experienced in the period between *The Hollow Men* and *Ash-Wednesday* would seem to have been necessary to free those memories and allow them, as Herbert Read puts it, to "expand in [the] mind" until remembering merges indistinguishably with imagining, and memory and imagination become virtually a single, creative faculty.

As I hinted a moment ago, I think it is a point of considerable relevance that Eliot composed several of the "landscape" poems while in America (and the others soon after returning to England), and it is probably equally relevant that many of the most pregnant remarks he had to make about the subject of memory—outside of the poetry that is—occurred in the lectures that he delivered at Harvard. In part at least, it was his return to America that reawakened and recharged his memories of early childhood. Nevertheless, if I had to point to one poem as *the* crucial poem in what I have termed Eliot's memorial progression, it would be "Marina," published two years in advance of his return to the United States. Writing in July 1930 to E. McKnight Kauffer, the designer who would later in that same year provide the illustration for the Ariel edition of "Marina," Eliot explained something of the theme and the scenery of the poem. "I hope you like it," Eliot wrote to Kauffer:

> I dont know whether it is any good at all. The theme is paternity; with a crisscross between the text and the quotation. The theme is a comment on the Recognition Motive in Shakespeare's later plays, and particularly of course the recognition of Pericles. The quotation is from 'Hercules Furens,' where Hercules, having killed his children in a fit of madness induced by an angry god, comes to without remembering what he has done . . . The scenery in which it is dressed up is Casco Bay, Maine. I am afraid no scenery except the Mississippi, the prairie and the North East Coast has ever made much impression on me.[11]

We might pause here briefly to return to a point made earlier: Reading this passage, one is startled to realize how void most of the early poetry is of anything to be called, in the sense of this letter, "scenery"; at the same time, one is impressed with how much "scenery" recalled from early childhood—particularly the scenery of the Mississippi and the North East Coast—there is in the late poetry. That Eliot should choose (or perhaps he did not choose—perhaps the matter is prior to conscious will or choice) or should be compelled to express what he calls "the Recognition Motive in Shakespeare's later plays" in imagery and scenery that had lain deep in his memory from childhood days is altogether significant. Recognition is the recovery of something (or someone) previously known but absent or lost to consciousness for a period of time; the recovery is effected by the connective act of memory, and recognition is thus the virtual equivalent of anamnesis. The scenery of "Marina"—and how different it is from the scenery of "Rhapsody on a Windy Night" or *The Waste Land* or *The Hollow Men*—is the scenery of "The Dry Salvages" and the imagery is the imagery of *Four Quartets* throughout. Because "Marina" is so central to the changes in the nature of memory that I am trying to trace in Eliot's poetry, I would like to quote the entire poem.

> What seas what shores what grey rocks and what islands
> What water lapping the bow

11. Quoted in *T. S. Eliot*, ed. James Olney (Oxford: Oxford University Press, 1988), 211. Shakespeare's Pericles recovers, in a way that seems to him miraculous, his daughter, Marina, and his wife, Thaisa, both of whom he had thought dead.

And scent of pine and the woodthrush singing through the fog
What images return
O my daughter.

Those who sharpen the tooth of the dog, meaning
Death
Those who glitter with the glory of the humming-bird, meaning
Death
Those who sit in the stye of contentment, meaning
Death
Those who suffer the ecstasy of the animals, meaning
Death

Are become unsubstantial, reduced by a wind,
A breath of pine, and the woodsong fog
By this grace dissolved in place

What is this face, less clear and clearer
The pulse in the arm, less strong and stronger—
Given or lent? more distant than stars and nearer than the eye

Whispers and small laughter between leaves and hurrying feet
Under sleep, where all the waters meet.

Bowsprit cracked with ice and paint cracked with heat.
I made this, I have forgotten
And remember.
The rigging weak and the canvas rotten
Between one June and another September.
Made this unknowing, half conscious, unknown, my own.
The garboard strake leaks, the seams need caulking.
This form, this face, this life
Living to live in a world of time beyond me; let me
Resign my life for this life, my speech for that unspoken,
The awakened, lips parted, the hope, the new ships.

What seas what shores what granite islands towards my timbers
And woodthrush calling through the fog
My daughter.

It is astonishing to me that "Marina,"—which is a poem of recognition, of anamnesis, of renewal, of recovery of memories that had been long buried or forgotten or denied—should be considered by Read the beginning of Eliot's "moralistic" poetry and outside the bounds of his "pure poetry." It was Read himself who wrote that "our memories make our imaginative life, and it is only as we increase our memories, widening the imbricated shutters which divide our mind from the light, that we find with quick recognition those images of truth which the world is pleased to attribute to our creative gift."[12] "What images return?" the poem asks, and one might extend the query to ask not only what images return but whence. Surely the answer is that they return from the realm of childhood and from the time when, in Read's own phrase, the eye was still innocent.

As I arrived at this point in composing this essay, I happened to be reading a splendid biography of Beethoven by Maynard Solomon. I want to emphasize that it was purely by chance that I was reading this biography: the book had been a birthday present, not of my choosing, and I began to read it with no intention at all of advancing my understanding of Eliot. But when I came to the point where Solomon describes those more or less minor works that in retrospect one can see were the necessary technical and thematic preparation for the late quartets, I seemed to feel that I was reading not only about Beethoven but also about Eliot and *his* late quartets. Critics of Eliot, acting on hints from the poet himself, have generally understood that the *Four Quartets* are in some sense intended to be analogous to the late Beethoven quartets (opuses 127, 130, 131, 132, and 135), but I am not aware that anyone has previously pointed out that works that preceded these two supreme achievements show striking similarities. I do not have space to develop these similarities in full, but what Solomon says of those Beethoven exercises in fugue, in variation, and in polyphony that prepared him for the great achievement of the late quartets is that "With the Bagatelles, op. 126, and the Diabelli Variations (Thirty-three Variations on a Waltz by Diabelli, op.120), Beethoven became a master miniaturist, capable of sketching a variety of emotional states in a few quick tone strokes."[13] It is perhaps not insignificant that Eliot called a group of minor poems of the early 1930s "Five-finger Exercises"; in any case, Solomon's description of Beethoven's Bagatelles and the Diabelli Variations could also serve as a description of "Marina" and the five poems gathered together as "Landscapes." Before glancing at a couple of the "Landscapes" and then going on to the culmination of what I have been trying to say with a brief consideration of *Four Quartets*, I want to read what Solomon says of variation, bearing in mind all the time that *mutatis mutandis* this could be said equally of the gradually developing technique of variation in "Landscapes" and *Four Quartets*.

12. *The Innocent Eye*, 11–12.
13. *Beethoven* (New York: Schirmer, 1977), 305.

Variation is the form of shifting moods, alternations of feeling, shades of meaning, dislocations of perspective. It shatters appearance into splinters of previously unperceived reality and, by an act of will, reassembles the fragments at the close. The sense of time is effaced—expanded, contracted—by changes in tempo; space and mass dissolved into the barest outline of the harmonic progressions and built up once again into baroque structures laden with richly ornamented patterns. The theme remains throughout as an anchor to prevent fantasy from losing contact with the outer world, but it too dissolves into the memories, images, and feelings which underlie its simple reality.[14]

"Memories, images, and feelings" sketched "in a few quick tone strokes": this is what the "Landscapes" are; but in *Four Quartets* these "fragments," as Solomon calls them, these miniatures and variations, will be combined and recombined, reassembled "at the close," and built up "once again into baroque structures laden with richly ornamented patterns." Here is "New Hampshire," the first of the "Landscapes":

> Children's voices in the orchard
> Between the blossom- and the fruit-time:
> Golden head, crimson head,
> Between the green tip and the root.
> Black wing, brown wing, hover over;
> Twenty years and the spring is over;
> To-day grieves, to-morrow grieves,
> Cover me over, light-in-leaves;
> Golden head, black wing,
> Cling, swing,
> Spring, sing,
> Swing up into the apple-tree.

Any reader of *Four Quartets* will know what Eliot does with the "Children's voices in the orchard," with the children covered "over, light-in-leaves," and with the children in the apple-tree, particularly what he does with them, these elements of variation, "at the close," as Solomon puts it. At the close of individual *Quartets*, elements from that poem are reassembled; at the close of the entire group, elements from all four are built up again "into baroque structures laden with richly ornamented patterns." "Cape Ann," the last of the five "Landscapes," begins:

> O quick quick quick, quick hear the song-sparrow,
> Swamp-sparrow, fox-sparrow, vesper-sparrow

14. Ibid., 303.

> At dawn and dusk. Follow the dance
> Of the goldfinch at noon.

It proceeds through the calls of a series of birds—the Blackburn-ian warbler, the quail, the bobwhite, the water-thrush, the purple martin, and the bullbat ("All are delectable. Sweet sweet sweet") to come at last to the sea gull whose cry remains when all the others are silent: "But resign this land at the end, resign it / To its true owner, the tough one, the sea-gull." These same bird calls will echo and reecho in *Four Quartets*, from "Burnt Norton" ("Quick, said the bird, find them, find them, / Round the corner" and "Go, said the bird, for the leaves were full of children, / Hidden excitedly, containing laughter" [I]) to "East Coker" (with its "petrel and por-poise" [V]) and "The Dry Salvages" (where the sea gull's is one of many sea voices [I]), to sound for the last time in "Little Gidding" with the same call as the first time in "Cape Ann" and "Burnt Nor-ton": "Quick now, here, now, always" (V).

Speaking in *The Use of Poetry* of the place memory has in the creative process, with particular regard to Coleridge and *Kubla Khan*, Eliot writes,

> The imagery of that fragment [*Kubla Khan*] . . . sank to the depths of Coleridge's feeling, was saturated, transformed there . . . and brought up into daylight again. . . . The re-creation of word and image which happens fitfully in the poetry of such a poet as Coleridge happens almost incessantly with Shakespeare. Again and again, in his use of a word, he will give a new meaning or extract a latent one; again and again the right imagery, saturated while it lay in the depths of Shake-speare's memory, will rise like Anadyomene from the sea.[15]

Eliot goes on to speak of an image that he borrowed from George Chapman, who had himself borrowed it from Seneca, an image that was saturated and transformed in the different memories of the different men to surface in the poetry of each with the variable value conferred upon it by the memorial context in which it had been saturated. "I suggest that what gives it such intensity as it has in each case is its saturation," Eliot wrote,

> but with feelings too obscure for the authors even to know quite what they were. And of course only a part of an author's imagery comes from his reading. It comes from the whole of his sensitive life since early childhood. Why, for all of us, out of all that we have heard, seen, felt, in a lifetime, do certain images recur, charged with emotion, rather than

15. *The Use of Poetry*, 146–47.

others? The song of one bird, the leap of one fish, at a particular place and time, the scent of one flower, an old woman on a German mountain path, six ruffians seen through an open window playing cards at night at a small French railway junction where there was a water-mill: such memories may have symbolic value, but of what we cannot tell, for they come to represent the depths of feeling into which we cannot peer.[16]

It was at just the time of this lecture, in the early 1930s, that such memories were beginning to return to Eliot—or perhaps we should say were being allowed to return. At any rate they are very much there in the late poetry as they are very much not there in the early poetry. In *Four Quartets*, for example, many such saturated memories from early childhood are, in Eliot's own phrase, "brought up into daylight again."[17] The richest passage comes "at the close," the end of ends, the final twenty-two lines of "Little Gidding":

> With the drawing of this Love and the voice of this
> Calling
>
> We shall not cease from exploration
> And the end of all our exploring
> Will be to arrive where we started
> And know the place for the first time.
> Through the unknown, remembered gate
> When the last of earth left to discover
> Is that which was the beginning;
> At the source of the longest river
> The voice of the hidden waterfall
> And the children in the apple-tree
> Not known, because not looked for
> But heard, half-heard, in the stillness
> Between two waves of the sea.
> Quick now, here, now, always—
> A condition of complete simplicity
> (Costing not less than everything)
> And all shall be well and
> All manner of thing shall be well
> When the tongues of flame are in-folded
> Into the crowned knot of fire
> And the fire and the rose are one.

The return is to early memories and, through early memories, to

16. Ibid., 147–48.
17. See particularly "Burnt Norton," I and V; "East Coker," III; "The Dry Salvages," I and V; and "Little Gidding," V.

childhood. "He almost became a schoolboy," Mrs. Eliot says, "as the train approached the station," returning him, returning them, to his boyhood in St. Louis. Elsewhere, Mrs. Eliot is quoted as saying that there was "a little boy in [Eliot] that had never been released."[18] According to my reading, it was T. S. Eliot himself who, in the early poems, refused to release—or perhaps was incapable of releasing—the small boy; he refused until the time came when the child would no longer be denied and then, whether actively released or not, with the prompting of the actual American landscapes, the little boy insisted on coming through in the memories of early experience presented by the later poems.

I conclude as I began with a memory of a memory of a memory, and fittingly it is a memory of Eliot recalling an earlier time that Mrs. Eliot recounted to me one evening in London. She said that shortly after they were married they moved into the flat where Mrs. Eliot continues to live. The first evening that they were there her husband locked the door behind them and turned to her and said, "This is the first home I have had since I left St. Louis." Eliot had lived in many places, of course, in the years between, but only at the end of his life, as at the end of his poetry, did he, in memory and in fact, return to and arrive at home: "And the end of all our exploring / Will be to arrive where we started / And know the place for the first time." Oscar Wilde maintained that life imitates art rather than the reverse. For T. S. Eliot this seems to have been miraculously true, for "Little Gidding" was published in 1942 and it was not until 1957 that he married Valerie Fletcher and arrived where he had started some sixty-eight years earlier, to "know the place for the first time."

18. Quoted in Peter Ackroyd, *T. S. Eliot: A Life* (New York: Simon and Schuster, 1984), 320.

T. S. Eliot: The American Strain

A. D. Moody

Eliot was an American, and a poet. But was he an *American* poet? In his origins and his upbringing he could hardly have been more American. His mother was descended from one of the original members of the Bay Colony, and his father was descended from an Eliot who settled there in 1667. His grandfather had been one of the founding fathers of St. Louis, and was especially noticed by Ralph Waldo Emerson when he visited the city in 1852: "This town interests me & I see kind adventurous people; Mr. Eliot, the Unitarian minister, is the Saint of the West, & has a sumptuous church, & crowds to hear his really good sermons. But," he added, in a comment to which time has lent its ironies, "I believe no thinking or even reading man is here in the 95000 souls. An abstractionist cannot live near the Mississippi River & the Iron Mountain."[1] We know that at least one "abstractionist" was born in St. Louis, on 26 September 1888, and did much of his growing up there. And then his northeastern roots carried him back to the Massachusetts coast, where the family spent their summers, and to Harvard University, with which they had strong connections. Given all this, how could Eliot *not* be an American poet?

Yet William Carlos Williams, with his commitment to creating a poetry from the local conditions of American life and from the speech of Americans, was quite sure Eliot was not with American poetry, but against it. In "Prufrock" and in *The Waste Land*, he saw Eliot finding his inspiration in literature, and in foreign literature at that.

In 1987 Richard Poirier renewed Williams's attack on Eliot in his "Emersonian Reflections." The gist of his argument was that Eliot's tradition was not in the American tradition. In his view—and it is an old charge which Poirier hardly bothered to prove—

---

1. *The Letters of Ralph Waldo Emerson*, ed. Ralph L. Rusk (New York: Columbia University Press, 1939), 4:338–39.

Eliot had an excessive reverence for the literature of the past and supposed it to be "a storehouse of values and wisdom . . . even more so when imagined as an alternative to some present day chaos." Poirier recommended Emerson as an exemplary American, citing his belief that "we are here not to read but to 'become' Dante," that is, to rediscover within ourselves the origins of such works as the *Vita Nuova* and the *Divine Comedy*, and to not let them be "obscured within the encrustations of acquired culture."[2]

Poirier's invocation of Emerson helpfully shifts the ground beyond the too simple implication that the authentic American poet must write about American life to the issue of originality versus derivativeness whatever the material. But I think both charges can be rebutted. I will argue that Eliot's American experience is the most vital strain in his poetry. And I will argue that his use of the literature of the past was original in exactly the way Emerson demanded. Moreover, these two things work together and constitute in their combination the peculiarly American character of his poetry.

My concern, then, is Eliot's American experience and his American way of handling it. It has to be said at once that his American experience is not the most obvious component of his poetry. There is "The Dry Salvages," of course. But otherwise only a few minor poems are conspicuously American. There are the early satirical vignettes—"The *Boston Evening Transcript*," "Aunt Helen," and "Cousin Nancy"—and the relatively late landscapes—"New Hampshire," "Cape Ann," and "Virginia." Eliot's only other Americana are the caricatures in "Mr. Apollinax," "Lune de Miel," "Burbank with a Baedeker," and possibly the Sweeney poems. With the sole exception of "The Dry Salvages," these are not the poems for which he is remembered. But even in the celebrated early poems, written when he was closest to his American origins, it is possible to find little or no trace of an American accent or of American life. It was long assumed, at least by English and other foreign readers, that "The Love Song of J. Alfred Prufrock" and "Portrait of a Lady" were set in London, not St. Louis or Boston. After all, when Prufrock listens for the mermaids' singing, he could well be on Arnold's Dover Beach, where the tide of Romantic faith is forever ebbing. And the yellow fog, which rubs its back upon the windowpanes,

2. *The Renewal of Literature: Emersonian Reflections* (New York: Random House, 1987), 18, 45.

could well be taken for a London peasouper as seen by Dickens and Lewis Carroll.

But Eliot's St. Louis had its own fogs which were yellowed by its own factories. By his own account, his "urban imagery was that of St. Louis," though with descriptions of Paris and London superimposed. He spent his first sixteen years in St. Louis, "in a house at 2635 Locust street, since demolished."[3] Because his grandmother lived nearby, in a house built by his grandfather, his family preferred to live on in a "neighborhood which had become shabby to a degree approaching slumminess. . . . And in my childhood, before the days of motor cars, people who lived in town stayed in town. So it was, that for nine months of the year my scenery was almost exclusively urban, and a good deal of it seedily, drably urban at that."[4] Given that hint we can find definite indications of an American locale in the early urban poems.

The third section of "Preludes" is a particularly interesting case, since Eliot wrote it in Paris in 1911 and took much of its imagery from Charles-Louis Philippe's *Bubu de Montparnasse*, a novel which for Eliot "stood for Paris as some of Dickens's novels stand for London."[5] Still, Eliot's evocation of the morning vision when "the light crept up between the shutters" could just as well be an American scene, an Edward Hopper perhaps:

> You curled the papers from your hair,
> Or clasped the yellow soles of feet
> In the palms of both soiled hands.

When all four "Preludes" are considered together, they reveal quite specific American traces. *Lot*, as in "newspapers from vacant lots" (I), is one American usage, and *block*, as in "skies / That fade behind a city block" (IV), is another. *Shades*, in "One thinks of all the hands / That are raising dingy shades / In a thousand furnished rooms" (II), is used in the American way. In England, those shades

---

3. Quoted in "The Eliot Family and St. Louis," appendix to T. S. Eliot, *American Literature and the American Language: An Address Delivered at Washington University.* Washington University Studies, New Series, Language and Literature, no. 23 (St. Louis: Washington University Committee on Publications, 1953), 29.

4. T. S. Eliot, "The Influence of Landscape upon the Poet," *Daedalus, Journal of the American Academy of Arts and Sciences* 89 (Spring 1960): 421–22.

5. Eliot, Preface to *Bubu of Montparnasse*, by Charles-Louis Philippe, trans. Laurence Vail (Paris: Crosby Continental Editions, 1932), x–xi.

would be called *blinds* (*shades* would be lampshades). But Eliot's blinds are on the outside: "The showers beat / On broken blinds and chimney-pots" (I). I have it from Cleanth Brooks that *blinds* is the Southern usage for what others call shutters. Such American-isms disappear after Eliot's first collection, apart from a few delib-erate effects. *Dooryard* occurs unselfconsciously in "Prufrock": "After the sunsets and the dooryards and the sprinkled streets." When it appears again, in "The Dry Salvages" ("the rank ailanthus of the April dooryard"), it is consciously associated with America and with Whitman.

But there is more to words than their variant meanings. Before meaning, there is sound; and there is the rhythm set up by a se-quence of sounds. Eliot once said, with his mind on the problem of translating from one language to another, that it was in the rhythm of a language, in its natural speech patterns, that the vital national character was expressed.[6] The specific national character is not so easily detected when spelling conventions make the two languages appear nearly identical. In fact, British and American English can be pronounced very differently and can have quite distinct speech patterns. American English rhymes *potato* and *tomato*, and *hur-ricane* rhymes not with *American*, but with *Cain*. Such differences of accentuation are frequent, and they give American English a dis-tinctive rhythm. The American tendency, to generalize, is to make more of the vowels by giving them more weight and duration; while the English tend to clip their vowels short with more defined con-sonants. As a consequence, the English of England has a more reg-ular measure, falling more readily into the iambic beat. When Robert Frost writes to the measure of the English iambic pentam-eter, one can feel the tension between his natural speech rhythms and the more regular English speech. It is the vowels that are most affected, and in his recordings one can hear him clipping his vowels to keep the meter. That is just what Eliot did *not* do, except in his thoroughly English *Practical Cats*. Even in his latest recordings, made when he had long been resident in England, the weights and lengths of his vowels and the rhythm of his speech are not in the English measure. His versification was always a departure from the iambic pentameter, stretching and contracting the conventional line into another measure altogether, called *vers libre* for want of a better name. He did this, presumably, simply by following his own

6. "A Commentary," *Criterion* 14 (July 1935): 611.

American speech rhythms. "Portrait of a Lady," for example, is written for an American voice, and sounds slightly "off" rhythmically when read by a standard English voice. A poet whose ear had been formed by English speech patterns would not have written in just that way. What had happened was a quiet takeover of the English verse line.

There is at least one other American quality in Eliot's work which should be recognized. This is his habit of skepticism, which surely has its roots in the American tradition. The "American Doubt" is set against the "American Dream," as in the concluding lines of part II of "Portrait of a Lady," where the street piano's "worn-out common song" and "the smell of hyacinths . . . Recalling things that other people have desired" leave the narrator musing, "Are these ideas right or wrong?" This combination of romantic feeling with a skeptical questioning of it is the source and driving force of much of Eliot's poetry. The skepticism is more a questing than a questioning. If it begins as a questioning of his own youthful romanticism, it rapidly develops into a quest for something beyond what any experience can offer, a quest that carries his work from *The Waste Land* to "Little Gidding." Perhaps there is no accounting for this habit of skepticism. It is simply there, deeply ingrained in Eliot's temperament. Eliot himself observed it in Henry Adams and called it the "Boston Doubt."[7] His own family background gave him a connection with the "Boston Doubt," specifically through its Unitarianism. "Are these ideas right or wrong?" seems to catch its tone exactly. Eliot's temperament, then, as well as his rhythm, is more American than it first appears.

Yet the question remains, how can *The Waste Land*, with all its "encrustations of acquired culture," be an American poem? In the drafts there were two long passages, one dealing with Boston nightlife, the other with the fate of the crew of a Gloucester fishing boat, which would have connected it explicitly with America. But their cancellation meant that the setting of the poem, along with its great range of cultural reference, became exclusively English and European. The only authentically American detail left in the poem is the hermit thrush.

Critics from William Carlos Williams on have noticed all the non-American and "undemocratic" culture in the poem, but they

7. "A Sceptical Patrician," review of *The Education of Henry Adams: An Autobiography, Athenaeum* 4647 (23 May 1919): 362.

have not adequately attended to what Eliot was doing with it. They have not noticed that he was dealing with it in his own speech rhythms, and from his own point of view; and that, above all, he was displaying it, subversively, as a heap of broken images, as stony rubbish that did not answer to his need. It has too often been said, as by Richard Poirier, that Eliot was setting up images of a glorious past to put down the sordid present. It is rather the case that he collapses the past and the present into each other in such a way as to suggest that they are much the same. Both are looked at from the viewpoint characterized as "Tiresias," the viewpoint of someone who has seen it all before. There may be a covert pun in its being a typist that he particularly regards, since for him everything is typical. His cynical, disillusioned view of human experience and history is of course an element in the European cultural tradition; if Eliot is to be charged with being too attached to that tradition, it should at least be on account of his disillusionment, and not on the false ground that he glorified the past. From his point of view, there has always been a desert at the heart of the romantic garden, and as in *The Waste Land*, passion always ends in desolation and despair:

> "What shall we do to-morrow?
> "What shall we ever do?"
> . . . .
> . . . we shall play a game of chess,
> Pressing lidless eyes and waiting for a knock upon the door.
>
> (ll. 133–34, 137)

In its search for a way out of that predicament—the permanent and universal predicament as the layers of cultural allusion imply— the poem offers intimations of a new life in what Eliot called the "water-dripping song." Eliot thought the thirty lines of "What the Thunder Said" which culminate in the hermit thrush's singing in the pine trees were the only *good* ones in *The Waste Land:* "the rest is ephemeral."[8] They are in fact not only the most vital lines in the poem, but also the most specifically American contribution to it.

I have argued elsewhere, in a paper on Eliot's formal inventiveness given at the Orono T. S. Eliot Centennial, that the "water-dripping song" completes the form of the poem by breaking out of the dramatic into the lyric mode, and that this was in effect a break-

---

8. *The Waste Land: A Facsimile and Transcript of the Original Drafts Including the Annotations of Ezra Pound*, ed. Valerie Eliot (New York: Harcourt Brace Jovanovich, 1971), 129.

ing out of a dead world represented there by the European past.[9] What I would add here is that it is the recourse to the American experience which effects the recovery. Eliot had heard the hermit thrush in Quebec Province, as his note indicates, and he would have been able to recognize and describe it because his mother had given him for his fourteenth birthday Chapman's *Handbook of Birds of Eastern North America*. But then it is likely that this personal experience would have been reinforced, possibly at a later date, by his reading of Whitman,[10] the Whitman who gave a vital function to American birdsong in "Out of the Cradle Endlessly Rocking" and "When Lilacs Last in the Dooryard Bloom'd." This is the Whitman that Eliot admired and deeply responded to:

Then with the knowledge of death as walking one side of me,
And the thought of death close-walking the other side of me,
And I in the middle as with companions, and as holding the hands of
    companions,
I fled forth to the hiding receiving night that talks not,
Down to the shores of the water, the path by the swamp in the dimness,
To the solemn shadowy cedars and ghostly pines so still.
And the singer so shy to the rest receiv'd me,
The gray-brown bird I know receiv'd us comrades three,
And he sang the carol of death, and a verse for him I love.[11]

When Eliot introduced the same birdsong into *The Waste Land* (and followed it with what must be read as a further allusion to Whitman's poem: "Who is that third who walks always beside you?" [l. 360]), he placed himself quite firmly in the American tradition.

The importance of the "water-dripping song" for Eliot's further development as a poet can hardly be overstated. It is the point at which he detaches his poetry from the desert witnessed to by the "Mind of Europe" and enters upon the new life of *Ash-Wednesday* and "Marina," a new life rooted and founded in his New World experience. It is not that America gave Eliot the answer to the death

9. "Eliot's Formal Invention," in *T. S. Eliot: Man and Poet*, ed. Laura Cowan (Orono, Me.: National Poetry Foundation, 1990), 1:21–34.

10. See Eliot, "Whitman and Tennyson," review of *Whitman: An Interpretive Narrative*, by Emory Holloway, *Nation and Athenaeum* 40 (18 December 1917): 167.

11. "When Lilacs Last in the Dooryard Bloom'd," in *Leaves of Grass*, ed. Harold W. Blodgett and Sculley Bradley (New York: New York University Press, 1965), 334.

of the Old World. For that answer, something more had to be added to his American experience, something which he found in Dante and Catholicism. There is another presence besides Whitman in the "water-dripping song," that of Dante and of Dante's Arnaut Daniel whose songs also are filled with birdsong.[12] One might say that the surface of *The Waste Land* is largely given by European culture. Beneath that surface there is another life, which finds expression in the American hermit thrush. But the full realization of that inner life will only come with the conscious explication of it.

Consider these lines from part VI of *Ash-Wednesday*, lines which are a distillation of the American strain in Eliot's poetry:

> though I do not wish to wish these things
> From the wide window towards the granite shore
> The white sails still fly seaward, seaward flying
> Unbroken wings
>
> And the lost heart stiffens and rejoices
> In the lost lilac and the lost sea voices
> And the weak spirit quickens to rebel
> For the bent golden-rod and the lost sea smell
> Quickens to recover
> The cry of quail and the whirling plover
> And the blind eye creates
> The empty forms between the ivory gates
> And smell renews the salt savour of the sandy earth

This is a time and place of tensions, as the next lines reveal. The white sails are flying seaward—toward the granite shore. The *lost* heart rejoices, in the *lost* lilac and the *lost* sea voices—the stress falls regularly upon "lost." And the heart, as it rejoices, *stiffens.* The *blind* eye creates *empty* forms, shades or phantoms; and smell renews the salt savor, not of the sea, but of the sandy earth. Thus, the images of sensual life have been patterned to insist upon mortality. Eliot's American experience is being shaped by a Catholic understanding. He is, in his own fashion, "becoming" Dante.

At the same time, the American experience remains the ground of the Dantescan understanding. "A writer's art," Eliot once wrote,

---

12. Dante's line for Arnaut Daniel's purgation—"*Poi s'ascose nel foco che gli affina*" ("Then he hid himself in the fire that purifies them")—will signal Eliot's next move: he reproduced the last line of Canto XXVI of the *Purgatorio* verbatim as line 428 of *The Waste Land.*

"must be based on the accumulated sensations of the first twenty-one years."[13]

> There might be the experience of a child of ten, a small boy peering through sea-water in a rock-pool, and finding a sea-anemone for the first time: the simple experience (not so simple, for an exceptional child, as it looks) might lie dormant in his mind for twenty years, and re-appear transformed in some verse-context charged with great imaginative pressure. There is so much memory in imagination . . .[14]

We find such memories surfacing in "Rhapsody on a Windy Night." Eliot considered it his business as a poet to express and to interpret "the deeper, unnamed feelings which form the substratum of our being, to which we rarely penetrate," and he relied particularly on images laid down in his childhood to bring those mysterious feelings to consciousness. Eliot could say quite justly, therefore, that "in its sources, its emotional springs," his poetry "comes from America."[15]

But again there is the paradox, that the range of imagery drawn from his American experience is very limited. There is the urban imagery, which I have already noticed, and the Mississippi River "as it passes between St. Louis and East St. Louis in Illinois . . . the most powerful force in Nature in that environment." There is what he called his "country landscape," "that of New England, of coastal New England, and New England from June to October." There, Eliot said, "I missed the long dark river, the ailanthus trees, the flaming cardinal birds, the high limestone bluffs where we searched for fossil shell-fish; in Missouri I missed the fir trees, the bay and goldenrod, the song-sparrows, the red granite and the blue sea of Massachusetts."[16] To complete the list we should add the memories of children in an orchard, playing and laughing in the foliage of an apple-tree, as in "New Hampshire" and *Four Quartets*. And that is about all. It is really only a small handful of childhood memories: certain birds and their songs, the children's voices, some trees and flowering shrubs, the Big River, the Massachusetts coast. And of

13. Review of *Turgenev*, by Edward Garnett, *Egoist* 4 (December 1917): 167.
14. *The Use of Poetry and the Use of Criticism: Studies in the Relation of Criticism to Poetry in England* (London: Faber, 1933), 78–79.
15. *The Use of Poetry*, 155; "The Art of Poetry I: T. S. Eliot," interview with Donald Hall, *Paris Review* 21 (Spring/Summer 1959): 70.
16. "The Influence of Landscape," 422; Preface to *This American World*, by Edgar Ansel Mowrer, quoted in "The Eliot Family and St. Louis," 28.

course there is nothing in the way of an adult experience of American life and manners.

But having recognized how limited the range of his American material is, we must be all the more struck by how far he made it go and how vital it was in his poetic development. Out of such slender resources he fashioned a first version of his urban hell, a purgatorial sea, and a glimpse of paradise. From those few childhood memories, he fabricated the framework of his poetic universe.

Possibly the most purely American of Eliot's poems is "Marina." Its images are closely associated with the lines from *Ash-Wednesday* that I looked at earlier; in fact, "Marina" originated in the drafting of *Ash-Wednesday*. Significantly, and appropriately, the poem uses its New England coastal imagery to announce a new world and a new life, though not without an undertone of paradox. It begins:

> What seas what shores what grey rocks and what islands
> What water lapping the bow
> And scent of pine and the woodthrush singing through the fog

It ends wishing to resign the known life for the new life announced by the woodthrush calling through the fog upon granite islands, though there have been also "Whispers and small laughter between leaves."

The meaning of these images becomes explicit in "The Dry Salvages." This quartet begins with Eliot's big river, the only time he used the Mississippi in his poetry in spite of his saying that it had had such a powerful effect upon him. There are two remarkable features. Although Twain's treatment of the Mississippi in *Huckleberry Finn*, which Eliot deeply admired,[17] is referred to, most recognizably in "the river with its cargo of dead Negroes, cows and chicken coops," "the brown god" is not really Twain's river at all. And that is Eliot's point. The river has been bridged, controlled, "sivilised," as Huck would say, and Eliot evidently wants it to be destructive of the merely human order. The other odd thing, if this river is the Mississippi, is that it should appear to come out on the coast of Massachusetts. This is the geography of the imagination, in which local fact is dissolved in universal meaning.

17. See Eliot, Introduction to *The Adventures of Huckleberry Finn*, by Mark Twain (London: Cresset Press, 1950); and Eliot, "American Literature and the American Language," in *To Criticize the Critic and Other Writings* (London: Faber, 1965), 54.

The sea is the major image in "The Dry Salvages." Introduced in the closing lines of "East Coker," it effectively dismisses the Old World and its sense of history:

> Here or there does not matter
> We must be still and still moving
> Into another intensity
> For a further union, a deeper communion
> Through the dark cold and the empty desolation,
> The wave cry, the wind cry, the vast waters
> Of the petrel and the porpoise.

This theme is taken up in "The Dry Salvages" after the opening river passage, and it is sustained and developed through to part IV ("Lady, whose shrine stands on the promontory"). The two quartets in effect form one continuous meditation, with the sea of the New World carrying us beyond the earth of the Old World, toward the "life of significant soil." Both the river and the sea are made to mean death, and then that meaning is altered so that death becomes the annunciation of another order of life. In this Eliot is shaping his American experience into a significant pattern, at one point by adapting the pattern of Arnaut Daniel's sestina, but more radically by following the inner form of Dante's Catholic sensibility. In "The Dry Salvages," the translation of the secular sea of Massachusetts into that of the "Lady, whose shrine stands on the promontory . . . Figlia del tuo figlio" (IV) is effected by the attempt to conceive the inconceivable in these lines from the third section:

> At the moment which is not of action or inaction
> You can receive this: 'on whatever sphere of being
> The mind of a man may be intent
> At the time of death'—that is the one action
> (And the time of death is every moment)
> Which shall fructify in the lives of others . . .

This passage is not only an annunciation of what the Incarnation might mean in the lives of individuals, but also an attempt to have the mind actually conceive the meaning.

"The Dry Salvages" might be called Eliot's *New World Quartet*, not only because it returns to his American sources, but because it discovers a new meaning in them, a meaning which goes back to the religious origins of New England. It goes back with a difference, because it seeks a world that is new in every moment. When Eliot goes on to speak of history in "Little Gidding," it is no more the history of America than of the Old World of "East Coker" that he has in mind. It is the history of the spirit which would find and create a new world, and which is defined in the tongues of fire and in other images of fire. It is intimated also in the hidden laughter of children in the foliage, children associated with birds and taking the place of the hermit thrush. The children's voices are heard in "Burnt Norton" (I) and again in the closing lines of "Little Gidding" ("At the source of the longest river / The voice of the hidden waterfall / And the children in the apple-tree") telling of a "condition of complete simplicity." That complex and mysterious condition is what Eliot has been seeking, and it is his American imagery that promises it and leads toward it. The coda of "Little Gidding" is deeply American, with just the significant addition of the tongues of flame and the crowned knot of fire. The rose, though it symbolizes several things, is at root the rose of memory, though its flowering in flame is metaphysical. It is in the end Dantescan, but in its source, it is American.

There are many ways of being American. *E pluribus unum:* the Union is made of many and diverse strains. In putting the word "strain" in the title of this paper, I was thinking of two of its meanings in particular. The first refers to the musical aspect, the melody, the lyric strain which is the vital principle of Eliot's poetry. The second is the genetic and genealogical aspect, the idea of an inherited quality. It is his American genes that make Eliot the kind of poet he is, and they show most markedly in the most vital parts of his work. His quest for a new life can surely be connected, through his family line and tradition, with the quest that brought his ancestors to New England in order to be, as Emerson was to put it, acquainted "at first hand with the Deity." One of the generic qualities of America, after all, is to seek the firsthand experience, to be original and independent. Emerson, the prophet, or at least the preacher of that spirit, might have been calling for Eliot as much as Whitman when he declared in the "Divinity School Address" that the "divine sentiment . . . cannot be received at second hand."[18]

Eliot's poetry is a practical application of Emerson's declaration of cultural independence: "The foregoing generations beheld God and nature face to face; we, through their eyes. Why should not we

18. "An Address Delivered before the Senior Class in Divinity College, Cambridge, July 15, 1838," in *Nature/Addresses and Lectures* (Boston: Houghton Mifflin, 1903), 146, 127.

also enjoy an original relation to the universe? Why should not we have a poetry and philosophy of insight and not of tradition, and a religion by revelation to us, and not the history of theirs."[19] Eliot meditated more deeply and more darkly upon the word "original" than Emerson, and connected origins and ends in a more ultimate sense; but even that was going on *from* Emerson, not going against him. Furthermore, the language which Eliot found best served his vision was the one Emerson recommended when he said "Nature always wears the colors of the spirit" and provides a language to express our minds. That is, nature does this for the poet who "conforms things to his thoughts, [who] invests dust and stones with humanity, and makes them the words of the Reason."[20] In "Difficulties of a Statesman," the small creatures of Eliot's first world serve him in that way, and serve to measure the great world of public affairs:

Fireflies flare against the faint sheet lightning
What shall I cry?
. . . .
Mother
May we not be some time, almost now, together,
If the mactations, immolations, oblations, impetrations,
Are now observed
May we not be
O hidden
Hidden in the stillness of noon, in the silent croaking night.
Come with the sweep of the little bat's wing, with the small flare of the
    firefly or lightning bug,
"Rising and falling, crowned with dust," the small creatures,
The small creatures chirp thinly through the dust, through the night.

With lines such as these, Eliot makes American nature a language of the spirit.

Eliot, clearly, is not an American poet in the sense that Whitman and Williams and Olson are. His poetry is as much English and European as it is American. It aspires to a vision and a wisdom not of any one nation or culture. But Eliot's is an English and European poetry that only an American could have written, and it is the American component that makes the difference.

---

19. "Nature," in *Nature/Addresses and Lectures* (Boston: Houghton Mifflin, 1903), 3.
    20. Ibid., 11, 53.

Actual Times and Actual Places in T. S. Eliot's Poetry
Leonard Unger

One of the more familiar features of T. S. Eliot's poetry is the interrelationship of parts. There are numerous and various examples, many of them of Eliot's deliberate making. When we read in part VI of *Ash-Wednesday*, "The place of solitude where three dreams cross / Between blue rocks," we recall from *The Waste Land*, "Come in under the shadow of this red rock" (1. 26). It eventually became apparent that the five parts of "Burnt Norton" correspond to and contrast with the five parts of *The Waste Land*, and later it was evident that the later of the *Four Quartets* were modeled on "Burnt Norton." Other relationships are claimed by readers and critics, not always with absolute consensus. The "sea-girls" at the end of "Prufrock" may be seen as having experienced a sea change if one regards them as prefiguring the daughter addressed in the Ariel poem "Marina," as well as "Sister, mother / And spirit of the river, spirit of the sea," from part VI of *Ash-Wednesday*. When we read in part V of "East Coker," "one has only learnt to get the better of words / For the thing one no longer has to say," we may justifiably recall Prufrock's frustrated lament, "It is impossible to say just what I mean"—although it is implausible that Eliot intended this association. But such association leads readily to a relevant facet of meaning in the first and last words of "East Coker": "In my beginning is my end" and "In my end is my beginning." This connection is significant even though the meaning relevant here is not the primary meaning.

Between the beginning and the end, among all of Eliot's writings—poems, plays, prose—there is the complex interrelationship of parts which I have documented briefly and selectively as preparation for attending in some detail to a particular subject. The subject occurred to me when I recalled these lines from part I of *Ash-Wednesday*:

> Because I know that time is always time
> And place is always and only place
> And what is actual is actual only for one time
> And only for one place
> I rejoice that things are as they are . . .

The lines are quoted out of context in order to isolate the elements that I have given, in order to emphasize actual times and actual places, as well as periods of time, as in the opening of "Burnt Norton": "Time present and time past." These are the material, or a material, of his poetry, and of the local and cumulative effects produced by this material. Already showing such effects is an early poem which Eliot chose to exclude from the canon. I refer to "Spleen," published in *The Harvard Advocate* in January 1910:

> Sunday: this satisfied procession
> Of definite Sunday faces;
> Bonnets, silk hats, and conscious graces
> In repetition that displaces
> Your mental self-possession
> By this unwarranted digression.
>
> Evening, lights, and tea!
> Children and cats in the alley;
> Dejection unable to rally
> Against this dull conspiracy.
>
> And Life, a little bald and gray,
> Languid, fastidious, and bland,
> Waits, hat and gloves in hand,
> Punctilious of tie and suit
> (Somewhat impatient of delay)
>   On the doorstep of the Absolute.[1]

The poem has been recognized as closely associated with better known poems, especially "The Love Song of J. Alfred Prufrock."

I would attend here first to the aspects of time and place. At the opening it is Sunday morning, and there is an account of persons in their Sunday finery, going to or returning from church. The poem shifts to evening, to teatime. And it ends with the personification of Life, and with a characterization of that person. That person, the church-goers, and the takers of tea represent the genteel society, which includes so many figures of the early poems, such as Pru-

1. *Poems Written in Early Youth* (New York: Farrar, Straus and Giroux, 1967).

frock, the man and woman of "Portrait of a Lady," the deliverer and readers of the *Boston Evening Transcript*, Aunt Helen, Cousin Nancy, the dowager Mrs. Phlaccus, and Mrs. Cheetah. Alongside the genteel society presented here, "Children and cats in the alley" signifies the second party of the dull conspiracy against which dejection is unable to rally. The alley and the alley cats prefigure the squalid urban scene that extends through so much of the poetry. I shall be dwelling at some length and in some detail on the urban scene. If the dejection was Eliot's, it obviously did rally, or to speak more correctly, the poet rallied and expressed the dejection in poems that are witty, vivid, and memorable.

The poems of *Prufrock and Other Observations* are rich with the details of time and place. They are in large part an account of particular details as they are perceived at particular times. The first section of "Preludes" provides a ready example:

> The winter evening settles down
> With smell of steaks in passageways.
> Six o'clock.
> The burnt-out ends of smoky days.
> And now a gusty shower wraps
> The grimy scraps
> Of withered leaves about your feet
> And newspapers from vacant lots;
> The showers beat
> On broken blinds and chimney-pots,
> And at the corner of the street
> A lonely cab-horse steams and stamps.
> And then the lighting of the lamps.

The opening statement tells the time of year (winter) and the time of day (evening) and of a place—"passageways," no less specific for being plural, especially since "evening" is singular. As for the "smell of steaks," that too is a perception of place, an olfactory perception made by a smeller who is situated where the smell is available or inescapable.

Like much of the poetry in the *Prufrock* group, "Preludes" is a catalogue of sensory perceptions. This consideration of sensory meaning gives a fine accuracy, as well as complexity, to the title *Prufrock and Other Observations*. The accuracy lies in the fact that one meaning of *observation* is the act or the instance of noticing or perceiving. To read that part of the title in that sense gives valid emphasis to a recognition of the poetry as an account of things immediately experienced, an account of actual times and actual places. There is also, of course, the other appropriate meaning, as when the speaker of the earliest poem in the volume, "Conversation Galante," says:

> I observe: "Our sentimental friend the moon!
> Or possibly (fantastic, I confess)
> It may be Prester John's balloon
> Or an old battered lantern hung aloft
> To light poor travellers to their distress."

The "I observe" here means not that he witnesses the moon, but that he makes the comment, giving expression to his thoughts, and that comment is enclosed in quotation marks. On the subject of such words, it is interesting to notice (even to observe) in part II of "Portrait of a Lady" a statement made by the speaker of the poem when he is in the park reading the morning newspaper: "Particularly I remark / An English countess goes upon the stage." Equally interesting are these words from the fourth stanza of "Rhapsody on a Windy Night":

> Half-past two,
> The street-lamp said,
> "Remark the cat which flattens itself in the gutter,
> Slips out its tongue
> And devours a morsel of rancid butter."

In these instances *remark* means "observe," "notice," "witness." This last synonym, witness, sharpens and defines *Other Observations* with the meaning I have chosen, because the poetry is a poetry that gives more than ordinary attention to particulars, details, instances of time and place.

   In turning to the poems, I shall assume that place is also understood as space, so that when I use the word *spatial*, the idea and the fact of place are contained within my meaning. The first six poems of *Prufrock and Other Observations* take up most of the pages of the entire collection and constitute a discrete group. They are, among other things, a suite of movements or of variations on a theme of time and place. In each poem it is a specific detail of time which is found in the opening or the title. "Let us go then, you and I, / When the evening is spread out against the sky" is the opening of the most famous poem of the *Prufrock* volume. "Portrait of a Lady" begins "Among the smoke and fog of a December afternoon." "The winter evening settles down" is the first line of the first of the

"Preludes." "Rhapsody on a Windy Night," "Morning at the Window," and "The *Boston Evening Transcript*" are the titles of the next three poems. Evenings, three of them, prevail among the openings and titles, as they do among the poems generally, and morning, afternoon, and night occur at the outset in the other poems.

I have attended to openings and titles for the purpose of emphasis, but as readers familiar with Eliot's poetry already know, these poems are rich with such details and effects. As we shall see, in recalling details the effects are of various kinds. Prufrock sometimes describes the temporal with a spatial metaphor, such as "the evening . . . spread out against the sky." The feline yellow smoke is made to lick "its tongue into the corners of the evening." Prufrock recalls that this particular evening "was a soft October night," an example of frequent reference in the poetry to months and seasons of the year. About midway through his reflections, Prufrock becomes aware that time has been slipping by:

> And the afternoon, the evening, sleeps so peacefully!
> Smoothed by long fingers,
> Asleep . . . tired . . . or it malingers,
> Stretched on the floor, here beside you and me.

This makes the second time that Prufrock describes the evening with a temporal-spatial metaphor, sensing the evening as a condition extended in space. For another such metaphor—in this case a simile—with a difference, I move to "The *Boston Evening Transcript.*" Bringing the newspaper to his cousin Harriet, the speaker reports,

> I mount the steps and ring the bell, turning
> Wearily, as one would turn to nod good-bye
>   to Rochefoucauld,
> If the street were time and he at the end of the
>   street, . . .

Imaginatively, phantasmally, historical time is here compared to the length of a city street.

But it is the time of evening that is especially associated with the city street, a spatial-temporal association, if not always a metaphor. Prufrock's invitation, we recall, as he observes the evening sky, is to go "through certain half-deserted streets." The same yellow smoke, whose tongue licked "into the corners of the evening," also "slides along the street." Prufrock considers whether he should say, "I have gone at dusk through narrow streets." He considers whether a certain something would "have been worth while, / After the sunsets and the dooryards and the sprinkled streets." The street is vividly present in each of the four "Preludes": "the corner of the street" (I) at evening; "the sawdust-trampled street" (II) in the morning; "a vision of the street" (III) in the morning; "a blackened street" (IV) at evening—in that order. In "Morning at the Window," while the rattling of breakfast plates is heard, housemaids are seen "along the trampled edges of the street." The brief action of "The *Boston Evening Transcript*" occurs as "evening quickens faintly in the street." In "Rhapsody on a Windy Night," the street is the scene of the entire action, which is a walk along city streets through the small hours of the night, and it is the voice of the personified muttering, sputtering streetlamps that speaks much of the poem, as well as *for* the poet.

If "Rhapsody on a Windy Night" is impressively a poem of nocturnal streets and streetlamps, it is no less impressively a poem that develops by precise details of time—time of the clock. At the opening of the poem, the exact hour is stated: "Twelve o'clock." Then successive strophes open by reporting the course of the night: "Half-past one," "Half-past two," "Half-past three," and finally, "The lamp said, / 'Four o'clock.'" Giving the half hours contributes to the effect of precise chronology, as the time passes and the time is reported.

The development of "Portrait of a Lady" is marked by another kind of time—not the clock, but the calendar. Roman numerals divide the poem into three sections, and as already noted, the first section opens "Among the smoke and fog of a December afternoon," the month and the course of the day. It is lilac time at the opening of the second part, "Now that lilacs are in bloom." In this same opening strophe of part II, the lady refers to "these April sunsets," adding the crepuscular image of sunsets to the month. At the opening of part III we find "The October night comes down." By these references, we know that the narrator has reported the account of a relationship over the course of most of a year. Turning again to part II, we find the narrator making a revealing analogy with the lady's persistent and insistent conversation: "The voice returns like the insistent out-of-tune / Of a broken violin on an August afternoon." Although Prufrock's time of year and time of day are somewhat indeterminate, it is appropriate to recall that the motions of the yellow smoke and fog occur on "a soft October night."

It has been convenient to attend to actual times in the poetry of this period because times are limited to a few kinds of references: time of the clock, a period of the day (such as evening), a month or season of the year, and historical time. Actual places are another matter, a matter to which it is far more difficult to attend. There are degrees of time, but there are no degrees of place, for by place I mean not only location, such as a street, but any *thing*, any object that can be seen, smelled, heard, and so on. It is especially the world of things seen which makes for difficulty, because such things are both numerous and various. Yet this difficulty supports my argument that within the entire corpus of Eliot's poetry *Prufrock and Other Observations* is singularly rich with things of this world. If there is not a scale of things, as there is of times, there are categories. This is a subject I considered in the essay, "T. S. Eliot's Images of Awareness," which I contributed to the Eliot memorial number of *The Sewanee Review* edited by Allen Tate.[2] The images discussed at some length there are stairs, smell, and music—images which, as I noted then, are among those that prevail especially in the *Prufrock* group of poems. In that case, *stairs* made a single category, but I will note here that this image is but one item among others, such as room, floor, wall, window, door. Equally prevalent are the atmospheric images of smoke and fog, and the anatomical images of arms, hands, fingers, legs, feet, eyes, head, and hair.

That is probably already an excess of images—my excess, because we do not find or feel any excess in our experience of reading the poems. Instead the poems give us the evocation of a world that is at once commonplace and vivid. What could be more commonplace than the components of a house (stairs, floors, windows), or the components of the body (arms and legs, hands and feet)? One reason I choose to say commonplace is to stress the immediacy and actuality of these objects in order to ignore any claim that some of them derive from an external source, or that they partake of some field of symbolism, even if it be a field of symbolism developed by Eliot's later career as a poet. There may be valid sources and symbolisms, but this poetry does not need these dimensions and extensions of relevance to produce a strikingly sufficient and effective quality. It had that quality for us on our first reading, and it deserves to be credited with that quality and to be appreciated for it, first and last.

2. *Sewanee Review* 74 (January–March, 1966): 197–224.

Well, what is this quality? I have chosen the second section of
"Preludes" to illustrate it:

> The morning comes to consciousness
> Of faint stale smells of beer
> From the sawdust-trampled street
> With all its muddy feet that press
> To early coffee-stands.
> With the other masquerades
> That time resumes,
> One thinks of all the hands
> That are raising dingy shades
> In a thousand furnished rooms.

Such poetry, as stated earlier, evokes a world that is at once commonplace and vivid. It is, of course, the vividness which gives
poetic effect, poetic quality, to the commonplace. The vividness is
achieved by stylistic devices. One of these is the density of references made within a strict economy of expression. From a single
statement made without pause in the first five lines, we learn that
in the morning there are smells of beer arising from the street
where many people are moving toward coffee stands. The flowing
statement compresses and unites the details into a single scene—
into a "consciousness" of that scene. Contained in the flow and in
the scene are the implicit descriptions: smells of beer are faint and
stale, the street is trampled with sawdust, the people's feet are
muddy, and the coffee stands are early.

The locutions, "morning comes to consciousness," and "other
masquerades / That time resumes," are decidedly not commonplace. Allowing that they are somewhat enigmatic, but not impen-
etrably obscure, I will observe that in each case the locution intro-
duces, or prepares for, a scene. The second scene, in the last three
lines of the passage, moves from outdoors to indoors, and is composed of hands raising shades in rooms. Here again it is description
which enriches the vividness of the details: "all the hands / That
are raising dingy shades / In a thousand furnished rooms." The
scene is the more drab and the more dismal because the shades are
dingy and the rooms are furnished rooms, and because the same
unchanging scene is multiplied a thousand times, a good round
number for individuals whose described situation is, in a special
sense, commonplace, and the more vivid because it is so. Eliot's
versification is still another device for giving emphasis to details
and producing the effect of vividness. The final words of the last

three lines of the passage are *hands*, *shades*, and *rooms*, rhyming
a b c with the preceding three lines and thus contributing to the
vividness of the details, as well as to the verbal music which we
recognize as Eliot's poetic voice.

If I believe that vividness gives poetic quality to the commonplace, do I also believe that it gives such quality to the drab, the
dismal, even the distasteful? Yes, I do—but before exploring that
issue, I will consider another example of Eliot's use of the commonplace. "Prufrock" begins:

> Let us go then, you and I,
> When the evening is spread out against the sky
> Like a patient etherised upon a table;
> Let us go, through certain half-deserted streets,
> The muttering retreats
> Of restless nights in one-night cheap hotels
> And sawdust restaurants with oyster-shells:

The "you and I" and the etherized patient have been much discussed, and they have been routinely footnoted in textbook anthol-
ogies. But I do not recall any close reading or footnoting of the
streets, hotels, and restaurants. Why should there be any? If these
are not merely commonplace, they are unquestionably familiar as
parts of a certain kind of urban neighborhood, a slummy skid row,
the more familiar for being vividly portrayed. Streets that are half-
deserted have their own atmosphere, different from those that are
empty or crowded. Hotels that are cheap and are typically occupied
on a one-night basis suggest troubled vagrancy, as well as illicit or
professional sex. The restaurants have sawdust strewn on the floors
for the purpose of sanitation, to absorb the wet and dirt brought in
from the street and the spillage of food and drink, which may
include oyster shells. I attend to this passage not only because it
illustrates Eliot's compactness of wording, the strict economy of
expression, but also because it contains an obscurity that has, to
my knowledge, gone unnoticed. I refer to "muttering retreats."
Some appropriate atmosphere derives from "muttering." But what
are the "retreats"? They could be the streets, for the two words are
equated by apposition. By grammatical analysis, they could also be
the "restless nights" and "sawdust restaurants." The purpose of my
quibbling is to illustrate the readiness with which we overlook the
lack of grammatical and syntactic clarity. The vividness and clarity
of atmosphere, the actuality of the scene, are so persuasive and

engaging that the technical ambiguity is left unnoticed. In the same poem there is a comparable passage, a superb vignette:

> Shall I say, I have gone at dusk through narrow streets
> And watched the smoke that rises from the pipes
> Of lonely men in shirt-sleeves, leaning out of windows?

This, too, is a vivid, engaging, and memorable image, the more so because of the rhythm and tone of its language. The language and the image share a lyrical quality which each gives to and takes from the other. And here again the impact of the imagery transcends and obscures the literal statement. For the literal statement is that Prufrock "watched the smoke." But as readers and listeners, we do not watch the smoke, or even the pipes from which it rises. We watch the "lonely men in shirt-sleeves, leaning out of windows," windows which, in effect, become one window that frames a picture of a lonely shirt-sleeved man smoking a pipe. The difference between the literal statement and the actual effect marks that economy of expression by which the effect is produced.

It is not likely that one can discuss the opening lines of "Prufrock" without giving some attention to the famous simile of "the evening . . . spread out against the sky / Like a patient etherised upon a table." The image is neither commonplace nor familiar. It is conspicuous and shocking, as it was intended to be. When an early critic called the simile a metaphysical conceit, he must have been influenced by Dr. Johnson's phrase describing a practice of some seventeenth-century English poets, who allegedly presented "heterogeneous ideas . . . yoked by violence together."[3] The evening sky and the etherized patient are certainly heterogeneous ideas. I recall John Berryman's pronouncement: "With this line, modern poetry begins."[4] And we should understand that "modern" here means modernist. The line had different effects on different readers. Louis Simpson has written: "To the first readers it must have been startling. . . . You could see the operating table and you could almost see the slops." Stephen Spender, a fairly early reader, has given a wholly different emphasis, associating "etherised" with

---

3. "Abraham Cowley," in *Lives of the English Poets*, vol. 1 (London: J. M. Dent, 1946), 11.

4. Ralph Ross, John Berryman, and Allen Tate, *The Arts of Reading* (New York: Crowell, 1960), 342. A prefatory note indicates that the remark is Berryman's.

ethereal. For him the image suggested "the head of the dreamer, full of the night sky and stars," and he felt that the image is made to "float, witty, dreaming."[5] My own speculation is that a survey of readers of any period would show the prevailing response to be in a middle ground between slops and stars.

I no longer find the image of the etherized patient as exciting as I once did. As an analogy, it is not as effective and persuasive as Prufrock's comparing himself to "a pair of ragged claws / Scuttling across the floors of silent seas." It is possible to speculate that the etherized patient image was inserted at a later stage of composition. It is already figurative to say that "the evening is spread out against the sky," just as it is would be to say that the evening is "stretched on the floor." Such figurativeness lacks the effect of extreme shock, and it lacks the potential for distracting readers, or, more strictly, editors and critics, into farfetched and irrelevant associations. A final point about the image is that it seems strikingly fresh because it is a scientific and therefore seemingly unpoetic reference. Although ether had been used as an anaesthetic since the middle of the nineteenth century, Eliot's vivid use of it as the opening of his poem is consistent with his purpose and his achievement of producing poetry which has the quality of contemporaneity. There is some irony on this score because the reference to ether is now historically dated, ether having been replaced by other anesthetics for several decades.

That the poetry of *Prufrock and Other Observations* is modernist and that it has the quality of contemporaneity are facts which have been stated by critics and which have long been a part of literary history. The point I wish to make is that the contemporaneity is an element in the modernism. The early description of the poetry as *vers de société*, meant as a pejorative characterization, may be cited as evidence that it is a poetry of the here and now, of actual times and actual places. It is also evidence that the poetry is modernist, though early critics were in a sense too early to recognize it as modernist poetry, as serious and important poetry. Many of the techniques and effects of *The Waste Land* are already present in the *Prufrock* poetry.

A number of details in the poetry are at once signs of contempo-

5. Simpson, *Three on the Tower: The Lives and Works of Ezra Pound, T. S. Eliot and William Carlos Williams* (New York: William Morrow, 1975), 104; Spender, *T. S. Eliot* (New York: Viking, 1975), 37.

raneity and of historical distance from the time the poetry was written. The "patient etherised upon a table" is one of these. The "sawdust restaurants" may be another. Several are more strictly dated—contemporary, but of an actual time that has receded into the past. One of these is Prufrock's remark, "I shall wear the bottoms of my trousers rolled." In one anthology a footnote explains, "Prufrock is eager to keep up with the latest fashion, which was to wear cuffs on trousers." That tells us something about the history of cuffs, a history which is still ongoing. Except for the military, cuffs prevailed for most of a century, but the word *rolled* in that sense was short-lived. The final lines of the first section of "Preludes" are relevant here:

> And at the corner of the street
> A lonely cab-horse steams and stamps.
> And then the lighting of the lamps.

There are still horse-drawn carriages in places like New York's Central Park, but they are deliberate antiques, whereas Eliot's cab-horse is a precursor of the "taxi throbbing waiting" in *The Waste Land.* As for the taxi, does it still throb as urgently as it used to? "And then the lighting of the lamps" is clarified, if it needs to be, by the streetlamp that provides the guided tour in "Rhapsody on a Windy Night," as it (first one lamp and then another) mutters, sputters, and hums throughout the small hours of the night. In both poems the lamps are gas lamps. They mutter and sputter and "beat like a fatalistic drum" because at an early stage in the history of gas illumination the gas jet did audibly, as well as visibly, throb and pulsate. But Eliot, in the opening stanza of "The Dry Salvages," recalled with nostalgia "the smell of grapes on the autumn table, / And the evening circle in the winter gaslight." Young readers today might have some trouble with these lines near the end of "Rhapsody":

> The bed is open; the tooth-brush hangs on the wall,
> Put your shoes at the door, sleep, prepare for life.

There was a time, earlier in our century, when, even at modest hotels, returning to one's room after dinner, one would find that somebody had turned down the bed covers in preparation for the night's sleep. Before retiring, one put one's shoes outside the door, expecting to find them shined in the morning, and they would be. There was no tipping of the unseen persons who had attended to the bed and shoes.

Even *The Waste Land*, with its variety of allusions to and echoes from different periods of history, contains some details which have become dated since the poem first appeared. Relevant on this score is the expression in "A Game of Chess": "a closed car at four" (l. 136). In the original unabridged manuscript the expression is "the closed carriage at four." Eliot was obviously moved to make the change by Ezra Pound's editorial notations. Pound drew a circle around "closed carriage," wrote in the left-hand margin, "Why this Blot on Scutchen *between* 1922 & Lil," and in the right-hand margin the date "1880."[6] There is a fine irony here. We no longer speak of *closed cars* because we no longer have *open cars*, that is, cars with roofs but otherwise open on both sides, unless one snapped on the isinglass panels to keep out the rain.

I have attended to these few dated references in order to indicate the contemporaneity, the actuality of time and place, which marks Eliot's early poetry. But the poetry has a quality of the here and now that abides into our own time for other reasons than specific references. One of these reasons is that the language of the poetry is genuinely conversational. It is conversational, but with a difference. The difference lies in the cadence, inflection, and tone with which the language is properly expressed. Combining with rhythm and rhyme, the meaning of the language calls for a meaningful cadence and tone, for a speaking voice that is silently heard as incantation, or is spoken and heard as incantation. In "The Music of Poetry" Eliot declared that "poetry must not stray too far from the ordinary everyday language which we use and hear." He declared also that "the music of poetry is not something which exists apart from the meaning."[7] The meaning is not just in the flat semantic statement, but also in the intimation of sensibility and emotion which attend the statement. Any passage from Eliot's early poetry is evidence of ordinary language endowed with the music of poetry and with Eliot's distinctive voice, as in this passage from "Prufrock":

> And would it have been worth it, after all,
> Would it have been worth while,
> After the sunsets and the dooryards and the sprinkled streets,
> After the novels, after the teacups, after the skirts that
>   trail along the floor—

6. *The Waste Land: A Facsimile and Transcript of the Original Drafts Including the Annotations of Ezra Pound*, ed. Valerie Eliot (New York: Harcourt Brace Jovanovich, 1971), 13.

7. "The Music of Poetry," in *On Poetry and Poets* (London: Faber, 1957), 21.

And this, and so much more?—
It is impossible to say just what I mean!

In the matter of contemporaneity, Eliot has been charged by some critics with presenting a dismal and degraded present in contrast with a glorious and splendid past, as if he were of the party of E. A. Robinson's Miniver Cheevy, who

> sighed for what was not,
> And dreamed, and rested from his labors;
> He dreamed of Thebes and Camelot,
> And Priam's neighbors.[8]

Such a charge is based on a simplistic view of *The Waste Land*, where there is recurring collage of references from different periods of history, including the present. But there is nothing of that kind in the early poems. When Prufrock twice observes, "In the room the women come and go / Talking of Michelangelo," the effect is a blunt caricature of modern society women talking affectedly about art. There is hardly the evocation of a glorious past. It is true enough that an atmosphere of gloom and melancholy pervades this poetry, an atmosphere created in large part by the recurring images of gloomy weather, of grubby, sordid, repugnant scenes and situations from modern urban life. Such weather and such scenes were the materials that engaged Eliot's sensibility and entered into a small body of poetry that has been read admiringly by several generations. A different sensibility would respond differently to such materials. Consider the statement, "I have seen your painted women under the gas lamps luring the farm boys." This is Carl Sandburg celebrating Chicago, robustly accepting "this my city . . . so proud to be alive and strong and coarse and cunning." "Chicago" was first published in 1916, a year before the *Prufrock* poems were published.[9]

When in *The Waste Land* Eliot says, "Unreal City, / Under the brown fog of a winter dawn," he is referring to London, but the very real city of the early poems is *his* city, Eliot's city, whether it be St. Louis or Boston or London, or a composite of these. It is his city, portrayed with its smoke and fog, its sawdust-trampled streets, its vacant lots, its muttering street lamps. Why this material appealed

8. "Miniver Cheevy," in *Collected Poems* (New York: Macmillan Co., 1946), 347.
9. *The Complete Poems of Carl Sandburg* (New York: Harcourt Brace and World, 1969), 3.

to Eliot, why it obsessed him as the stuff of poetry is a matter which
is relevant to some remarks he made in his essay on Tennyson's *In
Memoriam* after quoting the seventh part of that poem.

> Dark house, by which once more I stand
> Here in the long unlovely street,
> Doors, where my heart was used to beat
> So quickly, waiting for a hand,
>
> A hand that can be clasp'd no more—
> Behold me, for I cannot sleep,
> And like a guilty thing I creep
> At earliest morning to the door.
>
> He is not here; but far away
> The noise of life begins again,
> And ghastly thro' the drizzling rain
> On the bald street breaks the blank day.[10]

Having quoted this passage, Eliot comments: "This is great poetry,
economical of words, a universal emotion related to a particular
place; and it gives me the shudder that I fail to get from anything in
Maud."[11] By "universal emotion" Eliot surely meant grief over the
death of a very dear friend. To experience the shudder is to recognize that the poetry is great. It is obvious, I believe, that the poetry
produced a shudder because the emotion is related to a particular
time, a particular atmosphere, a particular place: "earliest morning," "drizzling rain," "the bald street," "the blank day." There is
nothing so openly and directly personal in Eliot's early poetry as
there is in Tennyson's lines, but that poetry is rich with particulars
comparable to those of Tennyson. It is "economical of words," so
economical that it does not reveal an emotion as specific as the
emotion of grief. It implies emotion, of course, and it acknowledges emotion, as in these lines near the end of the fourth section
of "Preludes":

> I am moved by fancies that are curled
> Around these images, and cling:
> The notion of some infinitely gentle
> Infinitely suffering thing.

There is a respect in which I have always found these lines some-

10. *In Memoriam* (New York: Norton, 1973), 8.
11. "In Memoriam," in *Selected Essays* (New York: Harcourt Brace, 1950),
291.

what puzzling. And they remain puzzling, but in a different way, after learning from a footnote in Valerie Eliot's edition of Eliot's letters that the poet had his brother Henry in mind when he wrote them.[12] In any case, the "infinitely gentle / Infinitely suffering thing" is itself an image in extreme contrast with those that precede it, and with those that follow it, in the final lines of the poem:

> Wipe your hand across your mouth, and laugh;
> The worlds revolve like ancient women
> Gathering fuel in vacant lots.

Like "Preludes," "Rhapsody on a Windy Night" ends with a statement that implies emotion, a suffering. The final line, set off by itself is "The last twist of the knife." Both poems present bleak and gloomy images of particular times and particular places, the most distasteful features of modern urban activity. Eliot has included at the end of each poem the kind of shudder he experienced upon reading the stanzas of *In Memoriam*.

Tennyson's poem tells of the poet's presence in "the long unlovely street." Until the later *Quartets*, Eliot's poetry is not so directly personal. He had, in "Tradition and the Individual Talent," proposed an "impersonal theory of poetry." But he must eventually have been aware that his poetry, while not directly personal, was indirectly personal. Eliot was to acknowledge as much in a later essay, with this statement: "In one's prose reflexions one may be legitimately occupied with ideals, whereas in the writing of verse one can only deal with actuality."[13] What was Eliot's actuality? It was times and places: "the smoke and fog of a December afternoon," "the smell of steaks in passageways," "the sparrows in the gutters." One could make a concordance of all the evenings and mornings, rooms and streets, smoke and fog, and one could indicate the frequency with which such actualities occur in Eliot's verse. That would provide some impressive information. But Eliot said "one can only deal with actuality." There is no analysis that can wholly explain how the poet did deal, in the writing of verse, with his material, with unlovely actuality, so as to make lovely poetry of it. Is *lovely* not quite the appropriate word? Maybe not.

12. *The Letters of T. S. Eliot*, (1898–1922), ed. Valerie Eliot (San Diego: Harcourt Brace Jovanovich, 1988), 1:54n.

13. *After Strange Gods: A Primer of Modern Heresy* (New York: Harcourt Brace, 1933), 30.

I. A. Richards called *The Hollow Men* "the most beautiful of Mr. Eliot's poems."[14] I don't think Richards used the word as in the expression "beautifully crafted" (although it may be that). He meant that the poem, which is about an unlovely subject, is a very beautiful poem. And he implies that Eliot's other poems are more or less beautiful. Is that a better term than *lovely*? Perhaps they are equally good, insofar as they are appropriate. I just referred to Eliot's material and almost wrote "his chosen material." But it occurred to me that the material had chosen the poet, for that is the meaning of his avowal that "in the writing of verse one can only deal with actuality." We should understand, I think, that the actuality is also the poet himself, with his temperament and sensibility, at the time he responded to the objective material.

The actuality, the contemporaneity, of Eliot's response is nowhere more positively and more clearly recorded than in the poetry of *Prufrock and Other Observations*. Because this is so, it is appropriate to recall his comment on this subject: "the best contemporary poetry can give us a feeling of excitement and a sense of fulfillment different from any sentiment aroused by even very much greater poetry of a past age."[15] The contemporaneity of Eliot's early poetry is now that of a past age. He wrote other kinds of poetry in later stages of his development. But he was never again to write a poetry in which actual times and actual places so abundantly, so sharply, and so lucidly exist. "I rejoice that things are as they are" in this poetry.

14. *Principles of Literary Criticism* (New York: Harcourt Brace, 1925), 294.
15. "The Music of Poetry," in *On Poetry and Poets*, 24.

II. T. S. Eliot Centennial Celebration Lectures

The Serious Poet in a Secularized Society: Reflections on Eliot and Twentieth-Century Culture
Cleanth Brooks

Though T. S. Eliot was a man who influenced my life very powerfully, he was not a man that I ever knew very directly or well. I met him personally on two occasions and both of these were late in his life. The last of the meetings actually was only a few weeks before he died in London. It would be very pleasant to be able to chat a little about what he said and did in these personal meetings, but I remember not a great deal about either of them. At the first there were too many people to allow very much intimate talk. The setting was a room in the apartment that the Allen Tates were renting in New York. Their other guests were my wife, myself, and Robert Lowell, the young poet, then coming along very fast. The evening was pleasant, charming, affable and friendly. We got into a few matters of Eliot's literary style but not much of any great consequence.

My second and last meeting with Eliot was even briefer. I had at that time settled in for two years at our embassy in London and had made my way over to have a talk with Eliot at his office at Faber and Faber. He could not have been kinder or more pleasant in his reception, but he was obviously having much trouble in talking. By that time his emphysema had got so bad that I shortened the interview, pleading that something had come up that demanded my presence elsewhere, because I felt that I was putting too much strain on him. Later I heard through a friend of his that he was in a nursing home, and then very shortly thereafter I learned of his death.

The real impact of the man on me, however, had occurred much earlier, in 1929 when I first came to Oxford. I knew something of Eliot's poetry but I knew nothing of his criticism until I found myself that fall reading *The Sacred Wood*, his first collection of essays. It was a transforming experience. I felt that I was listening to a man speaking with authority, not someone who was simply pleasant, gracious, and learned, but with a little more in what he had to say than the other more accomplished critics. Here was a man who loved poetry and knew something about it and was able to talk about it. Deliberately, graciously, but with a powerful sense of something actually there. I came to know Eliot's poetry later on after becoming thoroughly convinced of his knowledge of literature through that powerful, though never savage, mentality with which he discussed literature, what it was, and what it could accomplish.

I made no attempt, however, to see Eliot while I was in Oxford as a student. I felt that I was not up to that kind of authority. I did write to him later on from Baton Rouge, where I was teaching at Louisiana State University, in order to ask him to read my account of *The Waste Land.* By this time Eliot had become an important figure in my life, a figure who determined a great deal of my own thinking, and so it was with special satisfaction that I received his kind and prompt reply.[1]

I have spoken of Eliot's impact on my life but I have not indicated that it came not at once through the poetry but through his prose. Yet it is his poetry that matters most to me. It immediately showed itself to be a poetry attempting to make its case by cutting against the grain. The poetry is obviously a journey and soon enough shows itself to be a journey toward religion. *The Waste Land,* the poem that made his reputation, is a work which trembles with the concern for religion, and after *The Waste Land* most of the poetry actually has to do with religion and religious matters. Since ours is a secularized society, Eliot's poetry was frankly moving against the hard currents of such a society. In view of this fact, he deserved special credit as a man who had to win his way against difficulties and perhaps his basically non-Christian audience deserves some credit too for as much tolerance as it accorded him. But his intellectual position encountered and continues to encounter a powerful resistance.

---

1. Brooks's essay, "*The Waste Land:* Critique of the Myth," appeared first in *Southern Review* (1937) and then in *Modern Poetry and the Tradition* (1939; reprint Chapel Hill: University of North Carolina Press, 1967). Eliot's response (15 March 1937) to Brooks's letter (25 February 1937) is reprinted in its entirety in "*The Waste Land:* A Prophetic Document," *Yale Review* 78 (September 1989): 318–32. Eliot says that Brooks's analysis seems "on the whole excellent" and "perfectly justified." [Editor's note]

Whether the reader's personal position in this matter may be pro-Christian or non-Christian, it may be useful to find out what Eliot's criticism of the modern world actually amounts to—the real and not the imagined basis for that criticism of the world. It may also be useful to note that Eliot was not alone in his response to what has been called the "present crisis in culture." Other writers, prominent literary figures such as some of them are, made related responses, for they too were highly sensitive to the basic problems of our time. William Butler Yeats, Ezra Pound, James Joyce, William Faulkner, Saul Bellow, Allen Tate, Flannery O'Connor, and Walker Percy—though I make no pretense of calling the whole roll—have to be counted in this group. The responses were varied, of course, particularly in their implied solutions, but the diagnoses of the cultural situation are strikingly alike.

Yet for one of the clearest brief accounts of that situation, I think that it would be useful for me not to invoke the writings of a literary critic, but those of a political scientist, a specialist in cultural history, those of the late Eric Voegelin. In *From Enlightenment to Revolution* Voegelin wrote that:

> The eighteenth century has been variously characterized as the century of the Enlightenment and Revolution or alternatively as the Age of Reason. Whatever the merit of these designations, they embody a denial of cognitive value to spiritual experiences, [they] attest to the atrophy of Christian transcendental experiences and [they] seek to enthrone the Newtonian method of science as the only valid method of arriving at truth.[2]

The result of this process, begun in the eighteenth century according to Voegelin, has been to produce a basically secularized society by denying more and more completely that a whole area of human experience is a possible source of truth about the human condition. Voegelin's analysis of the darkness of enlightened reason is helpful in approaching Eliot's work.

One notes that in "Choruses from 'The Rock'" (III) Eliot uses the phrase "wretched generation of enlightened men." But Eliot did not borrow the phrase from Voegelin: *The Rock* was published before Voegelin's *From Enlightenment to Revolution* had appeared; nor do I see any reason to suppose that Voegelin borrowed from Eliot. The concept of an enlightenment which darkened the other

2. *From Enlightenment to Revolution*, ed. John H. Hallowell (Durham: Duke University Press, 1975), 3.

areas of experience is an integral and long-term part of Voegelin's whole notion of European intellectual history. My point in juxtaposing these two statements is to stress the point that Eliot's phrase was not the hyperbole of a religious crank or fanatic but a view that could be held by students of culture of the widest reading and most profound historical and philosophical learning.

So it is with another quotation from Voegelin's *From Enlightenment to Revolution.* He observes that the "contemplative critics of Western civilization . . . discerned the disintegration of society behind the facade of progress."[3] Eliot was clearly one of these contemplative critics. So also was Yeats, for all of his tinkering with the Hermetic lore, his trafficking with spirit mediums and his elaborate symbolism of the phases of the moon to account for the rise and fall of civilizations.

I could go on to add the various accounts given by other writers on this subject, but I think it will suffice if I simply spell out in more detail what Voegelin, Yeats, and Eliot all mean by what they are saying here: that is, that the Newtonian sciences have to do only with process, with how things come to be, with how things work out, with *means*; and that none of them is capable of dealing with ends, purposes, and values. Thus, the enlightenment which began at least in a notable form in the eighteenth century has gone on to achieve one technical triumph after another in our own day and there is no end yet in sight. Yet all the triumphs have to do with means, how to do this particular thing, how to achieve that. It was, for example, a splendid and brilliant feat to work out in detail how to put people on the moon, and how to recover them from the moon and bring them safely back to earth. Yet brilliant as all of this work was, it does not have anything to do with saying why one should go to the moon. That is to say, with why it is worthwhile to go there. The question put by the exact scientist is: tell me what you want to do and I can perhaps provide the quickest and most economical means by which you can do this particular thing. But do not ask me whether I can give you a scientific validation for doing this or that thing. Matters of this sort lie outside the realm of science.

These are matters, however, with which the person in the street is imperfectly acquainted; so he asks in full faith and fairness that

3. Ibid., 112.

since we can put people on the moon, why can't we solve the problem of poverty or why can't we put together a truly just society?

Eliot puts the matter very well in "Choruses from 'The Rock'" (VI):

[The Church] tells them of Evil and Sin, and other unpleasant facts.
They constantly try to escape
From the darkness outside and within
By dreaming of systems so perfect that no one will need to be good.

Karl Marx was also one of these many sectarians who dreamed of the perfect state and who thought that in a perfect state the choice of good rather than evil could be made sure. Voegelin, in *From Enlightenment to Revolution*, says that Marx believed that for such to occur, a change of heart would be necessary; and Marx believed that once the bourgeoisie had been overthrown, the revolutionists would automatically experience such a change of heart. That dream has, however, been shattered on the rock of experience. Consider the history of the last hundred years.

In short, Eliot's concerns about the future of our culture are not anachronistic platitudes, pious generalizations that are merely holdovers from the past. What Eliot has to say challenges assumptions that have been adopted without having been thought through. If Eliot's challenges have to take their chance under rigorous intellectual scrutiny, so do the assumptions which Eliot has called in question.

Yet I do not want to substitute Eliot the philosopher for Eliot the poet; so let me cite a passage again from "Choruses from 'The Rock,'" III. With what I have just said in mind, the poetry itself becomes much more powerful.

O weariness of men who turn from GOD
To the grandeur of your mind in the glory of your action,
To arts and inventions and daring enterprises,
To schemes of human greatness thoroughly discredited,
Binding the earth and the water to your service,
Exploiting the seas and developing the mountains,
Dividing the stars into common and preferred,
Engaged in devising the perfect refrigerator,

. . . .

Turning from your vacancy to fevered enthusiasm
For nation or race or what you call humanity;
Though you forget the way to the Temple,

> There is one who remembers a way to your door:
> Life you may evade, but Death you shall not.
> You shall not deny the Stranger.

The darkness of enlightened minds is also suggested in "Choruses from 'The Rock,'" I:

> All our knowledge brings us nearer to our ignorance,
> All our ignorance brings us nearer to death,
> But nearness to death no nearer to God.
> Where is the Life we have lost in living?
> Where is the wisdom we have lost in knowledge?
> Where is the knowledge we have lost in information?

We are told today by every radio and television station that this is the age of information; and in view of the billions of dollars invested in communications of every kind, from the transmission of picture and voice by copying machines and computers, who would have suggested that information cannot save us? Can you imagine the president putting such a question to the nation? And what would have happened to his campaign if he had suggested that we had need for wisdom as well as information? The voters honestly wouldn't have known what he was talking about. A practical, go-getting country needs knowledge that can be put to direct use. Wisdom? That's a rhetorical term and means practically nothing—that is, it means practically nothing to most of us.

This last statement is not simply cheap rhetoric. Hitler's Germany, whose population was one of the best educated in Europe, particularly in scientific and technical lore, showed that it could be swept by barbaric racist passions. Stalin's Russia, which was to be a rationally organized utopia brought down to this earth, committed its own crimes against humanity. Our own beloved country itself can provide examples: we have a perfect right to be immensely proud of our technological achievements, but cities like Los Angeles, not too far from Silicon Valley, admit that they have lost control, that some of their streets are now given over to what amounts to tribal warfare. And New York has not been able yet to free its neighborhoods of drug merchants who kill their rivals as a matter of course.

Eliot's poetry treats the present situation not only as an empirical fact but indicates its causes. But his analysis of the situation is not one likely to be reported in the *New York Times* or on any other editorial page and is even less likely to be taken up by any politi-

cian. In fact, even the so-called conservative politicians would re-
coil from such an analysis.

A searching look at the daily public experience of our quotidian
world would more often than not yield what Eliot in "Burnt Norton"
(III) has described as a finally inhuman world, one in which we see

> Only a flicker
> Over the strained time-ridden faces
> Distracted from distraction by distraction
> Filled with fancies and empty of meaning
> Tumid apathy with no concentration
> Men and bits of paper, whirled by the cold wind
> That blows before and after time,
> . . . .
> . . . in this twittering world.

Eliot is no Manichean. He does not believe the world is evil and
nature is unwholesome. Nor is he asking the usual citizen to be
what Yeats called "the Saint," God's athlete, and live always at the
highest and holiest pitch. But Eliot does find our culture in serious
trouble. Moreover, he has penetrated to the heart of the malaise—a
positivistic naturalism that has emptied the world of any spiritual
meaning. Most human beings, rich and poor alike, feel that life has
no real meaning, though for many the feeling remains at the level of
a vague hunger and restlessness. A superb technology has provided
(at least to those with sufficient funds) all manner of creature comforts but such are all it can provide, for humans are curious creatures who cannot live by bread alone, even on food served up by
Escoffier himself. I realize most of us think we could survive on
bread alone. The advertising industry tenderly reinforces that belief, but it just has not worked out that way.

Eliot, I repeat, was not alone among our poets in seeing what had
gone wrong. Yeats wrote some great prophetic poems on the subject,
such as "A Prayer for my Daughter" and "The Second Coming," poems
in which he described the breakup of our age. But Yeats also wrote
such squibs as the following in which he taunted our age:

> Locke sank into a swoon,
> The Garden died;
> God took the spinning-jenny
> Out of his side.[4]

4. *The Poems*, ed. Richard J. Finneran, vol. 1 of *The Collected Works of
W. B. Yeats* (New York: Macmillan, 1989), 214.

Such is the scoffing account that Yeats gives us of the creation of the new secularistic world in which we now live, a world in which the new Adam was John Locke, the seventeenth-century British philosopher. Perhaps the reader ought to be reminded that the spinning-jenny was the first of the instruments of the new mechanized society.

In a similar squib, Yeats jibes at science as the "opium of the suburbs."

> Should H.G. Wells afflict you
> Put whitewash in a pail;
> Paint, 'Science—opium of the suburbs'
> On some waste wall.[5]

Both squibs operate on the same key: scientific and technological progress do not create a social order which is based on what men believe in community with others. Science deals with how the world works when considered as a machine; it cannot as science determine what things the machine ought to produce.

I might quote apt examples from other twentieth-century poets, but I shall choose only one more, W. H. Auden. As a student at Oxford, Auden recognized that Eliot had truly diagnosed what was wrong with the culture of the West. Auden's poem, dated 1948, is entitled "To T. S. Eliot on his Sixtieth Birthday." It is not one of Auden's best and he wisely refrained from including it in any of his collections of selected poems. But I am not concerned here with its quality as a poem, but with Auden's sense of what Eliot had done.

The analogy with which the poem opens makes use of a murder mystery, a kind of "who-dun-it," placed in an English country house with, one supposes, guests assembled for a long weekend, somewhere in Sussex or Hampshire, perhaps. Strange things began to happen—inconveniences, wanton, senseless uglinesses, and finally murder itself, most foul. Auden casts Eliot in the role of the talented amateur sleuth whose sharp eyes, sensitive observation, and sound intellect allow him to solve the mystery and to point out to everyone's shocked surprise the real culprit.

How can I be so sure that this is what Auden meant to say? Well, there is the reference to "the unheard of drought," which clearly points back to Eliot's characterization of our present world as a

---

5. *Wheels and Butterflies* (New York: Macmillan, 1934), 69.

great wasteland, but is a reference that as a matter of fact has little to do with the opening scene of a murder mystery in a pleasant South English countryside. As part of the opening metaphoric scene, we get references to what Eliot, the poet, literally did, his finding an "appropriate language for thirst and fear," the means through which the horror could be identified and, thus, done away with. If you still have any doubt about my claim that in this poem Auden has in mind Eliot's discovery and unmasking of the source of the crime in our culture, I suggest that you read some of the other poems that Auden included in the volume (entitled *Nones*) in which his birthday tribute to Eliot appeared. Read, for example, "The Fall of Rome," "Memorial for the City," "The Chimeras," and especially "A Walk After Dark." The last four and a half lines of "To T. S. Eliot on His Sixtieth Birthday" may need special explication. Let me quote them:

> It is the crime that
> Counts, you will say. We know, but would gratefully add,
> Today as we wait for the Law to take its course,
> (And which of us shall escape whipping?)
> That your sixty years have not been wasted.[6]

Why does Auden imagine Eliot saying, "It is the crime that / Counts"? Simply because, like the modest man that Eliot is, he will deprecate his own ingenuity in solving the mystery. He would say, in effect: "Never mind me. It's the situation that's important and that is what all good men must concentrate upon." Auden then would reply, if I am interpreting the poem correctly: "Yes, we know." We know that the criminal will be punished; "we wait for the Law to take its course."

What law? Presumably the law of God, or if this seems too theo-logical, the law of history or the law of the universe. Auden then adds parenthetically "And which of us shall escape whipping?" This Shakespearean quotation is no mere rhetorical flourish. All of us have participated in the crime. Society has allowed it to happen. We must not try to find others to blame. That would surely be Eliot's own view also. He once twitted his friend Ezra Pound for having described a hell to be inhabited purely by other people. Eliot is not self-righteous. We are all involved. The hell that he imagines will be filled with the likes of ourselves.

6. *Nones* (New York: Random House, 1950), 71.

In conclusion, I return to Voegelin's *From Enlightenment to Revolution*:

> The interrelation of science and power and the consequent cancerous growth of the utilitarian segment of existence have injected a strong element of magic culture into modern civilization. The tendency to narrow the field of human experience to the area of reason, science and pragmatic action, the tendency to overvalue this area in relation to the *bios theoretikos* and the life of the spirit, the tendency to make it the exclusive preoccupation of man, the tendency to make it socially preponderant through economic pressure in the so-called free societies and through violence in totalitarian states—all these tendencies are part of a cultural process that is dominated by the idea of operating on the substance of man through the instrumentality of [the] pragmatically planning will. The climax of this is the magic dream of creating the Superman, the man-made Being that will succeed the sorry creature of God's making. This is the great dream that first appeared imaginatively in the works of Condorcet, Comte, Marx and Nietzsche and later pragmatically in the Communist and National Socialist movements.[7]

T. S. Eliot would have understood these lines all too well, for his poems contain a similar diagnosis. "Your sixty years have not been wasted," Auden says to his master, and in this assessment, we can all agree. Certainly, Eliot's labors have not been wasted.

7. *From Enlightenment to Revolution*, 301–2.

Some Complexities of European Culture(s) as Manifest in French and German Translations of *The Waste Land*
Armin Paul Frank

I

"**I**t is the final perfection, the consummation of an American to become, not an Englishman, but a European—something which no born European, no person of any European nationality, can become." In this endearingly dialectical observation, worthy of a specialist in the philosophy of F. H. Bradley, Eliot, in 1918, made elegant use of Randolph Bourne's concept of an American "transnationality,"[1] possibly in order to counteract any blame he might have incurred for having turned trans-Atlantic backtracker. While Europeans have discovered political, economic, and other practical reasons that make it worth their while to strive for some kind of transnationality, there are also intellectual and epistemological respects that nevertheless recommend nationality—and I do not mean nationalism, emphatically not—for special attention. It is not for nothing that Goethe, when he worked out his concept of world literature, was not really concerned with the best works that somehow exist, worldwide, in a neutral global context, as some makers of textbooks seem to think these days. As Fritz Strich has argued in some detail, world literature for Goethe meant, first and foremost, *inter*-national acts of literary understanding.[2] Nations obviously differ, for instance in the habits and traditions of their nationals, including habits and traditions of literary thought. Therefore, foreign responses, both critical and translational, bring to the literature of one's own country perspectives that are not likely to be had at home. This is why genuine acts of understanding across

1. "In Memory of Henry James," *Egoist* 5 (January 1918): 1–2; Bourne, "Trans-National America," *The Radical Will: Selected Writings 1911–1918,* ed. Olaf Hansen (New York: Urizen, 1977), 248–64.
2. *Goethe und die Weltliteratur,* 2d ed. (Bern: Francke, 1957), 15–30, 369–72.

national boundaries can provide startling insights that can hardly be obtained in any other way.

Possibly, this is a European perspective based on the national experiences of Europeans. Certainly Eliot, after having lived in Britain for decades, came round to this position, in his talks on *Die Einheit der europäischen Kultur*,[3] designed for broadcasting in Germany shortly after the Second World War, and in his reflections on the unity and diversity of culture, published in 1948 as part of his *Notes Towards the Definition of Culture*. The motto he selected from Alfred North Whitehead is quite in the tradition of Goethe, but hardly consistent with his own position of thirty years earlier:

> A diversification among human communities is essential for the provision of the incentive and material for the Odyssey of the human spirit. Other nations of different habits are not enemies: they are godsends. Men require of their neighbours something sufficiently akin to be understood, something sufficiently different to provoke attention, and something great enough to command admiration.[4]

Seen from this vantage point, Eliot's 1918 claim that it is the final perfection of an American to become a transnational European—so well understandable as a strategic argument for coping with the rather difficult circumstances of his life after he had decided to stay on in England—clearly is not a European ideal. I wonder whether it is an American dream. It is (as is much in the writings of Eliot, both critical and poetical) a trans-Atlantic perspective.

The trans-Atlantic perspective, as A. D. Moody indicates, is evident in the poem "Preludes," and not merely by circumstances of its genesis. The images of "Marina" suggest, among other things, an unconscious trans-Atlantic journey westward.[5] There is also a trans-Atlantic perspective in "East Coker," the first section of which strikes me as among the most clearly recognizable personal poetry Eliot has ever written. What is the location of the speaker

---

3. *Die Einheit der europäischen Kultur* (Berlin: Carl Habel Verlagsbuchhandlung, 1946).

4. Quoted by Eliot in *Notes Towards the Definition of Culture* (London: Faber, 1948), 50.

5. For Moody's comment, see "T. S. Eliot: The American Strain" earlier in this volume. On the westward journey, see Erika Hulpke, *Die Vielzahl der Übersetzungen und die Einheit des Werks: Bildmuster und Wortwiederholungen in T. S. Eliot, Collected Poems/Gesammelte Gedichte*, Neue Studien zur Anglistik und Amerikanistik, vol. 32 (Frankfurt: Lang, 1985), 85.

when, in the final lines of "East Coker," I, he says, "I am here / Or there, or elsewhere. In my beginning"? *Here:* in East Coker presumably, and particularly here and now. *There:* is this "Out at sea," as the previous line reads, or "In that open field" where we are so emphatically invited to eavesdrop on the archaic rustic community enjoying their earthy dance? Taken together with "In my beginning," the phrase might also point across the Atlantic, as might the later sentence from the fifth section of "East Coker": "Home is where one starts from." *Home:* for him personally, St. Louis, and historically for the Eliot family, East Coker. Eliot's decision to have his ashes immured in St. Michael's church, East Coker, certainly invites this simultaneously personal and familial reading, which does not, of course, exclude the other aspects of the poem.

II

The Waste Land, as originally written, was also a trans-Atlantic poem. This dimension was virtually lost in the drastic cuts suggested by Ezra Pound. Pound was intent on the poetry and on the quality of the poetry. But gone is the Cambridge, Massachusetts, opening which recounted the adventures of Tom the barfly, and gone too is the entire sea adventure off the coast of Maine and Nova Scotia and north of Cape Breton Island, an episode which is in itself trans-Atlantic, seeing that it is written in a Tennysonian mode. What survived the revisions is a poem in which two structural lines intersect: the decline of a city civilization, set in, and symbolized by, London, and an eastward hike through "this stony rubbish" and through an "arid plain" at whose distant shore the speaker of the concluding section sits, contemplating whether he should set his lands in order.

The poem has been a favorite with translators. For the period of slightly less than the first half-century of its existence, Donald Gallup recorded fifty-seven translations in twenty-eight languages.[6] There are seven entries for Japanese, and three each for Bengali, modern Greek, Italian, Polish, Castilian Spanish, South American and Mexican Spanish, and Urdu—which gives one a nice sense of the balance of interest in Eliot worldwide. But that was the count twenty years ago, and I do not know of a more recent survey of similar scope. My observations are based on a complemented and

6. *T. S. Eliot: A Bibliography,* rev. ed. (New York: Harcourt Brace and World, 1969).

updated segment, the two French and the five German translations that have come to my notice, not counting translations of excerpts.

The first three translators have at least one important trait in common with their author: like him, they are cultural mugwumps, straddling at least one intercultural boundary.[7] As far as Eliot is concerned, the layers of cultural complexity in his various backgrounds need not be detailed here. It may suffice to remember some of the tensions that were part of the early history of his native St. Louis, for instance between the "nativists" and the immigrants, or between the Northern and Southern loyalties during the Civil War—tensions which, in each case, also involved friction between the Anglo-American and German-American contingents of the city's population. On a wider scale, there was Eliot's own sense of being a New Englander in St. Louis, and a "South Westerner" in New England, and I have already mentioned the trans-Atlantic dimension of his later life. The author of the world premiere translation of *The Waste Land*, Jean de Menasce, who published a French version in 1926, was also caught between cultures, but in a different way, having been born in Egypt into a family of Francophone Jews.[8] He, too, studied at Oxford. He converted to Roman Catholicism, and later became a priest in the Dominican order; he gained international fame as a specialist in religions of the Near East.

In the same year of 1926, the first German translation of *The Waste Land* was completed by another man who had grown up at a cultural periphery, among the German-speaking Jewish minority of Rumania. He studied in Vienna, became a Communist during the First World War, lived with the Dadaists in Paris, and spent a few years in New York City, where he worked for a time in a bank, until, in the early 1920s, a serious illness forced him to return home. There he continued his career as journalist, poet, and translator of poetry. His name is Alfred Margul-Sperber, and his translation, about which he corresponded with Eliot, remained unpub-

---

7. For biographical facts, see Armin Paul Frank, "T. S. Eliot's frühe 'Wüste Länder,' französisch und deutsch . . . ," in *Formen innerliterarischer Rezeption*, ed. Wilfried Floeck et al., Wolfenbütteler Forschungen, vol. 34 (Wiesbaden: Harrassowitz, 1987), 481–504.

8. On St. Louis history, see James Neal Primm, *Lion of the Valley: St. Louis, Missouri*, Western Urban History, no. 3 (Boulder, Colo: Pruett, 1981). On Eliot's identification with place, see his preface to *This American World*, by Edgar Ansel Mowrer (London: Faber, 1928), ix–xv. See also Eliot, "La Terre mise à nu," trans. Jean de Menasce, *Esprit* 1 (May 1926): 174–94.

lished for more than forty years (apparently because that of Ernst Robert Curtius appeared in print in 1927); it was not published until 1968, posthumously, and for a German text, in the cultural diaspora, so to speak—in Bucharest, Rumania.[9]

Curtius was between cultures in yet a different way: his father was a Protestant who had a prominent church position in Catholic Alsace-Lorraine, or Elsass-Lothringen, that double province west of the Rhine which, time and again, bounced back and forth between Germany and France, depending on who had won the most recent war. I know a family from those parts. During the last war, the father was drafted into the German army; the son fought on the side of the French resistance; today, they run the family vineyards and winery together, and Frenchmen and Germans are among their customers. That's cultural complexity of yet another sort, and this dangling Alsatian situation surely was an incentive for Curtius to become a Romanist intent on promoting cultural understanding between Germany and France.[10]

On the French side, which was studied by Joan F. Hooker,[11] the early translation by de Menasce was supplanted by that of Pierre Leyris, published in 1946–1947. Leyris, a dedicated translator, had much help from John Hayward, and the additional notes make his revised version of 1969, which continues in print, a useful commentary. The half-decade around 1970 saw not only the publication of Sperber's translation just mentioned, but also a prose version by Karl Heinz Göller, a university professor, who included it in his interpretation in a popular German guide to English poetry published in 1968, and Eva Hesse's new translation in the 1972 volume of poems in the German four-volume collected Eliot.[12] Ms. Hesse, who had made a name for herself as a Pound scholar and translator, felt that the only way to keep interest in Eliot alive was to puncture his public image, and, consequently, in *her* translation, the poem is

9. "Ödland," trans. Alfred Margul-Sperber, in *Weltstimmen: Nachdichtungen* (Bucharest: Literaturverlag, 1968), 74–86.

10. Curtius's version, "Das wüste Land," was first published in *Neue Schweizer Rundschau* 20 (1 April 1927): 362–77.

11. *T. S. Eliot's Poems in French Translation: Pierre Leyris and Others* (Ann Arbor: University Microfilms, 1983).

12. "La Terre vaine," in *Poésies: Edition bilingue*, 2d ed., trans. Pierre Leyris (Paris: Éditions du Seuil, 1969), 54–103; "Das wüste Land," trans. Karl Heinz Göller, vol. 2 of *Die englische Lyrik*, ed. Karl Heinz Göller (Düsseldorf: Bagel, 1968), 344–50; *Gesammelte Gedichte, 1909–1962*, ed. Eva Hesse, vol. 4 of *Werke* (Frankfurt: Suhrkamp, 1972), 83–127.

confessional, suggesting a homosexual element in the poet. Her detailed interpretation, a year later, which, to my mind, is as forced as is James E. Miller's, has the advantage of antedating the latter's effort by four years.[13] The translation by Curtius, which Suhrkamp kept in print until the publication of *Collected Poems*, was revived in 1975, so that now one can obtain two quite different German versions of *The Waste Land* from the same publisher. The most recent prose translation is part of a 1988 dissertation by Klaus Junkes-Kirchen, surveying his predecessors, though from a somewhat antiquated philological vantage point.[14]

III

These, then, are the French and German translators of *The Waste Land*. How is the state of European culture reflected in their work? A look at two details must suffice—and can suffice because they exemplify some of the most characteristic findings. It is part of the urban apocalypse theme of *The Waste Land* that we find many references to a city, or *the* city, in decline. Thus, for instance, early on, there is the invocation: "Unreal City, / Under the brown fog of a winter dawn, / A crowd flowed over London Bridge, so many" (ll. 60–62). The city, obviously, is London. But the use of the capital *C* opens the word to additional, "symbolic" meaning. We are invited to think of something larger, perhaps of *civitas* as a key concept of human consociation. As such, it forms part of the myth known as "The Course of the Empire," the rise and fall of a civilization, the decline from *civitas Dei* to *civitas Dis*.[15]

Now this broader meaning of *City* as the focal point and representative of civilization clearly transcends any national culture or even what we call Western culture. Even so, the idea as such is not unaffected by translation. The German writer, for instance, who complies with the norms of his language, must do without the expressive use of capital letters, because in German capitalization

13. See Eva Hesse, "Afterword," in Eliot, *Werke*, 4:397, and her *T. S. Eliot und "Das wüste Land": Eine Analyse* (Frankfurt: Suhrkamp, 1973). See also James E. Miller, *T. S. Eliot's Personal Waste Land: Exorcism of the Demons* (University Park: Pennsylvania State University Press, 1977).

14. *T. S. Eliot's "The Waste Land" Deutsch: Theorie und Praxis einer Gedichtübersetzung nach literatur- und übersetzungswissenschaftlichen Gesichtspunkten*, Trierer Studien zur Literatur, vol. 17 (Frankfurt: Lang, 1988).

15. I understand myth to be the interpretation of cultural phenomena that is conventional and, as it were, time-hallowed among the respective cultural group; I understand cultural phenomena as anything man-made.

is a standard orthographic device simply signaling that a noun is coming. Besides, the etymology of German *Stadt* does not point to *civitas*. The phrase *Unwirkliche Stadt* was selected by all translators except Eva Hesse (who opted for a rather Wagnerian solution, *wahnschaffne Stadt*, that runs counter to Eliot's ideal of diction), but it is doubtful that *Stadt* will allow German readers to grasp the larger meaning. For this more comprehensive meaning, they will probably have to wait for a visionary passage some three hundred lines later in the poem, where it is suggested by the enumeration of a few ancient cities along the line of the *translatio Imperii*, the Course of Empire: "Jerusalem Athen Alexandrien / Wien London / Unwirklich."

Yet the semantic-poetic complexity of *City* in *The Waste Land* goes even further. There is, for instance, another invocation of London, phrased "O City city," and placed in context with a street direction: "along the Strand, up Queen Victoria Street" (ll. 258–59). The spelling with alternative upper case and lower case *C* was adopted for the first book edition as though the symbolic and the local meaning were now placed side by side—first London as the representative of a civilization, and then, simply, as a city located on the Thames river. But the street names mentioned in these passages point to yet another meaning, for to walk "along the Strand, up Queen Victoria Street" is to arrive at the very same spot which one reaches if, as in the first-mentioned passage, one starts from the location of "London Bridge" and continues through "King William Street." Both walks converge in front of a locality not referred to in the text (an ingenious kind of blank, or void, or indeterminacy, this!), the *Bank of England*, in the heart of the financial heart of the British Empire in 1922, the banking district of London, the City of the city (still capital, but lower case *c*). No German translator can hope to catch this triple-decker of cultural connotations. The readers of Leyris's French version, which offers "Cité, ô ma Cité" at least stand a real chance of identifying the transcultural meaning, *civitas*. But insofar as the capital *C* suggests a city district to a Frenchman, he will probably think of the picturesque medieval quarter, for instance of "L'Isle de la Cité," where he will find the cathedral of *Notre Dame*, but nothing as mundane as *Crédit Lyonnais* or some other bank. Thus, when it comes to culture-specific elements, a literal translation, British-French (and there is hardly anything more literal than "Cité" for "City," is there?) may, interculturally, lead to a considerable lateral shift.

Let's now move to the country. It's autumn at the beginning of "The Fire Sermon." The trees which in summer had shaded the narrow upper reaches of the river Thames have shed their leaves: "The river's tent is broken." Some commentators on "the river's broken tent" metaphor have been reminded of Old Testament texts in which the configuration of tent, river (or stream), and trees whose leaves never fade and fall are a prophecy of the eternal presence of God.[16] In Eliot's land laid waste, however, the river's tent is broken. The question as to whether this cultural reminiscence can also be felt in the translations is of more than merely local importance. For there are respects in which the Judeo-Christian (and, for similar reasons, the Greco-Roman) tradition cannot be taken as the firm and fixed foundation of all Western culture. And, as usual, it's the translators who were the mixer-uppers. In biblical matters, the obvious subtext of *The Waste Land* (in English) is the King James Version. In the relevant passages, the word in question is *tabernacle*, and it is literally fixed in its meaning of "tent" (Hebrew *ohel*) by stakes mentioned in the immediate context, and by the fact that it is described as being pitched near rivers and streams (see Isaiah 33:20–21). In Luther's version we find instead a cabin (*Hütte*), held together by nails (*Nägel*), and set up next to broad ditches or moats, I don't know which: *weite Wassergräben*.[17] And these bodies of rather stagnant water are not in the least reminiscent of the stream of living water next to which we find Ezekiel's indeciduous trees of perennial promise (Ezekiel 47:1, 12).

I do not criticize Luther as translator or theologian—I am not competent to do so—and I know from the Mosaic directions for setting up "the tabernacle, his tent" (Exodus 35:11, 39:33) that it is indeed a rather complex structure of planks, skins, cloth, etc (Exodus 25:1–9). But Luther consistently wrote *Hütte*, "cabin." That is to say, German Protestants brought up on Luther's text will hardly be able to catch this cultural allusion in any of the German translations of *The Waste Land*. Roman Catholics and Jews are in a better position, for their translations of the Scriptures do contain the configuration of tent, river, and trees.[18] Sperber, Curtius, and Göller

16. B. C. Southam, *A Student's Guide to the Selected Poems of T. S. Eliot*, 4th rev. ed. (London: Faber, 1981), 95–96.
17. See *Die Bibel oder die ganze Heilige Schrift*, trans. Martin Luther (Berlin: Bibelgesellschaft, 1885).
18. See *Die Heilige Schrift* (Stuttgart: Katholisches Bibelwerk, 1980), and *Die Heilige Schrift der Israeliten*, trans. Ludwig Philippson (Stuttgart: Hallberger, 1874).

also retained the image of the river's tent in their versions; Junkes-Kirchen chose *Zeltdach* and Hesse chose *Laubdach*.

Even though these examples are, in a sense, isolated cases, they permit one conclusion: when one traces the transformation that a poem—particularly if it is a culturally complex one, such as *The Waste Land*—undergoes in translational transfer, especially if one observes the crossing of more than one literature, language, and culture boundary, one begins to discover cracks and crannies in European culture which one never suspected and which make one wonder whether the plural might not be more appropriate: European cultures.

T. S. Eliot, Buddhism,
and the Point of No Return
Cleo McNelly Kearns

In a notorious and perhaps exaggerated remark overheard by Stephen Spender, Eliot mentioned once that at the time of writing *The Waste Land* he "almost became" a Buddhist. I suspect that this remark bears about the same relationship to reality as Eliot's other famous pronouncement that he had later become "classicist in literature, royalist in politics and anglo-catholic in religion," though the latter has oddly enough caused far more alarm.[1] Eliot always enjoyed the game of *épater le bourgeois* and these disconcerting declarations of allegiance were in part designed to do just that. In his youth, Eliot said, he had been delighted to find in Buddhism beliefs different from those of his (heavily Unitarian and upper-middle-class) family, and later, I am sure, he delighted in finding in Anglo-Catholicism beliefs different from those of many of his friends.

Nevertheless, we would be wrong to dismiss Eliot's interest in Buddhism as a phenomenon of his youth or simply a reaction against the liberal pieties and false consolations by which he so often felt surrounded. Buddhism was for him, both before and after his conversion to Christian faith, a source of profound contact with truths he deeply believed and sources of poetry he earnestly sought. With its radical critique of human nature, of the concept of deity, and of the illusions of transcendentalist escape, it represented for him both theologically and imaginatively that dimension of otherness and challenge without which thought, sensibility, and religion alike would fall into dereliction and decay.

In what follows I shall attempt first to sketch the basis on which I believe Eliot approached Buddhism and then to indicate the kinds of effects it generated in his poetry. I shall bracket here the question of his sources and indeed the greater question of his definition of

---

1. Spender, *T. S. Eliot* (New York: Viking, 1975), 20; Eliot, *For Lancelot Andrewes: Essays on Style and Order* (London: Faber, 1928), 15.

Buddhism, which I have treated extensively elsewhere.[2] Let me begin then by situating the first part of my discussion within what I take to be an emerging consensus in recent scholarship about the nature of Eliot's philosophical position. As books like those of Harriet Davidson, Sanford Schwartz, William Skaff, and Richard Shusterman have begun to show, Eliot was by no means either the unsystematic *littérateur* or the uncritical devotee of the Absolute he has sometimes appeared to be. Rather, he had a consistent, rigorous and closely reasoned view of texts and the realities to which they purport to refer that amounted to what today we would call a full-scale critical theory.[3]

That theory, however one articulates it, has borne and will, I think, continue to bear comparison with some of the richest textual approaches available to us today, from those of Heidegger and Adorno to Derrida and beyond. It is a theory which, as we have come to understand it better over the last few years, has three main characteristics: (1) an attraction to a realist position in philosophy stemming from Russell and Moore; (2) a radical critique of liberal humanism and of what was known in Eliot's time as "progressive" thought; and (3) a systematic and principled pragmatism, which underlay Eliot's embrace of any particular point of view, whether in philosophy, in religion or in aesthetics.

It is this latter point I wish to stress here, for I think Eliot's pragmatism explains a great deal about his attitude toward Buddhism. The word *pragmatism*, however, may be somewhat misleading. In its nontechnical sense, pragmatism seems to imply something adventitious, something *ad hoc*, something merely prudential in the worldly sense, a license, as it were, to the self-serving kind of thought which ignores rigor, consistency and principle in order to provide rationalizations for willful choice. Nothing could be further from Eliot's views. His pragmatism belongs rather to the extremely principled tradition he inherited from American philos-

---

2. See my *T. S. Eliot and Indic Traditions: A Study in Poetry and Belief* (New York: Cambridge University Press, 1987).

3. Harriet Davidson, *T. S. Eliot and Hermeneutics* (Baton Rouge: Louisiana State University Press, 1985); Sanford Schwartz, *The Matrix of Modernism: Pound, Eliot, and Early Twentieth-Century Thought* (Princeton: Princeton University Press, 1985); William Skaff, *The Philosophy of T. S. Eliot* (Philadelphia: University of Pennsylvania Press, 1986); and Richard Shusterman, *T. S. Eliot and the Philosophy of Criticism* (New York: Columbia University Press, 1988).

ophy in general and from Charles Peirce, William James, and Josiah Royce in particular. It involves the strong conviction that the proof of the pudding is in the eating, or to put it less colloquially, that one is entitled, in choosing a position, to take into account the practice to which it leads and, once embarked on that practice, to revise one's sense of reality in its light. Indeed, Eliot would say, one does this all the time, willy-nilly. To change one's point of view, then, is to change permanently the way one sees the world. Once in a new practice, one cannot simply return to the former state, in part because one can no longer conceive it without qualification.[4]

I raise this issue of pragmatism in the context of Eliot's approach to Buddhism because I think it sheds a certain light not only on his move toward this most pragmatic of religious paths, but, perhaps more important, on his move away from it. In choosing my title for this paper, I was thinking of the furthest point of this trajectory, its extreme margin, where Eliot met the thought of another culture and religious sensibility, recognized its claims, and then chose to meet them only in a highly qualified way. I confess that I was thinking as well of a wonderful proverb by Franz Kafka: "Beyond a certain point there is no return. *This point has to be reached.*"[5] Nowhere is this sense of extremity more necessary to understanding, I think, than in the case of Eliot's apprehension of Buddhism, which demands, or seems to demand, so little of its adherents in terms of dogmatic assent and so much in terms of those "forms of life" that permanently alter the consciousness of those who inhabit them.

Eliot fully realized the magnitude of these claims and realized as well their consonance with much already implicit in his own temperament and thought. He was capable of perceiving even in the most scholastic and complex of Buddhist texts and manuals precisely the same demand for a deliberate and quite clinical transformation of consciousness for which he himself felt the need. He fully understood the Buddha's insistence on the vanity and futility of liberal causes, personal accomplishments, and pious hopes and the necessity for some more basic recognition and eradication of evil than these could encompass. In a review of a history of Indic thought, for instance, Eliot wrote of what seems, in the Buddhist

---

4. On Eliot's pragmatism, see Walter Benn Michaels, "Philosophy in Kinkanja: Eliot's Pragmatism" *Glyph* 8 (1981): 170–202.

5. *Dearest Fathers: Stories and Other Writings*, trans. Ernst Kaiser (New York: Schocken, 1954), 35; my italics.

or Buddhist-influenced commentaries on Patanjali's *Yoga-Sutras*, "an arbitrary and fatiguing system of classifications." But Eliot points out that this apparent scholasticism conceals always an "extremely subtle and patient psychology." This psychology aims not to baffle the ignorant with a maze of fine distinctions between mental states, but to transform the perception of the engaged reader who attempts, in practice, to distinguish them.[6]

This very recognition of the demands for change made by Buddhist texts, however, helped to clarify for Eliot where he had to stop in their exploration. Two years, he explained, of studying Sanskrit under Charles Lanman left him in a state of "enlightened mystification." Half the problem lay in trying to "erase" from his mind "all the categories and kinds of distinction common to European philosophy from the time of the Greeks." This, Eliot went on, "for reasons both practical and sentimental," he did not wish to do.[7]

This explanation, made many years later in the weariness of middle age, is more than the dismissal of a philosophy. Like the perception that Henry James, "had a mind so fine that no idea could violate it," it concentrates an important idea. Underneath this passage is the recognition, which many poets in Eliot's own tradition had signally failed to attain, that Buddhism and Hinduism are neither comfortable affirmations of truths we hold to be self-evident nor exotic spices with which we may season an essentially domestic stew. They are highly evolved, historically conditioned, culturally rooted forms of life and religious practice. Those not born to them are by no means debarred from their adoption, but this adoption may well entail forfeiting the entire stock of wisdom which is their more immediate inheritance. There are good reasons—especially for a poet—not to do this (though good reasons *to* do so, too, as the names of Gary Snyder, Nathaniel Tarn, and Janet Rodney might remind us).[8] Eliot perhaps paid Buddhism a higher compliment in recognizing and rejecting its appeal than in ignoring or overriding its demands.

This, then, was Eliot's point of no return, the point at which he

6. Review of *Brahmadarsanam, or Intuition of the Absolute*, by Sri Ananda Acharya, *International Journal of Ethics* 28 (April 1918): 445–46.

7. *After Strange Gods: A Primer of Modern Heresy* (New York: Harcourt Brace, 1933), 34.

8. Eliot, "In Memory of Henry James," *Egoist* 5 (January 1918): 2. I am thinking of the formal commitment to Buddhism made by these writers, whose works often draw directly on Buddhist sources.

fully recognized the claims of Buddhism and yet chose for himself, partly in consequence, another path. This point, however, for Eliot as for Kafka in another sense, *had to be reached*, and its significance was by no means exhausted when he had turned another way. The appeal of Buddhism represented for Eliot one of the many situations in which he was made supremely aware of "The awful daring of a moment's surrender / Which an age of prudence can never retract." It is important to remember that, in this passage from *The Waste Land*, he went on to say:

> By this, and this only, we have existed
> Which is not to be found in our obituaries
> Or in memories draped by the beneficent spider
> Or under seals broken by the lean solicitor
> In our empty rooms.
>
> (ll. 406–10)

It is not recorded in Eliot's obituary that he "became" a Buddhist, nor even that these lines applied specifically to the problem of whether or not he should have done so. Nevertheless, we should recognize here that Buddhism was, for Eliot, the clear and definitive Other, the path not taken, which parallels and gives depth to more apparent commitments and concerns.[9]

For these and many other reasons, I find the most "Buddhist" moments in Eliot's work not always or only the ones where Buddhism is most explicit, but rather those, whatever the official frame of reference, where one senses the presence of a radical, a disturbing, a marginal and yet extremely powerful point of view. One of the problems of dealing with the influence of Buddhism on Eliot's work is that one always seems to be implying a more reductive, more one-on-one relationship than actually exists between the text and its so-called "source." Actually, I think the strongest Buddhist influence on Eliot lies not in local allusions, even very direct ones like those in "The Fire Sermon" section of *The Waste*

9. Most recent biographical studies are inadequate on this issue. Lyndall Gordon (*Eliot's Early Years* [New York: Oxford University Press, 1977]) cannot assimilate Eliot's interest in Buddhism into her view of his pursuit of sainthood, to which it has a complex and qualifying relationship (see my *T. S. Eliot and Indic Traditions*). Peter Ackroyd (*T. S. Eliot: A Life* [New York: Simon and Schuster, 1984]) is wrong to dismiss Eliot's early studies of Eastern philosophy and religion as untheoretical or unscholarly, and—inhibited by superficial views of Buddhism as a source of "great ideas"—he does not understand its persistent attraction for Eliot.

Land, but in his ever more refined sense of how the mind might actually be modified, in the very categories of its perception, by close, directed attention to experience—including the experience of reading. Such close attention tends, like a child's experimental squint, to render problematic many of the ontological categories that common sense takes for granted, destabilizing, one hopes creatively, our received ideas.

These moments occur throughout Eliot's work, not just in *The Waste Land.* They are characterized, I think, by a specific rhetoric, one marked by three characteristics: (1) a syntax that breaks down or renders ambiguous the classic subject-verb-object pattern by which many languages reinforce their notions of fixed identity and causality; (2) a full exploitation of the possibilities of double entendre and of the random accidents of language which are likely to undercut intentional meanings; and (3) a very subtle exploration of *différance* in the precise Derridean sense.[10] By this I mean the sense in which a gap that is at once frightening and liberating opens up between words or statements that seem clear, self-identical, non-contradictory and / or definitive—even dogmatic—and yet, by their very reiteration, are not quite any of these, or at least not at face value.

I think here of the classic instance of such an effect, the lines in "Little Gidding" (IV) which read "We only live, only suspire / Consumed by either fire or fire." It is the *différance,* the trace, between fire and "fire" that matters here, encoding the whole binary opposition we make between salvation and damnation and then in the next move eliding the distinction between them, which, from another point of view, seems precisely the error that had constituted them in the first place. Or, to cite another instance, there is the vexed line "I do not find / The Hanged Man" (ll. 54–55) spoken by Madame Sosostris in *The Waste Land.* From that point on, the absent presence of that card, the Hanged Man, most crucial of cards in the Tarot, hovers over the poem. We are not to seek him, or look for the "key" to his presence, for by such logocentric attempts at determination, the poem warns us, each of us "confirms a prison" (l. 415). And yet if we are not to look, why bring him up in the first place? Just so does Buddhist training treat the quest for some deter-

10. The clearest treatment of this concept in Derrida's work may be found in *Margins of Philosophy,* trans. and annotated by Alan Bass (Chicago: University of Chicago Press, 1982), 1–27.

minate state called enlightenment, a state which is both an ena-
bling goal and, so conceived, an ultimate illusion, to be pursued
and bracketed at the same time.

Indeed Buddhist training often has a "do not think of pink ele-
phants" quality which is part of its phenomenology, instilled by
such classic koans or questions for meditation as "what was your
face before you were born?" Eliot often captures this tantalizing,
mind-bending effect in his work. Take the question in the fifth part
of *The Waste Land*, "Who is the third who walks always beside you?
/ When I count, there are only you and I together / But when I look
ahead up the white road / There is always another one walking
beside you" (ll. 360–63). This question might be said to function
precisely as a koan does, to pose a conundrum apparently unanswerable, from which we get relief only by a sharper insight than
any provided by its initial terms of reference. In my view, the most
remarkable exercise in Buddhist syntax, double entendre, and *différance* in the whole of Eliot's work is the great passage in "Burnt
Norton" (I) about the lotus rising from the heart of light:

> So we moved, and they, in a formal pattern,
> Along the empty alley, into the box circle,
> To look down into the drained pool.
> Dry the pool, dry concrete, brown edged,
> And the pool was filled with water out of sunlight,
> And the lotos rose, quietly, quietly,
> The surface glittered out of heart of light,
> And they were behind us, reflected in the pool.
> Then a cloud passed, and the pool was empty.

It is difficult to ascertain positively, in a straightforward, declar-
ative, rational, and referential way, whether in the middle of this
passage the pool in question is full or empty and whether its full-
ness or its emptiness is in any case its most meaningful condition.
Whatever one's answer to this question, one will, I think, have
gone through some mental changes in the process of arriving at it.
It is to the significance and effect of these changes that a Buddhist
would probably wish to draw attention. He or she might also argue
that these lines are perhaps the best rendering we have in English of
the experience of *shunyata*, or divine emptiness, an experience
which for many lies at the very heart of Buddhism.[11]

11. *Shunyata*, I should say, which might be rendered "beatitude" or "grace"
or "acceptance," expresses at the conceptual level the Buddhist insistence that

These remarks are meant as suggestions and provocations for further study. In exploring them, I myself may already have reached my own "point of no return." Let me conclude, then, in the tradition of Buddhist rhetoric, with a paradox. It was, I think, in recognizing in Buddhism a point of *no* return that Eliot found himself able *to* return, again and again, with a fresh eye, to its fine distinction, its refusal of unmediated affirmations, its suspicion of false consolations, and its corrosive and cleansing power. In relation to Buddhism, his mind was always a "beginner's mind."[12] By never allowing himself the illusion of assimilation, or indeed of its cruder cousin, expertise, Eliot kept his sense of Buddhism alive and allowed it to flow into and modify his essentially Western sensibility and work. His clarity about the limits of his understanding and the economy and restraint with which he approached Buddhist texts actually strengthened, rather than weakened, his insight, so that, again perhaps paradoxically, it was precisely by *not* "becoming a Buddhist" that Eliot became the supreme expositor of Buddhist wisdom in our poetic tradition.

---

it is the perception of and reconciliation to nonbeing that matters, not the fulfillment of deferred hopes for plentitude. For a fuller discussion of the meaning of *shunyata* in Eliot's work, see my *T. S. Eliot and Indic Traditions*, 139–40, 158.

12. The phrase comes from D. T. Suzuki, the great expositor of Zen for the West, who liked to invoke the old aphorism "Zen mind, beginner's mind" to point to the nature of a true Buddhist sensibility.

Eliot's Christian Imagination
Russell Kirk

More than any other man of letters in this century, T. S. Eliot succeeded in persuading a good many educated and percipient people that the Christian religion might be regarded as a credible body of doctrines. It was not that Eliot fancied poetry could do duty for religion; he sternly rebuked that notion in Matthew Arnold, I. A. Richards, and others. But his religious imagination opened the eyes and comforted the souls of many who had been seeking for images of truth. His conscience spoke to a multitude of consciences, although not to the masses directly.

Let me commence with a passage on D. H. Lawrence by Eliseo Vivas:

> What the poet gives us is what he brings up from the depths of his creative imagination, in the ideal isolation of his perfected form and informed substance. True, the matter the poet works with is the stuff of his experience of life and of art; but if he is an artist, the act of creation *adds* to his experienced matter to make up a literally new product: the informed substance of his poetry. The addition makes this product more than an imitation or reflection of what exists; it is literally an addition, the manifestation of the freedom of his spirit. The vision the poet offers us has order and splendor, whereas the objects of our vision are incomplete, opaque, vague. . . . we do not see the world reflected in it, we see the world by means of it.[1]

Just so, we do not see Christian belief reflected in Eliot's poetry; rather, we perceive Christian dogmas by means of Eliot's poetry, especially in the *Four Quartets*. The reason why Eliot's poetry moves us to think deeply on the claims of Christianity, and why the typical pulpit sermon today does not so move us, is that Eliot possessed imagination in the highest degree, dreaming the high dream; and the average preacher, no matter how good, is not so endowed with imagination.

It seems desirable at this point to state what I mean by this term

1. *D. H. Lawrence: The Failure and the Triumph of Art* (Evanston: Northwestern University Press, 1960), 5–6.

imagination. The first definition in the old *Century Dictionary* will serve us here: "The act or faculty of forming a mental image of an object; the act or power of presenting to consciousness objects other than those directly and at that time produced by the action of the senses; the act or power of reproducing or recombining remembered images of sense-objects; especially, the higher form of this power exercised in poetry and art."[2] The same dictionary distinguishes between two types of imagination, the reproductive and the productive, the latter being "the creative imagination which designedly recombines former experiences into new images." (It is this latter "productive" imagination to which Vivas refers in the passage from his book on Lawrence that I already have quoted.) T. S. Eliot possessed both types of imagination almost to perfection—the reproductive type often to his unease, the productive type with a power that enabled him to pour new wine into the cobwebby bottles of dogma.

It should be understood that when I speak of Eliot's imagination, I do not mean that slippery word *intuition.* For Eliot was uneasy with the claims for intuition; though unwilling to expunge the word "intuition" from the dictionary, he wrote in reply to John Middleton Murry that "intuition must have its place in a world of discourse; there may be room for intuitions both at the top and the bottom, or the beginning and the end; but that intuition must always be tested, and capable of test, in a whole of experience in which intellect plays a large part."[3]

Eliot's creative imagination did not spring from private revelation or prophetic seizure. In large part, his remarkable imagination amounted to what John Henry Newman had called the "illative sense," which we may vulgarly term the jigsaw-puzzle capabilities of the intellect, a multitude of little evidences falling into place gradually, so that in the end one discovers "powerful and concurrent reasons" for belief, even though one cannot consciously trace the intricate process by which conviction was brought about.[4] It was no "Inner Voice," no computer-like private conscience, Eliot's imagination. Intuition had a part in that imagination, of course, as it has in the perceptions of every person of genius.

A passage in André Maurois's little book *Illusions* may help

2. *The Century Dictionary: An Encyclopedic Lexicon of the English Language* (New York: Century, 1904).

3. "Mr. Middleton Murry's Synthesis," *Criterion* 4 (October 1927): 342.

4. Eliot, Introduction to *Pascal's Pensées*, trans. W. F. Trotter (New York: E. P. Dutton, 1931), xii.

us here. Maurois describes the visit of Saint-John Perse to Albert Einstein at Princeton. The physicist had invited the poet there (both having received Nobel prizes in the recent past) to ask him a question:

> "How does a poet work? How does the idea of a poem come to him? How does this idea grow?" Saint-John Perse described the vast part played by intuition and the subconscious. Einstein seemed delighted: "But it's the same thing for the man of science," he said. "The mechanics of discovery are neither logical nor intellectual. It is a sudden illumination, almost a rapture. Later, to be sure, intelligence analyzes and experiments confirm (or invalidate) the intuition. But initially there is a great forward leap of the imagination."[5]

As Maurois adds, an intuition by a scientist "perhaps stems from an unconscious statistical recollection or from the sudden glimpse of an analogy." Similarly, the talented poet's "intuitions" may be the work of the reproductive imagination, or of the illative sense, rather than unique and inexplicable glimpses of transcendent reality. Eliot certainly never claimed for himself any powers of a preternatural character, nor even experience of "timeless moments," except for a few brief imperfect ones. But we know little of such mysteries, we moderns: some writers on the brain, in recent years, even suggest that consciousness does not exist—which seems to me a thesis wondrously self-contradictory. However that may be, Eliot's imagination, marvelously powerful though it was, ought not to be confounded with mystical vision or with that Inner Voice which, in the average sensual person, "breathes the eternal message of vanity, fear, and lust."[6]

Nevertheless, so piercing was Eliot's imagination that it still transforms men and women who have been born since the poet died. I received a letter from a medical student in Oklahoma, who declared that "Eliot, it seems to me, should comprise the cornerstone of modern literary education, especially for Christians concerned with regaining and preserving a proper world view." He went on to describe his introduction to Eliot's poetry at a conservative evangelical college:

> Eliot was dealt with by having us read "The Love Song of J. Alfred Prufrock" and excerpts from "The Waste Land" as examples of dis-

---

5. *Illusions* (New York: Columbia University Press, 1968), 35.
6. Eliot, "The Function of Criticism," in *Selected Essays* (New York: Harcourt Brace, 1950), 16.

jointed, fragmented, and alienated modern poetry (in contrast, say, to Milton and Donne). By any estimation, he was one of the bad guys, if not a bad-guy ringleader. An enigmatic statement to this effect was thrown in as an afterthought: "Eliot later became a Christian, and his poetry became less disjointed . . .", etc. Apparently he never quite redeemed himself in their eyes.

Since then, my correspondent remarks, he has read Eliot with eyes from which the scales have fallen. Even in his college days,

> The depth of thought in the "Love Song" captivated me in a way that no other modern poet did. . . . As near as I could tell, my professors must either have been unable to understand Eliot because of his Anglo-Catholic brand of Christianity or unwilling to accept him as a legitimate Christian because of it. The former may have played a role, but since in retrospect I find that I was almost systematically "protected" from the wide range of first-class Catholic scholarship, I believe the latter reason is more likely. This was unfortunate, but provincialism is alive and well in the evangelical world.

Here we have evidence to suggest that Eliot's Christian imagination, influential though it has been over the past half century, has not penetrated deeply into the Christian circles commonly called "fundamentalist." Yet why wonder at that? For the religious insights so movingly expressed in Eliot's poems have been rejected from a point of view distinctly not fundamentalist by some of Eliot's contemporaries among the poets and by some of his more eminent critics.

I suppose that many of my readers will have seen *The Mysterious Mr. Eliot*, a television film produced under the sponsorship of the National Endowment for the Humanities. Several of the poets and critics interviewed in that film wondered condescendingly at Eliot's quaint attachment to the superstitions of the childhood of the race. William Empson was quoted solemnly to the effect that Eliot had possessed, or been possessed by, a medieval mind, believing in hell and damnation. Stephen Spender put in, "All these things people in the Middle Ages believed in were very real to him." And a disembodied voice declared reproachfully that "he believed in elites, he believed in class," and remarked that Eliot's "preachy role" had been inherited from his Unitarian background.[7] Some of

7. Stephen Cross (director), *The Mysterious Mr. Eliot* (New York: McGraw-Hill Films, n.d.). Incidentally, Eliot most certainly believed in classes, but he detested the notion of domination by elites, observing that the doctrine of elites "posits an *atomic* view of society," like that of Hobbes, whom Eliot called "an extraordinary little upstart" ("John Bramhall," in *Selected Essays*, 312).

the people on that television program seem to have read Eliot a long time ago—and not have wished very much, in those days almost beyond recall, to read him with an open mind.

For intellectuals whose minds were closed to Eliot from the beginning, because they had been reared on a diet of doctrinaire positivism and scientism (a very different thing from an apprehension of scientific theory), Eliot's Christian imagination was a strange and rather unpleasant survival from the Dark Ages. It was not such secular dogmatists, however, but men and women of a skeptical turn of mind, myself among them, who came to learn from Eliot's verses that one is not a fool to suspect the existence of a transcendent realm of being. When, as a freshman at Michigan State University, I first read *Murder in the Cathedral*, I wrote a long, scathing, presumptuous paper about that drama's absurdities; that was in my salad days. Now my judgment is rather different, for with the passage of the years certain great writers have helped to alter my convictions in such matters—notably Saint Augustine, Dante, Sir Thomas Browne, Samuel Johnson, John Henry Newman, and Thomas Stearns Eliot. Those commentators on the dead Eliot who proclaim that he had one of the finest minds of the thirteenth century remind me of a textbook in world history for eighth graders that I reviewed once upon a time. In this volume there were but two references to Christianity, the latter of which informed the young that there was a religion in the Middle Ages called Christianity, which caused the building of many churches. The Christian faith ended then, so far as readers of this textbook were instructed.

In truth, Eliot was no medievalist, aside from his love of Dante. The religious writers who moved him were those I named above, as well as the great English divines of the sixteenth and seventeenth centuries and the English religious poets of the Anglican tradition. As for his contemporaries, Christopher Dawson and Martin D'Arcy seem to me to have been chief among those who influenced his thought.

Eliot knew well the position of his adversaries among men of letters, even though they made little effort to understand his postulates. He was at least as well informed about nineteenth- and twentieth-century natural science as those who have sat complacently in judgment upon his intellect. Between him and them a great gulf was fixed, and it was this: Eliot's imagination could transcend the twentieth century in which he and they found themselves, while their imagination was confined by what Eliot considered to be "the provincialism of time."

It was not by any infatuation with the Middle Ages, nor through any abrupt flight of fancy, that Eliot came to declare himself an Anglo-Catholic. As Hoxie Neale Fairchild puts it, "One might say that he became a Christian on discovering that he already *was* one— a very common type of conversion." Clearly Eliot believed in "holy living and holy dying, in sanctity, chastity, humility, austerity." And Fairchild concludes that perhaps the strongest motive of all for Eliot's profession of Christian faith was his "horrified revulsion against the *absence* of belief in these values from modern society."[8]

I wish it were possible in this essay to trace the development of Eliot's religious imagination. We would examine his visions of hell in "Prufrock," "Gerontion," *The Waste Land*, and *The Hollow Men*. Then we might turn to his images of the purgatorial condition in *Ash-Wednesday* and *The Family Reunion*. We would proceed to redemption from fire by fire in *Four Quartets*, and would trace in those poems his endeavor to express, through poetry, acceptance of the dogmas of the Apostles' Creed. We would closely examine his imagery, which opens minds to ancient insights that positivism ignores. And especially we would try to apprehend his concept of the timeless moment, at which temporal and eternal intersect, his awareness that we are now in eternity, and the symbols and images by which he communicates this perception to us.

But as Yeats laments in "I am of Ireland"—"Time runs on, runs on." Let me then conclude with a succinct approach to Eliot's own observations on the imagination—the moral imagination, the idyllic imagination, the diabolic imagination. Eliot rejected with contempt the argument of Thomas Hobbes that imagination is nothing but decaying sense. With Joubert, he held that imagination is the eye of the soul. To apprehend Eliot on imagination, one turns to *After Strange Gods*, and especially to the third lecture in that slim book. In the context of a discussion of separation from tradition, Eliot condemns what he calls the "diabolic" imagination:

Here I am concerned with the intrusion of the *diabolic* into modern literature in consequence of the same lamentable state of affairs. . . . I

8. Fairchild, *Religious Trends in English Poetry*, vol. 6, *1920–1965: Valley of Dry Bones* (New York: Columbia University Press, 1968), 442; Eliot, "Christianity and Communism," *Listener* 7 (16 March 1932): 382–83; Fairchild, *Religious Trends*, 6:442.

am afraid that even if you can entertain the notion of a positive power
for evil working through human agency, you may still have a very
inaccurate notion of what Evil is, and will find it difficult to believe
that it may operate through men of genius of the most excellent character. I doubt whether what I am saying can convey very much to
anyone for whom the doctrine of Original Sin is not a very real and
tremendous thing.[9]

More people may apprehend Eliot's meaning, and concur in it, in
the present age than could have understood his reflections on sin
and evil in 1933 at the University of Virginia. Eliot's poetry and
prose have done more than a little to renew that painful awareness
of the Adversary and of feeble human nature, readily corrupted.

What he called "the fruitful operations of the Evil Spirit," Eliot
discerned in Lawrence and Hardy. What would he say to most popular authors of fiction in our day? Eliot set his face so sternly against
the diabolic imagination, as given expression by the unregenerate
personality, because he knew its abysmal power. The two Eliot
poems that I find most memorable and convincing are "Gerontion"
and *The Hollow Men.* Having reread "Gerontion" nocturnally, I
have meditated on what it is to "lose beauty in terror, terror in
inquisition"; in imagination at least, I too have plodded, at five
o'clock in the morning, round the prickly pear, with the other old
guys in the valley of fading stars. That imagery of spiritual anni-
hilation, linked to the dogma of original sin, does not merely *reflect*
Christian teaching: it *renews* that terrible truth for the modern
age. Eliot struck hard at the diabolic imagination among twentieth-century men of letters, for he knew the uses of the word to
corrupt. As he wrote, "the number of people in possession of any
criteria for discriminating between good and evil is very small; the
number of the half-alive hungry for any form of spiritual experience, or what offers itself as spiritual experience, high or low, good
or bad, is considerable."[10] And he never forgot the biblical reproof
of imagination: "The imagination of man's heart is evil from his
youth" (Genesis 8:21).

So it is Eliot's images of the infernal that we tend to remember
most vividly. Yet he gives us, too, images drawn from the idyllic
picture of the human condition, and quite different images expressing what Edmund Burke called "the moral imagination." It was
from Irving Babbitt that Eliot learned of the idyllic imagination,

9. *After Strange Gods: A Primer of Modern Heresy* (New York: Harcourt
Brace, 1933), 61–62.
10. Ibid., 66–67.

most successfully expressed by Jean-Jacques Rousseau. This is the sort of imagination that, ignoring the hard necessities of human existence, would have us surrender to appetites in primitive simplicity; it is the sort of imagination which, at second hand, captured the rising generation in many countries during the 1960s, and which works private and public disorder still. When Eliot assailed Romanticism, he was not flailing such romantics as Samuel Taylor Coleridge or Walter Scott; what Eliot fought was the school of Rousseau, depraved in its fancied Arcadia, a sordid paradise celebrated in the song of *Sweeney Agonistes*:

> *Under the bam*
> *Under the boo*
> *Under the bamboo tree.*

As for the moral imagination, some concept of that Eliot acquired through Babbitt, who took the phrase from Burke. For a long time Eliot and the *Criterion* crowd were ill at ease with those two words; Allen Tate endeavored to demolish what was called "the ethical imagination" because he found it bound up with fancies of private inspiration. For that matter, Eliot very rarely mentioned Burke until his later writings, presumably on the assumption that Burke was what Johnson had called his friend, "a bottomless Whig." Not until the 1950s does the name of Burke seem to mean much to Eliot. But after that, Eliot discerns what Burke meant by "the moral imagination" and reinforces him.

For the moral imagination is the power of descrying people, despite their weaknesses and proclivity to sin, as moral beings meant for eternity. Human beings, after all, are created in the image of God. The moral imagination expresses what Pico della Mirandola called "the dignity of man." It was this moral imagination, indeed, that Eliot had been exercising with such persuasive, innovative skill and success ever since "Prufrock." This moral imagination offers to us the images of Becket martyred in the cathedral and Celia martyred upon an African anthill. In the words of St. Paul, "O death, where is thy sting? O grave, where is thy victory?" (1 Corinthians 15:55).

Eliot's endowment with moral imagination made him "able to see beneath both beauty and ugliness; to see the boredom, and the horror, and the glory."[11] Abruptly, in a sensate era, there started up

---

11. "Matthew Arnold," in *The Use of Poetry and the Use of Criticism: Studies in the Relation of Criticism to Poetry in England* (London: Faber, 1933), 106.

the poetry of Eliot—exciting, alarming, and morally demanding. The rising generation read it. The strangest thing about this new poetry, people learned presently, was that it came to affirm the authority of Christian teaching, which the intellectuals of the twentieth century had fancied hopelessly senescent.

In the long run, it has been said, great poets shape the culture into which they are born. This may be less true today than it was in Virgil's time or in Dante's; yet surely Eliot will be read, and his imagination work upon minds and consciences, long after the literary foibles of the twentieth century have been well and thoroughly forgotten. Without bravado and without equivocation, Eliot restored religious insights to poetry, and restored imaginative power to formulas of faith. We are entering a new Dark Age, Eliot wrote repeatedly. If that be so, conceivably Eliot may survive in myth, as did Virgil after the collapse of the Latin culture.

The human race is governed by its imagination—so argued the master of the big battalions, Napoleon Bonaparte. T. S. Eliot was not at all Napoleonic; nevertheless, his imagination was of the kind that gives order to the commonwealth and order to the soul. The images he revealed to us help to chasten the ragged follies of the time.

I have in my memory his image in his later years, when we would meet at the Garrick, or the Travellers' Club, or at some private hotel in Edinburgh. His face and his manner reflected an easy dignity and a Christian resignation. He had suffered a profound personal tribulation—long before, true, but as he says early in "Burnt Norton" (I): "All time is unredeemable." He had spoken for causes that seemed lost; yet, after all, there are no gained causes. He was a man eminently sane, and nevertheless a man of vision. From Apeneck Sweeney to the Light Invisible, the images he bequeathed to us enliven our own imagination in an era when it seems, in the language of "Choruses from 'The Rock'" (VII), as if "men have forgotten / All gods except Usury, Lust and Power." T. S. Eliot will continue to mold our imaginations, for in the lines from "Little Gidding" (I) engraved upon his memorial in Westminster Abbey, "The communication / Of the dead is tongued with fire beyond the language of the living."

The Elder Statesman:
Its Place in Eliot's Theater
Carol H. Smith

The hundredth anniversary of a poet's birth inevitably leads us to the question of the end result of that beginning, the question of the value of a life of achievement. This is the question that Eliot himself addresses in *The Elder Statesman*, his last play. The play is Eliot's final dramatic statement and a personal testimony to his discovery of a transforming love late in his life that seemed to change the meaning of all that had gone before.

I would like to focus in this essay on the importance of Eliot's willingness to express this transforming experience, indeed to celebrate it. This artistic act, which would have been impossible for him earlier in his career, seems to have surprised him more than anyone else, and it should surprise us too, for it revises the "doctrine of impersonality" that is at the heart of Eliot's early literary judgments.

When we look over the long list of plays that Eliot wrote during his career, as well as the statements he made about them, we recognize that one of the things that attracted him to drama was its ability to *conceal* the author while it *revealed* his ideas. Eliot's fundamental ambivalence about self-revelation shaped his dramatic method, just as it shaped the form of many of his most celebrated poems. In his plays he tried out a variety of dramatic styles, including melodramas, farce, and romantic comedy, which were intended to produce a dramatic surface at odds with the deeper meanings hidden below. Eliot allowed his hidden meanings to surface at times—sometimes openly in lyric duets, sometimes covertly in wordplay, double meanings, and witty juxtapositions—but more and more he worked to create plays in which the modern situations were secular fables that concealed his Greek sources and sometimes mystical Christian doctrines.

In part this method was a translation into drama of the "mythical method" that Eliot so admired in Joyce and used so creatively in his own poetry. But at the same time, his insistence on a drama of layers reveals certain assumptions about his audience and himself that are very different from those that characterize *The Elder Statesman:* the assumption, for example, that lay audiences cannot understand and will reject in drama the portrayal of religious experience (a view Eliot held despite the enormous success of *Murder in the Cathedral*); the assumption that only a few will be able to see through the dramatic surface to the depths below, while the other, less-perceptive theater-goers must be entertained by the surface; and finally the assumption that the artist must cultivate a discipline of silence, or at most a carefully coded utterance in the face of private pain and horror. We have only to remember the epigraph of *Sweeney Agonistes*, in which Eliot translates the warning by Saint John of the Cross that "the soul cannot be possessed of the divine union, until it has divested itself of the love of created beings" into Sweeney's tale of the murderer who dissolves his mistress in a lysol bath. This is Eliot at his most negative when he suffered his own dark night of the soul; *Sweeney Agonistes* was a play so dark and so private that he could not finish it. Eliot maintained the same dramatic formula that he had developed in *Sweeney Agonistes* throughout his career until it was finally modified in *The Elder Statesman.*

It is interesting to note that Eliot clung to this distanced and hierarchical view of drama long after he had begun to write the more personal poetry of *Four Quartets*, which were published individually between 1936 and 1942, near the time of *The Family Reunion* (1939) and before *The Cocktail Party* (1949). In *Four Quartets*, Eliot was not only able to achieve a more personal voice, but to bring his private trauma and family history into harmony with broader cultural and philosophical speculations.

However, the flexible and direct voice that Eliot was able to achieve in *Four Quartets* was not easy to transfer to drama. Partly this was because of the literalness of his belief that West End audiences wanted entertainment, not religion. But it was also because drama requires a much more complex relationship between the author and the world of the play than lyric poetry requires. Eliot himself recognized this, sometimes to the point of despair. Drama requires the construction of a world, not a response to a world. It requires a certain tolerance of multiple perspectives and a flexibility in the creation of a distinctive "culture" within the dramatic world. But even beyond these attitudes of the playwright, it requires the recognition that drama is essentially, as Yeats says, character defined by action.[1]

As we can see from Yeats's own work, this precept does not limit all drama to naturalism; it simply insists that however character is defined, the dramatic action is the vehicle for its expression. In Eliot's model, the dramatic action does not reveal character. Instead it is a stylized modern fable which alludes to a Greek original, and the hero's role as spiritual sufferer in a hostile secular world is constructed to be at odds with the surface action. We know from Eliot's comments on his education as a dramatist that he recognized this problem and experimented with a variety of methods to make the poetic passages that expressed the real meaning of the plays seem less like dramatic interruptions. But since he honestly saw religious experience as "interrupting" daily life in the most profound sense, a dramatic method that expressed this message was bound to appear on stage as a lack of dramatic unity, for the plays had essentially been set up that way.

Eliot felt this problem to be most acute in *The Family Reunion* (1939), where Harry's experience of guilt and suffering seems merely confusing and unpleasant, despite Eliot's experiments with a chorus to explain the play's deep meanings and the appearance of the Eumenides on stage. With hindsight, we can see Harry's guilt about the drowning of his wife on shipboard as a version of Sweeney's message: "Any man has to, needs to, wants to / Once in a lifetime, do a girl in" ("Fragment of an Agon," *Sweeney Agonistes*). And we can also see that Eliot's obsessive use of this theme reflected his efforts to dramatize an intensely private and painful response to his first marriage, however symbolically it is represented. But he could find no way to resolve this dramatic and theatrical problem except to move further away from direct expression, to the world of comedy and finally farce. In *The Cocktail Party* (1949) he constructed a brilliant *tour de force* that develops the philosophical issue of the two paths to Grace (the Negative Way of martyrdom and the Affirmative Way of Christian marriage). By the time of *The Confidential Clerk* (1953) Eliot had modified his view of human love and presented it as at least an alternative path to happiness, if not to Grace. But he chose to present a dramatic surface modeled on the foundling child plot of high comedy. While the surface has few in-

1. "An Introduction for My Plays," in *Essays and Introductions* (New York: Macmillan, 1961), 529.

terruptions, none of the characters seems fully realized, even in the terms of comedy, and the religious message comes close to confusing the problem of religious vocation with that of artistic vocation.

It is from the perspective of this history that *The Elder Statesman* (1958) is an important play in Eliot's canon, if not a fully successful dramatization of his message of love. In it, he shows a willingness to leave behind some of the artifice of his earlier works and to step forward with a new directness as author/character. In this final play he builds on many of the themes and methods of the earlier plays, but departs from them in some fundamental ways.

When I first wrote about this play in 1962, Eliot was still alive. I then saw *The Elder Statesman* as the furthest step that he had been able to take towards the acceptance of human love and the Affirmative Way as a path to salvation.[2] Today, I see the play as a more personal statement, and I can appreciate more fully the risks that it represented for Eliot. It is quite literally the poet's personal thank you to his wife Valerie, and it extends to her his blessing, just as Oedipus blessed Antigone and Ismene at the end of *Oedipus at Colonus.* It can also be read as a farewell to the theater and to a life of artistic struggle amid public acknowledgment. Most important, it expresses in unusually direct terms the message that death, while near, is not to be feared. This attitude of acceptance of death is surprising, considering that we might expect a degree of bitterness at the irony of a love so long delayed being ended so soon by death. Again, Yeats comes to mind as a contrast. Eliot does not rail out at death, nor does he celebrate a defiant and lusty old age: his mood is one of acceptance and even joy for the happiness that remains.

One of the main themes of the play, a new theme for Eliot, is that selfhood, while destroyed by a life of pretense and role-playing, can be restored by personal confession to a truly accepting beloved. This is very different from the denial of the love of created beings of *Sweeney Agonistes.* It is not only a new view of human love but a new view of woman. In *Sweeney Agonistes* the bonds of woman had to be dissolved because she embodied the danger of man's own sensory desire. Eliot's representation of woman as an object of love after his acceptance of the Church was more positive but also more distant; she was the Mary figure, to whom one might

2. See my *T. S. Eliot's Dramatic Theory and Practice: From "Sweeney Agonistes" to "The Elder Statesman"* (Princeton: Princeton University Press, 1963).

pray for forgiveness. In this last play, the woman is a beloved daughter/wife to whom confession has a different meaning. It is her human understanding, not her divine pity, that qualifies her as the restorer of self. She is now a real woman, and marriage and parental love are portrayed as intimacy and caretaking, not as "the best of a bad job," as the Chamberlains say early in act 2 of *The Cocktail Party.*

The significance of this change is that now divine love is sought not outside the self, but inside, in the purification that the love of another human being can bring. The diagnosis of the human condition, as well as its cure, is offered at Badgley Court, the convalescent home where Lord Claverton will be cleansed in preparation for his mystic death under the great beech tree. This is the last of Eliot's many medical cures for the spiritual illnesses of his characters.

Lord Claverton must strip himself of his false roles of elder statesman and irreproachable father and husband and accept the truth about his real nature and his shabby past. When he can strip himself of illusions and risk being loved for himself alone, he can be free to give up control of others. In his moment of illumination at the end of *The Elder Statesman*, Lord Claverton says to his daughter Monica:

> Why did I want to keep you to myself, Monica?
> Because I wanted you to give your life to adoring
> The man that I pretended to myself that I was,
> So that I could believe in my own pretences.[3]

The greatest ordeal that Lord Claverton must endure is to witness the sacrifice of his son Michael to his enemies, with the recognition that he has forced Michael into the path he takes.

Eliot's Greek source for *The Elder Statesman* is Sophocles' *Oedipus at Colonus,* a choice that suggests the theme of expiation by suffering and devotion to the will of the gods. At the time of *The Family Reunion*, Eliot had written to his director, E. Martin Browne, that "Harry's career needs to be completed by an Orestes or an Oedipus at Colonus," another indication that the play represented to Eliot a final statement.[4]

In *Oedipus at Colonus* the exiled king has reached a state of

3. *The Elder Statesman* (London: Faber, 1959). All quotations from the play are from this edition.
4. See Browne, *The Making of T. S. Eliot's Plays* (London: Cambridge University Press, 1969), 107.

reconciliation with the gods, and he nears the sacred grove of the Eumenides, where it is ordained that he is to die. Because of his blindness, he is led by his faithful daughter Antigone. Oedipus receives asylum from the King of Athens, since his burial at Colonus was ordained by Apollo and will bring a blessing on the city. But his peaceful end is threatened by the attempt of Creon to bring Oedipus back to Thebes, and by his son Polynices, who asks his father's blessing for his war with his brother. Oedipus curses both his sons for their selfish disregard of him and the will of the gods. Thunder is heard and Oedipus bids a loving farewell to his daughters and obeys the divine summons which urges him toward his fated place of death.

In Eliot's version of Sophocles' play, Lord Claverton re-enacts the final purgation of the aged Oedipus. Like Oedipus he has been blind to his guilt; even his past sins parallel those of Oedipus. He has run over an old man, lived with his wife without recognizing her identity, and reared a son who is an outcast. Perhaps the most important identification is in the loving support of a beloved daughter.

There can be little doubt that Eliot identified the curative love of Monica in *The Elder Statesman* with the happiness he had found with his wife Valerie. But the Greek source cannot do the dramatic work of showing us transformative love in action. Nor can Monica's words or Lord Claverton's assertions. It is more honestly expressed in "To My Wife," the frank love poem that appears in the play's printed version as a dedication to Valerie Eliot.

> To whom I owe the leaping delight
> That quickens my senses in our wakingtime
> And the rhythm that governs the repose of our sleepingtime,
>   The breathing in unison
>
> Of lovers . . .
> Who think the same thoughts without need of speech
> And babble the same speech without need of meaning:
>
> To you I dedicate this book, to return as best I can
> With words a little part of what you have given me.
> The words mean what they say, but some have a further meaning
>   For you and me only. [Eliot's ellipsis]

I take this poem to be more than a literary dedication and more even than an announcement of his love for his wife. It announces something about words and the way they act in public and private.

The rhythm that is celebrated is not the rhythm of poetry; it is the rhythm of "our sleepingtime, / The breathing in unison / Of lovers." Words, in fact, are not needed by lovers, "Who think the same thoughts without need of speech / And babble the same speech without need of meaning." The public words, the play, is dedicated to his wife "to return as best I can / With words a little part of what you have given me." But it is the "further meaning / For you and me only" that is valued. This is an extraordinary statement from the poet who once endorsed "impersonality." It would be extraordinary coming from any poet, for that matter.

The theme of the poem is that, next to the "leaping delight" of human love, literature comes in a poor second. The poet has been "brushed by the wing of happiness" (*The Elder Statesman*, act 3), as Lord Claverton has, and that joy, like the saint's union, is ineffable. The struggle to speak and be understood takes place at a lower level of experience, much as we, the audience, might wish it otherwise. This then I take to be the combined message of Eliot's final play: that the physical and spiritual fulfillment of personal love goes beyond the temporary satisfaction of fame, beyond doctrines, programs, and finally beyond art. Eliot's life of high achievement and deep despair has been crowned by joy, and everything has changed for him.

If his play is Eliot's dramatization of the Affirmative Way, as I thought in my own theoretical youth, then it is because Eliot did not have the dramatic means to express his private joy and final peace. His complementary love poem seems a more direct and a more appropriate vehicle for the private message. And while we might wish for a more perfect play, we can all feel joy that a life of such high achievement ended with such happiness.

Voices That Figure in *Four Quartets*
George T. Wright

Was not writing poetry a secret transaction,
a voice answering a voice?
> —Virginia Woolf, *Orlando*

I see a voice: now will I to the chink,
To spy an I can hear my Thisby's face.
> —Bottom, *A Midsummer Night's Dream*

Why do you never speak.
> —*The Waste Land*

I

Because of Eliot's abiding interest in dramatic poetry and his unusual success in writing both plays and a verse frequently described as "dramatic," critics have often written about the voices in his work. His own criticism regularly addressed the problems of writing for the voice. Even formal verse, he claimed, "must not stray too far" from a plausible conversational style.[1] He could hear behind the dialogue of Jacobean plays the distinctive voice of each playwright, and within lyric poems in the English tradition he could discern three voices of the poet. "The first voice is the voice of the poet talking to himself—or to nobody. The second is the voice of the poet addressing an audience. . . . The third is the voice of the poet when he attempts to create a dramatic character speaking in verse."[2] These terms, which are familiar to every critic of the dramatic monologue, make a promising point of departure for discussions of point of view in poetry, even for recent critics who would invoke the "figure of voice" as a key to the postmodern understanding of poetry and who see *prosopopoeia* (personification

---

1. "The Music of Poetry," in *On Poetry and Poets* (London: Faber, 1957), 21.
2. "The Three Voices of Poetry," in *On Poetry and Poets*, 96.

or mask poetry) as a term to be preferred (perhaps because it's Greek) to the New Critical (and Latin) *persona.*

My own interest in Eliot's voices grows out of a longstanding fascination with Eliot's personae. Along with other critics, however, I have learned over the last two decades that the notion of persona by itself cannot do justice to the variety and frequency of what Rosenthal and Gall rightly emphasize as Eliot's tonal shifts (or Calvin Bedient calls his "polyvocalism" and "heteroglossia"), most conspicuous in *The Waste Land* but at the heart of his poetic strategy in all his best work.[3] But my thinking about these issues has benefited from reflection on the sound of Shakespeare's later dramatic verse, where two features in particular—the frequency of metrical lines with more or fewer syllables than we expect, sometimes in oddly deviant combinations, and the habit of running the sentence sense over the line endings—must have made the verse extremely difficult to hear as verse. Did Shakespeare's theater audience continue to hear the lines as lines, as they surely did in earlier plays and must still have done during the occasional bursts of rhyme in the later ones? Or did they hear nothing more than sentences floating down a generalized iambic current? Did they hear the meter just now and then, appearing and disappearing, and only intermittently offering the metrical order as an uncertain emblem of coherence for the increasingly problematical issues that Shakespeare takes up in his later plays?

To address this problem is to become aware of the profound chasm that separates a Shakespearean performance and a Shakespearean text, in which we see the verse lines in an entirely different light. We do *see* them; in effect, like Bottom, we see a voice. Because the lines are visually presented, we are at liberty to follow the beat with our inner and silent sense of rhythm, to give voice to a line or passage here and there, or to ignore its sound completely. But, however our nervous systems process the visible text, most of us will not experience the metrical anxiety that may trouble a careful listener in the theater. The "word of no speech" that we hear in some sense as we read the text bears little resemblance to the complex sounded rhythms and counter-rhythms that a first-rate per-

---

3. M. L. Rosenthal and Sally Gall, *The Modern Poetic Sequence: The Genesis of Modern Poetry* (New York: Oxford University Press, 1983), 156–83; Calvin Bedient, *He Do the Police in Different Voices: "The Waste Land" and Its Protagonist* (Chicago: University of Chicago Press, 1986), 9–10.

formance can give us. Still, when the verse is ineptly spoken on the stage, we may prefer to listen to the lines furnished by the visible page to our inward ear, though dubious editorial practices of spelling, punctuation, and lineation may help make our own verse-listening procedures as questionable as a tin-eared actor's speech.

Furthermore, Shakespeare's exclusive concern during his later years with the production, and not with the publication, of his plays may lead us to wonder about the extent to which Shakespeare's dramatic work should be understood as oral literature rather than as a hardly differentiated episode in the English poetic tradition. These are formidable questions, and some of them arise also for a reader of Eliot. After all, if Shakespeare's plays most acutely pose the problem of how differently we hear a play and a dramatic text, Eliot's poems most acutely pose the problem of how we hear (or take in) the play of voices or tones in nondramatic verse. To read Eliot at all, we have constantly to negotiate the shifting tones of allusion, quotation, question, and assertions of various weights and stances, to understand which self, or which part of a self, or a self in what guise, is speaking, and to what kind of audience— himself, nobody, us, God, another creature or character, or another point of view—the words are addressed.

In our efforts to identify these different speakers, selves, or tones, however, we sometimes lose sight of what we mean when we speak of voice in nondramatic poetry. We all use the term, and we know more or less what it signifies, but we seldom acknowledge that the voice we have in mind, the voice we suppose to be speaking from the page in any silent reading (which is our usual way of reading) is not really a voice; it does not speak, it makes no sound, it does not share with actual voices (or even whispers) the physical characteristics of pitch, volume, timbre, and accent. It is "unheard," like the music that hides in the shrubbery of "Burnt Norton" and echoes the unheard "melodies" played in absolute silence by the pipers on Keats's Grecian urn. Such melodies, Keats tells us, are "sweeter" than the ones we actually hear, because it is "to the spirit" that they "Pipe . . . ditties of no tone."

Keats's phrase gives a very high value to unsounded verse, even when the verse is as sensuous as Keats's own. Eliot's deliberate echo of Keats's passage reminds us that in his verse, too, the unsounded voice, a subvocal register, is central. This is the register that I want to explore in this paper, with some special but not exclusive reference to *Four Quartets*, the poetic sequence written just when this poet of many voices (and many gods) leaves the territory of lyric poetry and lights out for the real theater of the West End, where voices are not heard silently in private by a single reader, but sounded by actors and heard by living listeners.

II

In a well-known formulation, Barbara Herrnstein Smith tells us that poetry imitates natural utterance. For Susanne K. Langer, literature creates "virtual events": prose fiction, in Langer's terms, is "virtual memory," and "poetic reflections create the semblance of reasoning."[4] Poetry, we may infer, is virtual speech—in two senses: first, that the person whose words are presented is not speaking them here and now in the context offered by the poem; and, second, that, when the words are read silently from the page, they are not sounded, as speech is by definition.

The distinction between actually spoken poetry and poetry silently read is not one that informs Eliot's own three-voice classification, but he could hardly have been unaware of it when he began to write plays.[5] Even earlier, his professional interest in phenomenological philosophy is inseparable from his intense poetic presentation of streams of consciousness, streams that in actual life under normal circumstances are unlikely to be vocalized. His early poems usually imitate not speech but verbal thought—reverie, a speaker's silent wording of the world and his feelings about it, "subvocal" speech in Langer's terminology. From "Portrait of a Lady" on, this speech is contrasted with other voices referred to and quoted, and the contrast between them is one of the familiar "dramatic" resources of his nondramatic verse. We are frequently made aware of the difference between actual speech and words that are framed but remain unspoken, like those answers given in the first section of *The Waste Land* to the hyacinth girl, or in the second to the nervous woman. We infer that they are unspoken because, unlike the woman's words, they are printed without quotation marks. They are thought, they are ordered, but they are not voiced. It is one kind,

4. Smith, *On the Margins of Discourse: The Relation of Literature to Language* (Chicago: University of Chicago Press, 1978), 24–25; Langer, *Feeling and Form* (New York: Scribner's, 1953), 219.
5. Eliot's distinction is between verse written for his own voice and verse written for other voices—in both cases, he seems to say, actually sounded: "the way it sounds when you read it to yourself" ("Poetry and Drama," in *On Poetry and Poets*, 83).

the principal kind, of language that Eliot's poems imitate—not "utterance" but silent speech. This is not unusual for English meditative, reflective, or even narrative poems, but in Eliot what is remarkable is how "dramatically" this silent voice plays off other ostensibly audible voices. Through this technique, his poetry poses a world outside the "speaker," an outer world, for which the heard or remembered language of other speakers, often filtered through the poet's own voice, frequently serves as a notation, against a silent voice of continuous inner reflection. But the sharp difference between these two kinds of language tends to be obscured by our reading both of them silently from the page (the usual case) or by our *vocalizing* both of them in a public reading or a class discussion.

The outer world's voices are familiar to any reader of Eliot, though most of my examples are taken from *Four Quartets:* the shrieking, chattering, scolding, mocking voices; voices of temptation, of quiet-voiced elders; voices of distraction, the conversation in the underground that rises and slowly fades into silence; the empty voices of political or cultural sloganeering. These voices are generally the voices of others, the insensitive or wrongheaded ones, those against whom the agonizing first-person nonspeaker must manage to defend not only his wounded soul but also the sense of precision and purity of language through which whatever is of value in the tradition may be preserved. Eliot is as scornful of these voices as Shakespeare's Coriolanus is of the discordant voices of the people of Rome, and he is equally aware that these voices are also votes, that in modern democracy they represent not only an irritation but a political threat to the language, soul, and culture of the interior, silent protagonist.

But all these voices are mediated through the subvocal voice of the silent, unspeaking speaker, the man "explaining to himself."[6] Though unheard—in the fiction of the poem, that is—this voice is a very changeable one which imitates at various times the tones of an academic lecturer, or those of the personal reminiscer, the armchair philosopher, the agèd eagle, the historian, the critic, the reporter of others' words, or the guardian and extender of the tradition. Sometimes this voice seems that of the tradition itself, echoing its "moments of happiness," its ways of putting it, its "eminent

6. See Ronald Bush, *T. S. Eliot: A Study in Character and Style* (New York: Oxford University Press, 1984), 131.

men of letters." Such a voice had been central in Eliot's poems from the beginning, but its tones have altered, deepened, and been differently directed and modulated.

We know this ruminant voice, which presents and comprehends all the others, not only through our experience of unsounded but formulated thought but also through our acquaintance with printed English poetry, which has trained us to read poems silently. We do not need to say the words aloud to capture their rhythms, or move our lips to savor the words. When we speak of them as sounded by a voice, we probably mean, among other things, that as we follow the phrases and clauses on the page, our own vocal apparatus is at some low level *set* to speak them, and/or that our hearing apparatus is set to hear a voice actually saying the lines—our own voice, Olivier's, Burton's, or Eliot's. Such imagined speaking may include the imagination of variations of stress between syllables, pauses, hesitations, natural pacing, effective strategies of emphasis, shrewd management of pitch, along with paralinguistic gestures, facial expressions, and body language. We are tempted to think that we hear (or see) all this in our heads, but we actually hear (and see) none of it. We are only *prepared*, set, to hear it if a voice materializes and speaks it. Silent reading, however muscularly persevered in, is silent reading. When engaged in it, we are *ready* to perform an action (in this case, to speak words) or to perceive a sense-impression (in this case, to hear words) without actually doing it, though in reading poetry you may have the same experience I have of following the words silently for a time and then, occasionally, being so caught up in the eloquence of a passage that you actually voice a phrase or a word without quite having realized that you were going to do so.

For centuries this has been the usual mode of reception for the reader of poetry, and it is this subvocal speech register that Eliot is imitating—one which the tradition of reflective poetry in English since the sixteenth century has persuaded us to recognize as the common currency of consciousness. Despite the Victorian practice of reading long poems and even novels aloud in family groups, despite the enjoyment many readers have felt in declaiming verse to their friends or to themselves (one thinks of Mr. Ramsay in Virginia Woolf's *To the Lighthouse* marching up and down again to his own rendition of Tennyson's line, "Someone had blunder'd"), despite the popularity of the public poetry reading, despite our readiness in English classes to cite lines or passages of verse, most reading of printed English poetry for more than four centuries has gone on subvocally, in imitation not of spoken English but of this sound-less register that plays so large a part in our daily experience. To be sure, the subvocal register works with the same system of mus-cular tension and effort as the vocal one, but its silence—its in-completeness, the sense we have of its aspiring perhaps to the condition of performance or action—makes it different in feeling, perhaps even more poignant, more expressive, than speech of un-achieved possibilities or of possibilities achieved only in imagina-tion, including those two extremes of experience so important to Romantic sensibilities: the inexpressive and the unspeakable.[7]

The relevance of all this to *The Waste Land* (Eliot's first silent opera, as it were) is obvious enough. Indeed, one reason for the poem's force is that so many voices quoted from characters, from other poems and plays, from saints and songs and thunder, are imprisoned in the soundless voice we see on the speechless page. The hyacinth girl's companion's voice is not the only one that "could not speak"; that inability is built into the vocal structure of the poem, which in its final form presents all the remembered and desired voices as locked in the poem's essential silence.[8]

In *Four Quartets*, the title and Eliot's deliberate interweaving of themes invite comparisons between the way we listen to music and the way we listen to poetry—to that "music," as Eliot puts it in "The Dry Salvages" (V), "heard so deeply that it is not heard at all" (a line in which we hear an echo of Keats's "unheard melodies"). Poetry can be read in silence for hours, but I don't know anyone who can take pleasure in reading it aloud in solitude for many min-utes or in listening for hours to readings or recordings of verse (except of verse plays). The brevity that Poe required of poems does seem to be required at least of most poetry spoken aloud, and only the liveliness and visual (or subvisual) interest of dramatic conflict relieves verse drama, as once it may have relieved oral epic, from the need to be brief. Music is different. Music sounded seems unde-niably more impressive than when silently absorbed by a fluent

7. Eliot imitated English poetry's traditional subvocal register and ex-panded it to include not only well-formed sentences but the mutters, grunts, and half-formed phrases that compose much of our verbal inner life. In this respect he opened up a vast new territory that has continued to be explored by Auden, Berryman, Lowell, and by later colloquial poets.

8. "Why do you never speak" in *The Waste Land* II is less a question than an assertion, as the period after it shows.

reader of the score. The rich possibilities of the instruments, including the voice, are given fuller definition, are not merely imagined but sensuously experienced.[9]

But for the art of poetry, silent reading is a much more standard experience, whether for lovers of the art or beginners. It is probably also a less passive experience, for the reader must do the work of imagining the sound (even half-creating it) as well as visualizing the scenes, the characters, and the settings. The sounded poem is more definite, more determinate, and students on first hearing it may be surprised by its power or delicacy. When read by the author, it may seem especially effective or notably disappointing; trained actors may do much for some poems.

But the determinateness of oral performance incurs a cost: poems may be insensitively read by teachers and even by actors, and as everyone knows who goes to readings, for most poets the poem on the page is very different from the "same" poem recited before an audience. Poets usually think they must surround their poems with commentary and orchestrate them with gestures, to an extent that readers of their poetic texts would find intrusive. The lineation that is so prominent a feature of the printed poem may become wholly obscured in performance. And poets are often dismally unable to reproduce the tones of voice that are suggested by their own printed poems—in fact, most American poets make a practice, when reading, of reducing radically the number of pitches their voices would normally make use of (to perhaps as few as three). When they do this, they limit substantially the expressiveness of their poems. The voice of a poem thus spoken may seem much inferior to that of the "same" poem printed on the page and heard, half-heard, by an actively listening reader. An excellent reader, of course, can make his bad poem (his bad *page*-poem, that is) sound good in performance. For Eliot, incidentally, the sudden vogue of poetry recordings and readings that began in the 1940s resulted in the peculiar circumstance that we almost always hear the poems he composed in his twenties read by their sixty-odd-year-old author; in a literal act of impersonation, the poems of the young American are sounded through the voice of the aging Euro-

---

9. Langer, on hearing music from a score, observes: "Inward hearing is a work of the mind, that begins with conceptions of form and ends with their complete presentation in imagined sense experience. . . . [It] usually stops short of just that determinateness of quality and duration which characterizes actual sensation" (*Feeling and Form*, 137–38).

pean, with its acquired half-British accent, cracking timbre, and mournful intonation.

Another analogy to this process deserves mention. Subvocal reading works much like visual imagery. When we read silently, we have the opportunity not only to imagine the sound (to see a voice, like Bottom) but also, with the help of the (unheard) verse, to visualize at least some of the objects and people referred to—in effect, to hear a face.[10] Different readers do this differently, and so does the same reader during different readings, especially when returning to familiar works after many years. But, though in an ostensibly silent reading we have the option of sounding some of the words and rhythms, we do not normally have the same visual option. We see nothing, nothing but the printed page; we are set to see much, set to see everything. The unvoiced voices of poems read silently work very much like the unseen sights of poems read from the page. The play of images in a poem provides a parallel to the play of voices, and much of the intensity of poems read silently and in the study derives from the interest, pleasure, and creative satisfaction we take in performing the play of images and rhythms for ourselves, under the guidance of the poet's fairly general directions.[11] In drama, of course, the theater audience not only sees the action on the stage but imagines other action and images referred to in the speeches of the characters—the best of both worlds, perhaps.

In addition to the two kinds of voices already mentioned, the world's voices and that of the silent ruminant, we can find in Eliot's poetry another voice, one that usually emanates from urban objects in the early verse or from natural forces in *Four Quartets*, a voice that is trying to tell us something and that we may need special powers to hear and understand: the whisper of running streams, the river's rhythms, the wave cry and wind cry, the menace and caress of wave that breaks on water, the distant rote in the granite teeth, a voice descanting in the rigging and the aerial, and the voice of the hidden waterfall. There are musical messages, too: the music of "the weak pipe and the little drum" ("East Coker," I), "the sea bell's / Perpetual angelus" ("The Dry Salvages," IV), and "the still-

---

10. Bottom's situation, to be sure, is slightly different. Since Thisby's mouth is speaking into the chink from the other side, Pyramus, in putting his ear to wall, does literally hear her face.

11. I do not, *pace* the modern Marxist critic, see poetic reverie as a bourgeois capitalist technology, designed to isolate the individual from a community of listeners who would otherwise share an experience of images and voices.

ness of the violin, while the note lasts" ("Burnt Norton," V). And certain human voices have special resonance: children's laughter, rustic laughter, lacerating laughter; voices in prayer, the voices of Krishna and the compound ghost; and the communication of the dead, who can tell you more now than they could have when they were living.

In a longer paper, one could show how various subvocal voices succeed each other in these poems. The inner word-streams that imitate our own silent meditations include echoes of old poems and prose, descriptive and narrative segments, murmurs, directions to the self ("In that open field / If you do not come too close, if you do not come too close . . ." ["East Coker," I]), and summary phrases ("Feet rising and falling. / Eating and drinking. Dung and death." ["East Coker," I]). In other word-streams, we discern the manner of the quiet-voiced elder, the Miltonic preacher, the Homeric singer, and the tendentious silent speaker instructing himself in the paradoxes through which humility is to be achieved (ending: "And where you are is where you are not" ["East Coker," III]).

To my ear, all of these are silent speech, which imitates our inner verbal life and, of course, idealizes it, for the inner voice of none of us is as eloquent as this one, and neither, we may be sure, was Eliot's most of the time. Like speech itself, subspeech wastes words, chatters, deserves to have most of its language disappear without trace. But this silent register is essential to our lives and to our speech—as Sweeney might say, "I gotta use words when I talk to *me*"—and in Eliot's poems it becomes the mode of an impressive verbal art.

I don't mean to suggest that Eliot's verse should never be read aloud or that the words are better left unspoken. Voicing can give them an intensity they can rarely achieve without vocal speech—it is true of verse as it is with music, though to a lesser degree and in smaller scale. But it still seems helpful to recognize what sort of speech this is that Eliot is usually imitating and what sorts of voices we are mixing when we read them either silently or aloud. It may also help to explain why Eliot's drama is not so spectacularly successful as his poems.

Shakespeare, to bring him in again, had to deal with a similar problem and may have solved it almost by accident; he certainly didn't worry the problem as Eliot so consciously did in his critical writing as well as in plays and poems. When plague forced the theaters to close in 1592–1593, Shakespeare used the time to write his narrative poems, *Venus and Adonis* and *The Rape of Lucrece*. But he also probably wrote many of his sonnets at this time and in them developed that quiet but intensely reflective style, the voice of "sweet silent thought," that is one of their outstanding features. When the theaters reopened, he was able for the first time to give to some characters in virtually every play—men and women, villains as well as heroes—a language that seemed to spring out of memory and desire, from deep reflection on issues of common humanity.

When the characters in Eliot's plays try to do that, to give voice to the inner, the private, world (Colby Simpkins's "secret garden") that lies behind the public one we see, the result is not so happy. They sound pretentious, as if they had just stepped out of our common world into another realm of existence to which only they have the key. For all the virtues of the plays, Eliot did not wholly succeed in integrating in them these two kinds of language. It is difficult to say why, but the answers are probably in part technical, having to do with tone, syntax, imagery; in part cultural, having to do with language and power in the sixteenth and twentieth centuries; in part social, related to his apparent belief that only a gifted few have interesting inner word-streams.[12] But his lack of success in the plays in integrating kinds of language is also in part personal. For Eliot, the gap between the silent voice and public voices, between the intense inner word-stream and shared public speech, could never be resolved, as it had been by Shakespeare, through an art that lets the outer voice absorb and incorporate the rich inner one. In Eliot's best work, his poems, it is always the other way around.

12. His choral voices, thus, are most successful when the language Eliot finds for them breaks away from realistic idiom into a powerful symbolic dream-language: e.g., the Women of Canterbury in *Murder in the Cathedral*, as opposed to the Workmen in *The Rock* or the uncles and aunts in *The Family Reunion*.

Language as Plot in *The Family Reunion*
Linda Wyman

*T*he *Family Reunion* did not satisfy T. S. Eliot, and it has not satisfied many, perhaps most, of its readers. I say "readers" because I do not intend to deal with the issue of the play's theatricality (although in my experience it performs surprisingly well). I do want, however, to address myself to two observations that have been common among readers of the play and that have accounted in large measure for their disappointment in it. The first of these is that the language is dramatically deficient. As Denis Donoghue writes, "In *The Family Reunion* more than in any other play Eliot yielded to the temptation to be 'poetical,' indulging in purely verbal activity at the expense of dramatic relevance and propriety."[1] The second observation is that there is a "gulf" (more than one critic has used the word) between Harry, the central character, and the members of his family. These objections fall away, it seems to me, when readers open themselves to the proposition that *The Family Reunion* is a play in which the element of language—rather than the element of character, say, or of thought—is the chief imitator of the action. The reader who attends carefully to the very words of this play and discovers how Eliot has used them to make his meaning may very well find that *The Family Reunion*, far from being a disappointment, is a luminous success.

When I suggest that the meaning of this play is realized primarily in its language, I am fully aware that some of that language is at first disconcerting, some of it puzzling, some of it strange. None of it, however, is without purpose, none of it finally obscure. Even in a first reading, one notices that the speeches in *The Family Reunion* do not all seem to exist on the same level of meaning. One can identify three large categories of speech which, for lack of better terms, I will call "naturalistic" (indicated below by roman

1. *The Third Voice: Modern British and American Verse Drama* (Princeton: Princeton University Press, 1959), 98.

163

type), "overlaid" (indicated by italics), and "supra-naturalistic" (indicated by bold type). These three are exemplified in the opening speech of the play. The maid enters to draw the curtains, and Amy says:

> Not yet! I will ring for you. *It is still quite light.*
> *I have nothing to do but watch the days draw out,*
> *Now that I sit in the house from October to June,*
> **And the swallow comes too soon and the spring will be over**
> **And the cuckoo will be gone before I am out again.**
> **O Sun, that was once so warm, O Light that was taken for granted**
> **When I was young and strong, and sun and light unsought for**
> **And the night unfeared and the day expected**
> **And clocks could be trusted, tomorrow assured**
> **And time would not stop in the dark!**
> *Put on the lights. But leave the curtains undrawn.*
> *Make up the fire. Will the spring never come? I am cold.*

One might classify as naturalistic those speeches which are addressed to other characters and which (except for being in verse) sound most like the discourse of ordinary small talk, conversations, interviews, or instructions. That is, there are a number of lines in *The Family Reunion* which one can easily conceive of hearing in the drawing room of an actual "country house in the North of England," instead of in a play set in such a house. Examples are such lines as "My servants are perfectly competent, Gerald" (act 1, scene 1) and "We might as well go in to dinner" (act 1, scene 3).

The play contains certain speeches which, like naturalistic speeches, are parts of dialogue but which are either obviously metaphoric the moment they are spoken or are alluded to or repeated later in the play so that they take on the qualities of a metaphor or motif. One might classify such speeches as "overlaid": their meanings exist simultaneously on more than one level. They are likely to be spoken, and accepted, in conjunction with more wholly naturalistic, or one-dimensional, speeches. But their language is charged in such a way that their meanings occur in more than one dimension.

Agatha's remark about "the loop in time" (act 1, scene 1), for example, is clearly metaphoric from the moment it is uttered. More frequently, however, the metaphoric nature of overlaid speeches is not immediately apparent. When first encountering the following exchange, for instance, one has no reason to think of the phrase "all that has happened" as other than naturalistic:

Amy: This is a very particular occasion
       As you ought to know. It will be the first time
       For eight years that we have all been together.
Agatha: It is going to be rather painful for Harry
       After eight years and all that has happened
       To come back to Wishwood.

(act 1, scene 1)

Subsequently, however, the phrase "all that has happened" is repeated several times and made to stand opposite the word *events* so
that the first term comes to signify the inner, or spiritual, life while
the second signifies the life of circumstance. One will recall Amy's
exhorting the family to "behave only / As if nothing had happened
in the last eight years" and insisting to Harry that, at Wishwood,
"nothing has been changed." Harry's response to his family's behavior is an accusation: "You all of you try to talk as if nothing had
happened." He sees no way to explain himself to them:

All that I could hope to make you understand
Is only events: not what has happened.
And people to whom nothing has ever happened
Cannot understand the unimportance of events.

(act 1, scene 1)

The phrase "all that has happened" is used several times more, so that
it begins to have a ring to it when it comes around again. Eventually,
because of the meaning accruing to the phrase, Eliot can give Ivy a
line in the second part of the play that effectively dramatizes her
failure to understand what is going on: "We must carry on as if nothing had happened, / And have the cake and presents" (act 2, scene 1).

A great many speeches in *The Family Reunion* fit neither category discussed thus far, but share, nevertheless, certain characteristics with each other. Unlike naturalistic and overlaid speeches,
they are not parts of dialogue. If they occur when a character is on
stage by himself, they resemble choric speeches more than solilo-
quies; that is, the speaker is more likely to comment on the events
of the play than to talk about himself. If they occur when more than
one character is present, they have at least one of the following
characteristics: they are spoken in unison, they are spoken in
"duet," or there is evidence in the text that they are spoken out of
the hearing of the other characters. One may call such speeches
"supra-naturalistic" and discern four sorts among them: choruses,
runes, "lyrical duets" (Eliot's term), and speeches (such as the one
by Amy quoted earlier) that are supra-naturalistic only in part.

The significance to this categorizing lies in the fact that no character is limited to speeches of any one level. The aunts and uncles,
for instance, at least in their naturalistic speeches, seem to think
only of gardeners and newspaper stories and such. They reveal almost no understanding of the events of the play except when speaking in chorus. This fact suggests that the "spiritual awareness" of
the aunts and uncles is, ironically, below consciousness; they do
not, at any rate, communicate such awareness to any other character. Only in chorus do they express significant insight ("The past
is about to happen, and the future was long since settled" [act 1,
scene 3]) or admit that Harry's experience has in any great way
affected their own ("We have suffered far more than a personal
loss— / We have lost our way in the dark" [act 2, scene 3]). But in
chorus they are able even to use the word *happened* in a manner
consistent with Harry's use: "I am afraid of all that has happened,
and of all that is to come" (act 1, scene 3). One may point, similarly—and in fact more frequently than for the aunts and uncles—
to instances in which Amy, Agatha, and Mary speak on the supra-
naturalistic level. To say that Harry and the other characters share
in supra-naturalistic speech is a way of saying that they are alike, as
well as different.

There are differences, of course, between Harry and the members of his family. One of the great differences is that Harry can talk
quite openly, in conversation, about "spectres," "the cancer / That
eats away the self" (act 1, scene 1), and other things that trouble
him, whereas the other Monchenseys cannot. After an absence of
eight years he comes into the house haunted by the sight of "them"
(the Eumenides) and says to his family, "How can you sit in this
blaze of light for all the world to look at?" Amy, his mother, responds by reminding him that he is "at Wishwood, not in town
where you have to close the blinds." This is not the sort of consideration to give Harry comfort. Time and again, ironically enough,
he speaks of both his predicament and his inability to communicate. His experience is, he says, "unspeakable, untranslatable."
Charles, his uncle, moves to reassure him: "Of course we know
what really happened, we read it in the papers" (act 1, scene 1).
Needless to say, a comment such as this one only intensifies
Harry's pain as it places on him the added burden of being surrounded by people who are totally obtuse when he is experiencing
"the sudden extinction of every alternative" (act 1, scene 2). There
is, of course, considerable reason for Harry to think his insights

superior to those of his family. But the play makes clear that it is a great mistake for him to think of himself as completely separate from the people of Wishwood. The language of *The Family Reunion* discloses that even though the differences between Harry and his family are great and painful, they are not absolute, and since neither Harry nor any other character is represented as comprehending the full significance of the events of the play, one may say that that opportunity is reserved for the reader.

Harry and his family cannot meet on the level of drawing room conversation, but they do touch, upon occasion, and the significance of their "touching" is, in part, what this play is about. Though Harry makes no exceptions among members of his family when he says that he cannot explain to them the things most important to him, he is not equally distant from all of them. It is largely in encounters with Mary and Agatha that he comes to identify the Eumenides and to discover his spiritual election.

The scene between Mary and Harry is intensely dramatic; a number of highly charged and necessarily sequential events occur in a short period of time. One may interpret the events as follows: Harry takes hope from the discovery that there is someone at Wishwood with whom he has something in common, experiences a moment of deep communion with Mary, and falls off into despair as the Eumenides intrude upon that moment and he realizes that he is not yet free of them. The events themselves, however, are largely literal; the drama is accomplished in what the characters say: for one brief shining moment Harry and Mary speak the same language.

Harry's encounter with Agatha is even more significant than the one with Mary. From early in the play, Eliot has indicated a closeness between Harry and Agatha by having them use some of the same words and images. In act 2, scene 2, these characters enter most fully into relationship. Harry's questions about his parents lead Agatha to reveal the "deeper organisation" of her life, as her answers help him to discover the "deeper organisation" of his own. Agatha tells him of a "summer day of unusual heat," on which she and Harry's father fell in love. (Harry has remembered the uncomfortable emotions which the "summer day of unusual heat" brought him, but not its events.) When that autumn came, she says, "I found him thinking / How to get rid of your mother" (act 2, scene 2). That fact is, of course, the essential one which Harry must know, and his responding to it is perhaps the climactic moment of the play. As Agatha tells him,

> It is possible that you have not known what sin
> You shall expiate, or whose, or why. It is certain
> That the knowledge of it must precede the expiation.
>   (act 2, scene 2)

She suggests to Harry the possibility that he must embark on a long journey as the "consciousness" of his family. In this terrible moment Agatha and Harry experience some release from their burdens and draw close to one another in the play's second lyrical duet.

One may say that the duet provides, paradoxically, a means of dramatizing a moment in which two characters achieve a closeness that ordinary speech—even the ordinary, or naturalistic, speech of a poetic drama—cannot express. One means of dramatizing such a moment is for the playwright to suspend dialogue and to indicate, by means of stage direction, that two characters are to engage in a passionate embrace. Such a means is inappropriate, however, for dramatizing the great closeness, the intense communion of spirits, that Harry and Agatha feel after a dialogue which has been for them mutually liberating. To dramatize this communion, Eliot gives Harry and Agatha a meter used only rarely in the play, lets them share the metaphor of the single eye ("the unwinking eye" [act 2, scene 2]), and links their speeches by having the characters duplicate one another's syntax. (The poetry is passionate; only the description of it is not.)

One may say, then, that Harry's spiritual understanding is not a *given* in the play; he "discovers his election" progressively, helped by people with whom he can seldom talk and by whom he is only slightly understood. To use the terms to which I earlier made reference, he has known only "what happened," the spiritual side of experience. He moves toward salvation only as he faces certain "events" in the life of circumstance. Agatha and other members of his family help to effect Harry's enlightenment and then, to varying degrees, share in it. As Harry might say, they get a glimpse of "what happened." Or, as he does say, "Everything is true in a different sense," and "Everything tends towards reconciliation" (act 2, scene 2). In *The Family Reunion*, fully dramatic language is the key element of the plot: it enacts the saving reciprocity of human relationships.

Eliot and Yeats: A Personal View

Michael Butler Yeats

September 1988 marked the one hundredth anniversary of the birth of T. S. Eliot, and January 1989 the fiftieth anniversary of the death of William Butler Yeats. This juxtaposition of dates provides a convenient reason for having a look at the relationship between these great poets of the twentieth century.[1] They were not of course truly contemporary; Eliot was some twenty-three years younger than Yeats. But from 1915 onwards, Eliot was living in London, while Yeats also spent much of his time there until 1922, and returned there frequently in later years, even after he had come back to Ireland on the foundation of the new Irish State. There was ample opportunity for the two writers to meet, to exchange letters, and to establish at least a certain mutual familiarity.

However, so far as Eliot and Yeats are concerned, the most striking aspect of their mutual relations is that, except for one short period, these barely existed at all. They seem rarely to have met. In the main they impinged on each other by the use of long-range artillery, the publishing of critical comments about each other—though most of the bombardment came from Eliot's side.

They did indeed have two things in common: they both were avid readers of detective stories, and they both loved cats. But these mutual interests were a somewhat inadequate basis on which to build a complete human relationship. On a personal plane they had little else in common; on Eliot's side there was even for a while a mildly contemptuous dislike for Yeats. But they were kept apart primarily by their totally different—indeed opposite—views on the writing of poetry. As Stephen Spender once put it, Eliot "had listened to the machines and not to horses' hooves and chariots."[2]

---

1. Yeats's influence on Eliot's poetry was surveyed in an address of May 1988 by Grover Smith. This address, which Professor Smith shared with me in typescript, has been published under the title "Yeats, Eliot, and the Use of Memory," *Yeats Eliot Review* 9 (1988): 131–39.

2. "The Influence of Yeats on Later English Poets," *TriQuarterly* 4 (1965): 85.

Over the years there did come a radical change in Eliot's estimation of Yeats as a poet; from thinking about him as merely an out-of-date relic of the 1890s, he ended by describing him as the greatest figure of his time.

Yeats, on the other hand, never really changed his mind. From the first he disliked the poetry of Eliot; it was, he claimed, grey, cold, flat, bare. In time he came to accept Eliot as a major poet, and he commented in particular on his great influence on the young.[3] But on Eliot as a person, he seems to have had nothing to say.

But this lack of interest on Yeats's part in the personality of Eliot is perhaps not really surprising. Mrs. Yeats always maintained that her husband had no interest in people as such, only in what they did. The poetry of Eliot did not appeal to him; therefore Eliot as a man had no interest for him. Only in the mid–1930s, when they briefly became engaged in a common cause, did they achieve on a personal level some degree of mutual comprehension. What little we do know of relations between the two poets is one-sided. There is more of Eliot on Yeats than of Yeats on Eliot. In a 1919 review Eliot was negative, ranging from mild derision to outright hostility, but by the mid–1930s, he had come to appreciate Yeats's poetry. Writing in 1946, Eliot said that up to 1914, the year in which he arrived in England, the contemporary literary scene in America remained in his mind "a complete blank." "I cannot remember the name of a single poet of that period whose work I read: it was only in 1915, after I came to England, that I heard the name of Robert Frost. Undergraduates at Harvard in my time read the English poets of the '90s, who were dead; that was as near as we could get to any living tradition."[4] Yeats was well known, of course, but to Eliot at that period he did not appear to be anything but a minor survival of the 1890s.

In the years immediately following Eliot's arrival, Ezra Pound arranged that the two poets should meet. According to Richard Ellmann, these early meetings could hardly have been described as successful.[5] Eliot was bored, and claimed that Yeats's only two subjects of conversation were spooks and George Moore. Neither of these was of any particular interest to Eliot. The recently published

3. See Richard Ellmann, *Eminent Domain* (New York: Oxford University Press, 1967), 89, and *Letters of W. B. Yeats*, ed. Allan Wade (London: Hart-Davis, 1954), 833.
4. Eliot, "Ezra Pound," *Poetry* 68 (September 1946): 326.
5. Ellmann, *Eminent Domain*, 92.

edition of Eliot's letters shows, however, that these meetings were rather more successful than suggested by Ellmann. Eliot and Yeats seem first to have met at a meal in a Chinese restaurant in London with Ezra and Dorothy Pound in October 1914, and they may have met again in the following February. Eliot clearly enjoyed these early meetings; he wrote of his pleasure in meeting Yeats and his hopes for further meetings. Yeats, in his view, was a very agreeable talker.[6]

Yet Eliot seems to have remained ambivalent about Yeats's personality. Just two years later, in March 1917, they met again in a gathering at the Omega Club (described by Eliot as "a curious zoo of people"). He and Yeats sat on a mat discussing psychical research, the only thing, he claimed, that Yeats ever talked about except Dublin gossip.[7] It must have been this occasion that was the origin of Ellmann's anecdote about "spooks and George Moore."

It is not easy, therefore, to trace the development of Eliot's views on Yeats as an individual. Nor is it any easier to follow him step by step in his changing attitudes to Yeats as writer. It is clear that in later years Eliot did modify his early view of Yeats as a minor survivor of a former age. But when did this change happen? Writing in 1946, Eliot claimed that he saw Yeats "very differently" after 1917. "I remember well the first performance of *The Hawk's Well*, in a London drawing room, with a celebrated Japanese dancer in the role of the hawk, to which Pound took me. Thereafter one saw Yeats rather as a more eminent contemporary than as an elder from whom one could learn."[8] In a world where so much is obscure and complicated, it would be nice to be able to accept this simple statement at face value. One is presented with a picture of Eliot being dragged reluctantly to hear another play by a relic of the 1890s, and of him returning home that night convinced that he had now acquired a new and eminent contemporary. The reality is somewhat different. Eliot in 1946 was writing with the benefit of hindsight, and somewhat forgetful hindsight at that. It is fair to assume that he was indeed influenced by *At the Hawk's Well*, and still more so, a couple of years later, by *The Wild Swans at Coole*. But this influence must in fact have been a very gradual one, because it was many

6. *The Letters of T. S. Eliot*, (1898–1922), ed. Valerie Eliot (San Diego: Harcourt Brace Jovanovich, 1988), 1:58–59, 92, 95.
7. Ibid., 169.
8. Eliot, "Ezra Pound," 326.

years before his public attitude to Yeats underwent any fundamental change. Just a few months after that first performance of *At the Hawk's Well*, we find Vivien Eliot in a letter approving of a friend's dislike of Yeats. Yeats, she claimed, hated Eliot's poetry, and the two of them were at odds.[9] Although this letter was written by Vivien and not by Eliot himself, it seems likely that it did portray prevailing attitudes in the Eliot household.

Certainly in the following year, 1919, Eliot launched an attack on Yeats in *The Athenaeum*, in the guise of a review of *The Cutting of an Agate*, a book of collected essays and prefaces published that year. In this review, entitled "A Foreign Mind," Eliot has little to say about the book, but a great deal to say about its author:

> Mr. Yeats more than any of the subjects that have engaged his attention, is what engages our attention in this book. When we read it we are confirmed in the conviction . . . that its author, as much in his prose as in his verse, is not 'of this world'. . . . The difference between his world and ours is so complete as to seem almost a physiological variety, different nerves and senses. It is, therefore, allowable to imagine that the difference is not only personal, but national.[10]

Eliot then considers the possibility that Yeats was an eccentric, which would at least be comprehensible; but no, this answer must be rejected. So Eliot returns to his earlier theory that Yeats's primary interests are in "spooks."

> [W]hen we say 'not of this world,' we do not point to another. Ghosts, mediums, leprechauns, sprites, are only a few of the elements in Mr. Yeats's population, and in this volume they hardly appear at all. . . . Mr. Yeats on any subject is a cause of bewilderment and distress. The sprites are not unacceptable, but Mr. Yeats's daily world, the world which admits these monsters without astonishment . . . this is the unknown and unknowable. Mr. Yeats's mind is a mind in some way independent of experience; and anything that occurs in that mind is of equal importance. It is a mind in which perception of fact, and feeling and thinking are all a little different from ours.[11]

He goes on to speak of Yeats as being remote and "a little crude," with a mind "extreme in egoism." He notes that crudity and ego-

9. Vivien Eliot to Lady Ottoline Morrell, Humanities Research Center, University of Texas at Austin. My thanks to Donald E. Stanford, Baton Rouge, Louisiana, for bringing this letter to my attention.

10. "A Foreign Mind," review of *The Cutting of an Agate*, by W. B. Yeats, *Athenaeum* 4653 (4 July 1919): 552.

11. Ibid., 552.

ism are to be found in "what is called Irish literature," adding that Yeats's "crudity and egoism are present in other writers who are Irish." As if Eliot felt that in this review of Yeats's prose he had gone a little too far, he added: "It must always be granted that in verse at least Mr. Yeats's feeling is not simply crudeness and egoism, but that it has a positive, individual and permanent quality."[12]

It is not easy to understand the cause of this remarkable attack. One can understand that Eliot felt quite out of sympathy with Yeats's early poetry—a minor survival, in his view, of the 1890s. On the other hand, the book under review was written in prose, and contained no verse; and in any event, as he later claimed, Eliot was at this time (1919) in the process of changing his views about Yeats as a writer. One can understand also that Eliot was not enthused by Yeats's "spooks," and looked on them as suitable subjects for derision. But as he said himself, these spooks hardly appear at all in the book of essays he was reviewing. So what did impel Eliot to write this onslaught on Yeats, in particular on Yeats's own personality? Obviously no definitive answer is possible, but it appears that at least part of the solution may be found in Eliot's reaction to the society and environment in which at that period he found himself. It is difficult to think of Eliot as a man isolated from his surroundings. To understand his thinking, one must have regard also to his attitude toward those with whom he lived and worked. In his review in *The Athenaeum*, he remarked that "Mr. Yeats has spent altogether a great deal of time in England and acquired here a degree of notoriety without being or becoming an Englishman."[13] Is there reference here to Eliot's own view of life in England? Yeats, for all his many years of English residence, retained to the end his Sligo accent and never for a moment ceased to think of himself as an Irishman writing for his own people. Eliot, on the other hand, had some of the characteristics of the chameleon. For example, Peter Ackroyd claims that when Eliot arrived as a teenager at Milton Academy in Massachusetts, he "became self-conscious about his Missouri accent . . . and proceeded to lose it."[14] In turn, when in August 1914 he came to London, the city in which he was to spend the last fifty years of his life, Eliot appears to have embarked on the

12. Ibid., 553.
13. Ibid., 552.
14. Peter Ackroyd, *T. S. Eliot: A Life* (New York: Simon and Schuster, 1984), 28.

task of becoming a member of English society. Obviously this did not mean that he abandoned his American origins. No man can forget his roots, and Eliot never made the attempt to do so. He always kept in touch with his family and his American friends, several times revisited America, and he himself wrote that "St. Louis affected me more deeply than any other environment has done."[15] Yet he seems to have studied with attention the manners, deportment, and appearance of those members of English society that he met in country houses such as Lady Ottoline Morrell's Garsington Manor, near Oxford. In due course he lost his American accent, and adopted English-style clothes, including the traditional bowler hat and furled umbrella when at work in London. He immersed himself in London society, eating at traditional English restaurants where sherry was served before the meal and port afterwards. In an attempt to justify to his mother his decision to remain in England and work at the bank, he wrote to her about his improving social position.[16] Finally, in 1927 he joined the state Anglican Church, and in the same year became a British citizen.

Such efforts at assimilation can never wholly succeed, least of all in England, where in certain quarters to describe even once a "sitting room" as a "lounge" is enough to betray one as an outsider. Eliot did well at his self-imposed task, though he did make occasional errors. Richard Aldington reports, for example, that Eliot once raised his hat to a sentry outside one of the royal palaces in London. This harmless gesture, which would have been humorously meant, was considered shocking by Aldington and his friends. This showed, they felt, that Eliot did not understand the society he wished to join. Much later, he took to celebrating the anniversary of the fifteenth-century battle of Bosworth and the death of Richard III, whom he considered to be the last true English king. Taking his mild historical affectation more seriously than one suspects he did himself, one of Eliot's friends said that he "wasn't a bit like an Englishman."[17] Nor, in the final analysis, did Eliot himself feel that he was wholly an Englishman. There were times, certainly, when

15. "The Eliot Family and St. Louis," appendix to T. S. Eliot, *American Literature and the American Language: An Address Delivered at Washington University.* Washington University Studies, n.s., Language and Literature, no. 23 (St. Louis: Washington University Committee on Publications, 1953), 28.

16. See Ackroyd, *T. S. Eliot,* 89, and *The Letters of T. S. Eliot,* 1:280.

17. Ackroyd, *T. S. Eliot,* 166.

he spoke of "we English," yet on other occasions he described himself as merely being "always a foreigner."[18]

All this might be of only marginal interest were it simply Eliot's outward deportment that was at issue. It was inevitable, however, that in his efforts to blend into English society he would absorb at least some of the social and political thinking of the Tory environment in which he found himself. As a literary critic, he was of course entirely his own man; thus his negative views on Yeats's poetry were a natural reflection of his own anti-Romantic tendency. But when it comes to his criticism of Yeats as a man—and in particular of Yeats as an Irishman—one can sense other influences coming into play.

It must be remembered that Ireland at that time was still legally an integral part of the United Kingdom. The Irish might feel that they were an ancient nation with their own history and cultural traditions, but as seen from London they were provincials on the outer fringes of the British Isles. They were looked upon as poorer and more backward than other provincials and certainly a great deal more troublesome. The Irish, in English eyes, had no native culture, merely superstitions. The Easter Rising had taken place in Dublin in 1916; two years later the Irish republicans had overwhelmingly won a general election and had formed an underground parliament and government. All this could not fail to have had an effect on English public opinion.

It may be that Eliot absorbed some of the atmosphere around him. One senses this in the title of his *Athenaeum* review, "A Foreign Mind," and in his doubts as to whether an Irish literature in fact exists. There is a derisive tone that creeps in when he speaks of things Irish, as in the reference in the review to "a trick of the eye and a hanging of the nether lip that comes from across the Irish Channel."[19] That he held an unfavorable view of the Irish is evident also from his correspondence. Thus he wrote of meeting "two Irishmen," who have "rather raised my opinion of that race." About Desmond MacCarthy, he wrote that he "is of course an Irishman, that is to say he belongs to a race which I cannot understand."[20]

The 1919 review in *The Athenaeum* was the high point of Eliot's

18. *The Letters of T. S. Eliot*, 1:310.
19. "A Foreign Mind," review of *The Cutting of an Agate*, 553.
20. *The Letters of T. S. Eliot*, 1:92, 464.

onslaught on Yeats. He wrote no more on him for many years, though Ezra Pound did report in 1925 that "Eliot don't see either Yeats or Hardy."[21] The two poets did meet, however, at least once during the 1920s and on a more amicable plane than previously. Eliot had been anxious to obtain a contribution from Yeats for his literary periodical *The Criterion*, but he hesitated to ask him. Yeats, he confided to Ezra Pound in October 1922, did not particularly like him, so there seemed no reason why he should consent.[22] But when they did in fact have lunch together at the Saville Club in December 1922, all went well. Yeats was quite willing to like Eliot, and he wrote to his wife, George, that they had spent three hours talking about poetry, Joyce, and other matters. "I am charmed with Eliot," he wrote, "and find that I have a reasonable liking for his *Sacred Wood.*"[23]

Eliot, on his side, described the lunch with Yeats in a letter (12 December 1922) to Ottoline Morrell: "I enjoyed seeing him immensely; I had not seen him for six or seven years, and it was the first time that I have ever talked to him for any length of time alone. He is really one of a very small number of people with whom one can talk profitably about poetry, and I found him altogether stimulating."[24] It was just a few months after this meeting that Eliot sent him a copy of *The Waste Land* inscribed: "For W. B. Yeats, Esq., in admiration of his work." One result of this Saville Club lunch was that a prose passage of autobiography by Yeats appeared in the July 1923 issue of *The Criterion.*[25] More important, *The Criterion* a year later (July 1924) gave its first publication to Yeats's play *The Cat and the Moon.*

During the next ten years there seems to have been little if any further contact, but on 1 April 1932, Eliot sent Yeats a curious letter in which he asked for his advice. Vivien Eliot's family, he said, had some house property in Dun Laoghaire (near Dublin) of which he and his brother-in-law were trustees. One or the other of them would shortly be going to Dublin to inspect the property, and in advance of this event Eliot had procured introductions "to vari-

21. Ellmann, *Eminent Domain*, 92.
22. *The Letters of T. S. Eliot*, 1:585.
23. Yeats to George Yeats, 3 December 1922, Private Papers, Michael B. Yeats. My thanks to George Harper, Tallahassee, Florida, for bringing this letter to my attention.
24. *The Letters of T. S. Eliot*, 1:611.
25. Ibid., 610.

ous people of importance in Dublin." Unfortunately all these introductions were addressed to people in the Irish government that had
just been put out of office. "Now, to put it simply, do you know
anyone in the new Government whom it might be desirable or
useful—however indirectly—for us to know?"[26] He ended the letter
by saying that it was so rare for Yeats to be in London, and such a
pleasure, that he hoped he might come in the following night after
dinner for coffee.

It is not clear whether this invitation was accepted, but the
circumstances of their next meeting suggest otherwise. Later in
the same year, Eliot had gone to Harvard to spend a year there
lecturing, while Yeats was on an American lecture tour. On 8 December 1933, he lectured at Wellesley College on "The Irish National Theatre," and that evening there was a dinner at the college
at which he and Eliot were seated side by side. Richard Ellmann
related what took place, a story that he presumably heard from
Eliot himself:

> Among their various mild collisions, none was more defined than the
> dinner at Wellesley College when Yeats, seated next to Eliot but
> oblivious of him, conversed with the guest on the other side until late
> in the meal. He then turned and said, "my friend here and I have been
> discussing the defects of T. S. Eliot's poetry. What do you think of
> that poetry?" Eliot held up his place card to excuse himself from the
> jury.[27]

However unlikely it may seem, this story may well be true. Yeats,
who could be extremely efficient when it was a matter of managing
the Abbey Theatre or negotiating with publishers, could on other
occasions display a remarkable absent-mindedness. He was notori-
ously bad at recognizing people, even to the extent of asking his
own daughter when they arrived simultaneously at the family gate,
"Who is it you are looking for?"

This curious confrontation with Eliot did not leave Yeats totally
unmoved. A few weeks before the dinner at Wellesley College, he
had been asked by a journalist to comment on American literature
and the only name he could think of was that of Eugene O'Neill.

26. Eliot to Yeats, 1 April 1932, Private Papers, Michael B. Yeats. Although
Yeats had had close relations with the outgoing Cosgrave administration, he
had none at all with the new government led by De Valera, of which he strongly
disapproved.
27. *Eminent Domain*, 89.

Asked the same question the day after the dinner, Yeats said that he did not read much contemporary literature: "but you can mention T. S. Eliot as one I admire greatly."[28]

At this period Eliot gave a series of lectures at the University of Virginia, later published under the title *After Strange Gods.* They were strongly polemical in tone, so much so that Eliot never allowed the book to be republished; later on he suggested that some of the polemics may have been due to his having been ill at the time.[29] Under the circumstances Yeats escaped quite lightly. He had tried, Eliot said, to make poetry supplant religion and he had tried to invent his own religion. His supernatural world was provincial and eccentric. When it came to Yeats's poetry, however, Eliot was quite positive. He praised Yeats for having given up most of his eccentricity in his more recent, austere poetry. Yeats, he said, "has arrived at greatness against the greatest odds."[30]

Shortly after this, Yeats and Eliot did at last get to know each other. According to Peter Ackroyd, Eliot associated himself with Rupert Doone's attempts to establish a theatrical home for verse drama in London. A committee was formed of Eliot, Ashley Dukes, Auden, and Yeats, and discussions dragged on through 1934 and into 1935 without the plans evolving beyond the theoretical stage. Yeats was often not in London at the time of the meetings, and Eliot is alleged to have told Rupert Doone that he would like to kick Yeats down the stairs. Ackroyd gleaned this rather improbable story from an article written in 1981 by Robert Medley, the painter, who worked in the 1930s with the Group Theatre.[31] Writing nearly fifty years after the event, it is clear that Medley's memory was faulty in the extreme. In particular it does seem unlikely that Eliot, however exasperated, would have expressed a wish to kick an elderly fellow poet down the stairs.

Fortunately on this one occasion, we do have a detailed account of the whole affair, written by Yeats in a series of letters to his wife; these naturally reflect his own personal point of view. The story begins in October 1934.

28. Karin Strand, *W. B. Yeats's American Lecture Tours* (Ann Arbor, Mich.: University Microfilms International, 1978), 330, 336.
29. Ackroyd, *T. S. Eliot*, 201.
30. *After Strange Gods: A Primer of Modern Heresy* (New York: Harcourt Brace, 1933), 51.
31. Ackroyd, *T. S. Eliot*, 216.

A little gathering of friends at Dulac's last night decided that "The Group Theatre" should act and produce my plays but that a public theatre must be found for the performances. . . . They object to my working with Auden and Eliot as they say comparisons between rival schools prevent a proper understanding. I must have the assent of Eliot, Ashton, Ninette de Valois and one or two others.[32]

A couple of letters follow in which Yeats tells George of lunching with Eliot and meeting various people, all in connection with the project. This lunch with Eliot took place on 29 October 1934, the same day Eliot wrote to Ottoline Morrell that he had a growing admiration and liking for Yeats, who was one of those few of whom one could say without exaggeration that it was a privilege to know them.[33]

Finally, towards the end of 1934, Yeats writes an enthusiastic letter to his wife.

I am tired but triumphant. An attempt is to be made to form a poetic theatre. Ashley Dukes of the Mercury Theatre (a little theatre in Notting Hill) has undertaken all expenses. We will open with *Fighting the Waves, Player Queen* (costumes by Dulac) and my new version of *The Clock Tower* (music by Dulac). *Fighting the Waves* will have new music (drums, gong, flute and zither), and new masks, all suitable for a small theatre. The music will I hope be by [Constant] Lambert. I have insisted on the inclusion in the repertoire of the poetical left—3 evenings by me, then 3 evenings by Auden and T. S. Eliot. Tomorrow I meet Ashton and Ninette de Valois to arrange details. The Group Theatre (its representative has just left me) will do Auden and Eliot. My aim will be to get masks and music and costumes I can use in Dublin. . . . [In a postscript:] Organizing is like a bumble bee in a bottle. One flies in all directions until one finds the neck.[34]

Next comes a letter dated 17 December 1934, in which Yeats writes:

I am getting things arranged here. Our plays will in all likelihood be given April 29 to May 19. There will be a controlling board consisting of T. S. Eliot, Dulac, Ashton and myself. I shall probably give a programme consisting of *Resurrection, Player Queen, Full Moon in March*, to alternate (a week each) with T. S. Eliot's *Sweeney Agonistes* and a

32. Yeats to George Yeats, n.d. [late October 1934], Private Papers, Michael B. Yeats. Ashton was Frederick Ashton, who became one of the great figures of English ballet and died in 1981.

33. Yeats to Lady Ottoline Morrell, 29 October 1934, Humanities Research Center, University of Texas at Austin.

34. Yeats to George Yeats, n.d. [1934], Private Papers, Michael B. Yeats. It is unlikely, by the way, that Eliot, as a committed High Tory, would have relished being described as a member of the "poetical left."

new ballet play by Auden. My next work [will be] to get the committee to meet. . . .[35]

From this point problems begin to arise, as Yeats explains on 3 January 1935:

> Last Wednesday we had the first meeting of our dramatic committee. Edmund Dulac, Rupert Doone (ballet master and producer), T. S. Eliot, myself and Margot Collis's secretary. Ashton was away dancing somewhere. Next morning I phoned to Dulac: "I won't have Rupert Doone spreading mustard and molasses over my brown bread, I shall produce all my own plays." Result, a visit from Dulac to Ashley Dukes, who owns the theatre we are to play in and who supplies the finances, and to Ashton. General agreement that I don't know enough about London actors to cast my plays—somebody else has to be found. We are now in pursuit of that somebody else, and there is to be a committee meeting on Tuesday. It has been decided that the actual performances of the plays will be from April 29th to May 19th, or longer if we have a success, and the rehearsals will take about a month.[36]

A further committee meeting was held on 8 January 1935, but Yeats was ill and could not attend. They met again on 23 January after which Dulac wrote to Yeats saying: "We were distressed to hear that you had been ill. George tells me that another week will see you quite well again; we are looking forward to a line from you showing that all anxiety is past. 'The Council,' as T. S. Eliot calls it, send you their very sincere sympathy."[37] He then went on to describe the events of the meeting. Eliot had not been present, but they had been in touch with him by telephone. He was working at this time on *Murder in the Cathedral*, and there was some discussion at the committee as to whether it could be included in the season at the Mercury Theatre. Eliot told them that the play would not be ready before the end of March, but he promised to send them a scenario before that. Dulac went on: "The end of March leaves very little time to make any changes, should the finished play be unsuitable. We decided that, in that case, it would be better to postpone the season for a few weeks; you will be here in a few weeks, well in time to give your opinion on the question should it arise."[38]

35. Yeats to George Yeats, 17 December 1934, Private Papers, Michael B. Yeats.

36. Yeats to George Yeats, 3 January 1935, Private Papers, Michael B. Yeats.

37. Richard Finneran, George Harper, and William Murphy, eds., *Letters to W. B. Yeats*, (London: Macmillan, 1972), 2:570.

38. Ibid.

In fact, Yeats was ill for a further five months, and he took little further part in the Mercury Theatre project. There are just two short letters during this period. On 5 April 1935, he writes to Mrs. Yeats:

> I am well now but the doctor hates my going out, however I have his leave to dine at Dulac's tonight. These last two days have been packed with work, people coming and going about the theatre project. . . . Peak who will probably produce for us has just gone and taken T. S. Eliot's play—no play but magnificent speech. There are difficulties but I hope all will be right before I return to Dublin.[39]

In fact all was not right, and a few days later comes the end of the story. On 10 April Yeats writes that "the theatre project has I think broken down. Ashley Dukes has insisted on the Eliot play, and we do not feel that we could make a success with cuts, and in any case for Eliot's sake Canterbury should come first. Ashley Dukes has rejected all counter-proposals."[40] There was no Yeats-Eliot-Auden season at the Mercury Theatre. *Sweeney Agonistes* and Auden's *The Dance of Death* were duly performed by the Group Theatre, but at the Westminster Theatre and not at the Mercury as had been intended. *Murder in the Cathedral* had its first performance in Canterbury Cathedral on 19 June 1935, and later in the year went for a long run to the Mercury Theatre. Eliot expressed his regret at the collapse of the planned season of verse plays, and felt that had Yeats not been ill things might have gone better.[41]

It was obviously of this brief collaborative period that Eliot was thinking when he spoke of Yeats as a man in the course of his 1940 Memorial Lecture at the Abbey Theatre in Dublin:

> When [Yeats] visited London he liked to meet and talk to younger poets. People have sometimes spoken of him as arrogant and overbearing. I never found him so; in his conversations with a younger writer I always felt that he offered terms of equality, as to a fellow worker, a practitioner of the same mistery. It was, I think, that, unlike many writers, he cared more for poetry than for his own reputation as a poet. Art was greater than the artist: and this feeling he communicated to others; which was why younger men were never ill at ease in his company.[42]

39. Yeats to George Yeats, 5 April 1935, Private Papers, Michael B. Yeats.
40. Yeats to George Yeats, 10 April 1935, Private Papers, Michael B. Yeats.
41. Eliot to Rupert Doone, in Michael J. Sidnell, *Dances of Death* (London: Faber, 1984), 269.
42. "Yeats," in *On Poetry and Poets*, 296–97.

By 1935, Eliot had come to think more favorably of Yeats as an individual; he had also brought to completion his revaluation of him as a poet. In July 1935, on the occasion of Yeats's seventieth birthday, Eliot gave in *The Criterion* what he described as an appreciation of his services and an expression of gratitude, concluding:

> it should be apparent at least that Mr. Yeats has been and is the greatest poet of his time. . . . I can think of no poet, not even among the very greatest, who has shown a longer period of development than Yeats. At no time was he less out-of-date than today, among men twenty and forty years his juniors. Development to this extent is not merely genius, it is character; and it sets a standard which his juniors should seek to emulate, without hoping to equal.[43]

Yeats himself never really changed his views on Eliot's poetry. Even near the end of his life, he was writing to Dorothy Wellesley that "the worst language is Eliot's in all his early poems—a level flatness of rhythm." In a letter to another friend he wrote of his "bare poetry."[44] In 1936 he had in quick succession to give a major radio broadcast for the BBC, under the title "Modern Poetry," and then to write the introduction to his *Oxford Book of Modern Verse*. In a letter to Olivia Shakespeare he said: "My problem this time will be: 'How far do I like the Ezra, Eliot, Auden school and if I do not, why not?' Then this further problem 'Why do the younger generation like it so much? What do they see or hope?' "[45]

For the first time, perhaps, Yeats now read all the poetry of Eliot, but he did not change his mind about it.

> In the third year of the War came the most revolutionary man in poetry in my lifetime, though his revolution was stylistic alone—T. S. Eliot published his first book. No romantic word or sound, nothing reminiscent, nothing in the least like the painting of Ricketts could be permitted henceforth. Poetry must resemble prose, and both must accept the vocabulary of their time; nor must there be any special subject-matter. Tristam and Iseult were not a more suitable theme than Paddington Railway Station. The past had deceived us: let us accept the worthless present.[46]

He then recited a verse from Eliot's "Preludes," a poem that he in-

---

43. "A Commentary," *Criterion*, 14 (July 1935): 612–13.
44. *Letters on Poetry from W. B. Yeats to Dorothy Wellesley* (London: Oxford University Press, 1940), 48; *Letters of W. B. Yeats*, 792.
45. *Letters of W. B. Yeats*, 833.
46. "Modern Poetry: A Broadcast," in *Essays and Introductions* (New York: Macmillan, 1961), 499.

cluded in his anthology, adding the comment: "We older poets dislike this new poetry, but were forced to admit its satiric intensity."

He returned to the fray in his introduction to the *Oxford Book of
Modern Verse*, published late in 1936:

> Eliot has produced his great effect upon his generation because he has
> described men and women that get out of bed or into it from mere
> habit; in describing this life that has lost heart his own art seems grey,
> cold, dry. He is an Alexander Pope, working without apparent imagina-
> tion, producing his effects by a rejection of all rhythms and metaphors
> used by the more popular romantics rather than by the discovery of his
> own, this rejection giving his work an unexaggerated plainness that
> has the effect of novelty. He has the rhythmical flatness of the *Essay on
> Man* . . . later, in *The Waste Land*, amid much that is moving in sym-
> bol and imagery there is much monotony of accent.[47]

It was presumably this "monotony of accent" that prevented Yeats
from including any part of *The Waste Land* in his anthology.

"Not until *The Hollow Men* and *Ash-Wednesday*," he went on,
"where he is helped by the short lines, and in the dramatic poems
where his remarkable sense of actor, chanter, scene, sweeps him
away, is there rhythmical animation." Some of Yeats's friends, he
said, attributed the change to an emotional enrichment from religion, but he would have none of this. Eliot's religion, he claimed,
lacked all strong emotion: "A New England Protestant by descent,
there is little self-surrender in his personal relation to God and the
soul."[48] One wonders how Yeats came to be so well-informed about
Eliot's "personal relation to God and the soul"! He went on to
accept *Murder in the Cathedral* as a powerful stage play, but it was
clearly not a play that he liked. He acknowledged Eliot's position
as the most influential of all the contemporary poets, but nowhere
can one detect any element of enthusiasm for his works.

So far as Yeats was concerned, that was the end of the uncertain,
hesitant and often obscure relationship between the two great
poets. Eliot, however, had one last part to play, when he was asked
to deliver the Yeats Memorial Lecture at the Abbey Theatre in Dublin in 1940. In this lecture he maintained his views on Yeats's earlier poems. Some of these were as perfect of their kind as anything
in the language, but "Among all the poems in Yeats's early volumes

---

47. *The Oxford Book of Modern Verse: 1892–1935*, ed. W. B. Yeats (New
York: Oxford University Press, 1936), xxi.
48. Ibid., xxii, xxiii.

I find only in a line here or there, that sense of a unique personality which makes one sit up in excitement and eagerness to learn more about the author's mind and feelings." There were beautiful poems amongst them, but even these were only craftsman's work. Eliot continued:

> The poetry of the young Yeats hardly existed for me until after my enthusiasm had been won by the poetry of the older Yeats; and by that time—I mean, from 1919 on—my own course of evolution was already determined. Hence, I find myself regarding him, from one point of view, as a contemporary and not as a predecessor; and from another point of view, I can share the feelings of younger men, who came to know and admire him by that work from 1919 on, which was produced while they were adolescent.

Yeats, he finished by saying, "was one of those few whose history is the history of their own time, who are a part of the consciousness of an age which cannot be understood without them. This is a very high position to assign to him: but I believe that it is one which is secure."[49]

There is just one footnote to add to the story of the relationship of Eliot and Yeats; it is one provided by Ezra Pound, who had for many years been intimately associated with their lives. He had secured the publication of Eliot's early poems and had had a decisive influence on the creation of *The Waste Land.* Much later, after World War II, Eliot did his utmost to help Pound during the sad years in St. Elizabeths Hospital. Equally, Pound played an important part in Yeats's life. He had encouraged him to modernize his style and had introduced him to the Japanese Noh dramas. He was best man at his wedding, and there was a family relationship between his wife and George Yeats. He was far more closely associated, in fact, with each of the two poets than they ever were with each other.

When Eliot died in January 1965, Pound came from Italy to London to attend the funeral service in Westminster Abbey. The next day he came to Dublin without warning for a meeting with Yeats's widow. At this stage of her life she had given up answering the telephone, but on this one occasion something impelled her to lift the receiver. The message came that Ezra Pound was in town and would like to meet her. She at once called a taxi, and went to meet her old friend. Thus was forged one last symbolic link in the chain of relationships that joined the careers of those two great twentieth-century poets, T. S. Eliot and William Butler Yeats.

49. "Yeats," in *On Poetry and Poets,* 298–99, 295–96, 308.

Works Cited

I. Books by T. S. Eliot

For Lancelot Andrewes: Essays on Style and Order. London: Faber, 1928.

The Sacred Wood: Essays on Poetry and Criticism. 2d ed. 1928. Reprint. London: Methuen, 1960.

Selected Essays. New ed. (1st ed. 1932) New York: Harcourt Brace, 1950.

After Strange Gods: A Primer of Modern Heresy. New York: Harcourt Brace, 1933.

The Use of Poetry and the Use of Criticism: Studies in the Relation of Criticism to Poetry in England. London: Faber, 1933.

Notes Towards the Definition of Culture. London: Faber, 1948.

The Complete Poems and Plays (1909-1950). New York: Harcourt Brace, 1952.

American Literature and the American Language: An Address Delivered at Washington University. Washington University Studies, New Series, Language and Literature, no. 23. St. Louis: Washington University Committee on Publications, 1953.

On Poetry and Poets. London: Faber, 1957.

The Elder Statesman. London: Faber, 1959.

To Criticize the Critic and Other Writings. London: Faber, 1965.

Poems Written in Early Youth. New York: Farrar, Straus and Giroux, 1967.

The Waste Land: A Facsimile and Transcript of the Original Drafts Including the Annotations of Ezra Pound. Edited by Valerie Eliot. New York: Harcourt Brace Jovanovich, 1971.

Gesammelte Gedichte 1909-1962. Edited by Eva Hesse. Vol. 4, *Werke.* Frankfurt: Suhrkamp, 1972.

The Letters of T. S. Eliot. Vol. 1 (1898-1922). Edited by Valerie Eliot. San Diego: Harcourt Brace Jovanovich, 1988.

II. Other Writings by T. S. Eliot

Review of *Group Theories of Religion and the Religion of the Individual*, by Clement C. J. Webb. *International Journal of Ethics* 27 (October 1916): 115–17.

"The Noh and the Image." Review of *Noh, or Accomplishment, a Study of the Classical Stage of Japan*, by Ernest Fenollosa and Ezra Pound. *Egoist* 4 (August 1917): 102–3.

Review of *Turgenev*, by Edward Garnett. *Egoist* 4 (December 1917): 167.

"In Memory of Henry James." *Egoist* 5 (January 1918): 1–2.

Review of *Elements of Folk Psychology: Outlines of a Psychological History of the Development of Mankind*, by Wilhelm Wundt. *Monist* 28 (January 1918): 159–60.

Review of *Brahmadarsanam, or Intuition of the Absolute, Being an Introduction to the Study of Hindu Philosophy*, by Sri Ananda Acharya. *International Journal of Ethics* 28 (April 1918): 445–46.

"Tarr." Review of *Tarr*, by Wyndham Lewis. *Egoist* 5 (September 1918): 105–6.

"American Literature." Review of *A History of American Literature*, vol. 2, edited by William P. Trent et al. *Athenaeum* 4643 (25 April 1919): 236–37.

"A Romantic Patrician." Review of *Essays in Romantic Literature*, by George Wyndham. *Athenaeum* 4644 (2 May 1919): 265–67.

"A Sceptical Patrician." Review of *The Education of Henry Adams: An Autobiography*. *Athenaeum* 4647 (23 May 1919): 361–62.

"Beyle and Balzac." Review of *A History of the French Novel, to the Close of the Nineteenth Century*, vol. 2, by George Saintsbury. *Athenaeum* 4648 (30 May 1919): 392–93.

"A Foreign Mind." Review of *The Cutting of an Agate*, by W. B. Yeats. *Athenaeum* 4653 (4 July 1919): 552–53.

"Hamlet and His Problems." Review of *The Problem of "Hamlet,"* by J. M. Robertson. *Athenaeum* 4665 (26 September 1919): 940–41. Reprinted, with revisions, in *Selected Essays*.

"The Poetic Drama." Review of *Cinnamon and Angelica: A Play*, by John Middleton Murry. *Athenaeum* 4698 (14 May 1920): 635–36.

"The Romantic Englishman, the Comic Spirit, and the Function of Criticism—The Lesson of Baudelaire." *Tyro* (London) 1 (Spring 1921): 4.

"London Letter." *Dial* 70 (June 1921): 686–91.

"Contemporary English Prose." *Vanity Fair* (New York) 20 (July 1923): 51, 98.

"La Terre mise à nu." *Esprit* 1 (May 1926): 174–94. Translation by Jean de Menasce of *The Waste Land*.

"Whitman and Tennyson." Review of *Whitman: An Interpretive Narrative*, by Emory Holloway. *Nation and Athenaeum* 40 (18 December 1926): 426.

"Das wüste Land." Translation by Ernst Robert Curtius of *The Waste Land*. *Neue Schweizer Rundschau* 20 (1 April 1927): 362–77.

"Mr. Middleton Murry's Synthesis." *Criterion* 6 (October 1927): 340–47.

Preface to *This American World*, by Edgar Ansel Mowrer. London: Faber, 1928.

"The Literature of Fascism." *Criterion* 8 (December 1928): 280–90.

Letter to William Force Stead. 2 December 1930. Osborn Collection, Beinecke Library, Yale University.

Introduction to *Pascal's Pensées*. Translated by W. F. Trotter. New York: E. P. Dutton, 1931.

"Christianity and Communism." *Listener* 7 (16 March 1932): 382–83.

Preface to *Bubu of Montparnasse*, by Charles-Louis Philippe. Translated by Laurence Vail. Paris: Crosby Continental Editions, 1932.

Letter to W. B. Yeats. 1 April 1932. Private papers, Michael B. Yeats.

Letter to Lady Ottoline Morrell. 14 March 1933. Ransom Humanities Research Center, University of Texas at Austin.

"A Commentary." *Criterion* 14 (January 1935): 260–64.

"A Commentary." *Criterion* 14 (July 1935): 610–13.

Die Einheit der europäischen Kultur. Berlin: Carl Habel Verlagsbuchhandlung, 1946.

"Ezra Pound." *Poetry* 68 (September 1946): 326–38.

Introduction to *The Adventures of Huckleberry Finn*, by Mark Twain. London: Cresset Press, 1950.

"The Silver Bough." *Sunday Times* (London) (6 April 1958): 4.

"The Art of Poetry I: T. S. Eliot." Interview with Donald Hall. *Paris Review* 21 (Spring/Summer 1959): 47–70.

"The Influence of Landscape upon the Poet." *Daedalus, Journal of the American Academy of Arts and Sciences* 89 (Spring 1960): 420–22.

"American Literature and the American Language." In *To Criticize the Critic and Other Writings*. London: Faber, 1965.

Holograph outline of *Sweeney Agonistes*. In *The Stage Sixty Theatre Club Presents Homage to T. S. Eliot: A Programme of Po-*

etry, Drama and Music. 13 June 1965. Globe Theatre, London. 4–5.

"Ödland." Translation by Alfred Margul-Sperber of *The Waste Land.* In *Weltstimmen: Nachdichtungen.* Bucharest: Literaturverlag, 1968.

"Das wüste Land." Translation by Karl Heinz Göller of *The Waste Land.* In *Die englische Lyrik.* Vol. 2. Edited by Karl Heinz Göller. Düsseldorf: Bagel, 1968.

"La Terre vaine." In *Poésies: Edition bilingue.* 2d rev. ed. Translation by Pierre Leyris of *The Waste Land.* Paris: Éditions du Seuil, 1969.

"Das wüste Land." Translation by Eva Hesse of *The Waste Land.* In *Gesammelte Gedichte, 1909–1962.* Edited by Eva Hesse. Vol. 4, *Werke.* Frankfurt: Suhrkamp, 1972.

Letter to Rupert Doone. Quoted in Michael J. Sidnell, *Dances of Death: The Group Theatre of London in the Thirties.* London: Faber, 1984.

III. Works by Other Writers

Ackroyd, Peter. *T. S. Eliot: A Life.* New York: Simon and Schuster, 1984.

Aiken, Conrad. "King Bolo and Others." In *T. S. Eliot: A Symposium.* Compiled by Tambimuttu and Richard March. Chicago: Regnery, 1949.

Anonymous. *The Raigne of King Edward the Third.* Edited by Fred Lapides. New York: Garland, 1980.

Auden, W. H. "Yeats as an Example." *Kenyon Review* 10 (1948): 187–95.

———. *Nones.* New York: Random House, 1950.

Augustine, Saint. *The Confessions of Saint Augustine.* Translated by Rex Warner. New York: New American Library, 1963.

Aristophanes. *Aristophanis Comoediae: cum scholiis et varietate lectionis.* Edited by Immanuel Bekker. 5 vols. London: Whittaker, Treacher, and Arnot, 1829.

Baudelaire, Charles. "On the Essence of Laughter, and Generally of the Comic." In *Baudelaire: Selected Writings on Art and Artists.* Translated by P. E. Charvet. Harmondsworth, Middlesex, England: Penguin, 1972.

Beaumont, Francis, and John Fletcher. *The Maid's Tragedy.* Edited by Howard B. Norland. Lincoln: University of Nebraska Press, 1968.

Bedient, Calvin. *He Do the Police in Different Voices: "The Waste Land" and Its Protagonist.* Chicago: University of Chicago Press, 1986.

Bell, Robert H. "Bertrand Russell and the Eliots." *American Scholar* 52 (Summer 1983): 309–25.

Bergson, Henri. *Laughter: An Essay on the Meaning of the Comic.* Translated by Cloudesley Brereton and Fred Rothwell. New York: Macmillan, 1911.

Bourne, Randolph. "Trans-National America." In *The Radical Will: Selected Writings 1911–1918.* Edited by Olaf Hansen. New York: Urizen, 1977.

Bradley, A. C. *Shakespearean Tragedy.* London: Macmillan, 1904.

Bradley, F. H. *Appearance and Reality.* 1893. Reprint. Oxford: Clarendon Press, 1897.

Brooker, Jewel Spears. "The Case of the Missing Abstraction: Eliot, Frazer, and Modernism." *Massachusetts Review* 25 (Winter 1984): 539–52.

———. "The Dispensations of Art: Mallarmé and the Fallen Reader." *Southern Review* 19 (January 1983): 17–38.

———. "The Structure of Eliot's 'Gerontion': An Interpretation Based on Bradley's Doctrine of the Systematic Nature of Truth." *ELH* 46 (Summer 1979): 314–40.

Brooker, Jewel Spears, and Joseph Bentley. *Reading* The Waste Land: *Modernism and the Limits of Interpretation.* Amherst: University of Massachusetts Press, 1990.

Brooks, Cleanth. "*The Waste Land:* A Prophetic Document." *Yale Review* 78 (September 1989): 318–32.

———. "*The Waste Land:* Critique of the Myth." In *Modern Poetry and the Tradition.* 1939. Reprint. Chapel Hill: University of North Carolina Press, 1967.

Browne, Martin E. *The Making of T. S. Eliot's Plays.* London: Cambridge University Press, 1969.

Bush, Ronald. *T. S. Eliot: A Study in Character and Style.* New York: Oxford University Press, 1984.

Cross, Stephen (director). *The Mysterious Mr. Eliot.* New York: McGraw-Hill Films, n.d.

Davidson, Harriet. *T. S. Eliot and Hermeneutics: Absence and Presence in "The Waste Land."* Baton Rouge: Louisiana State University Press, 1985.

Derrida, Jacques. *Margins of Philosophy.* Translated and annotated by Alan Bass. Chicago: Chicago University Press, 1982.

Donoghue, Denis. *The Third Voice: Modern British and American Verse Drama.* Princeton: Princeton University Press, 1959.

Eliot, Valerie. "A Photographic Memoir, with a Note by James Olney." *Southern Review* 21 (October 1985): 987–99.

Eliot, Vivien. Letter to Lady Ottoline Morrell. 14 March 1933. Ransom Humanities Research Center, University of Texas at Austin.

Ellmann, Richard. *Eminent Domain.* New York: Oxford University Press, 1967.

Emerson, Ralph Waldo. "An Address Delivered before the Senior Class in Divinity College, Cambridge, July 15, 1838." In *Nature/Addresses and Lectures.* Boston: Houghton Mifflin, 1903.

———. *Letters of Ralph Waldo Emerson.* Vol. 4. Edited by Ralph L. Rusk. New York: Columbia University Press, 1939.

———. "Nature." In *Nature/Addresses and Lectures.* Boston: Houghton Mifflin, 1903.

Fairchild, Hoxie Neale. *Religious Trends in English Poetry.* Vol. 6, *1920–1965: Valley of Dry Bones.* New York: Columbia University Press, 1968.

Finneran, Richard, George Harper, and William Murphy, eds. *Letters to W. B. Yeats.* London: Macmillan, 1972.

Frank, Armin Paul. "T. S. Eliot's frühe 'Wüste Länder,' französisch und deutsch. . . ." In *Formen innerliterarischer Rezeption.* Edited by Wilfried Floeck et al. Wolfenbütteler Forschungen, vol. 34. Wiesbaden: Harrassowitz, 1987. 481–504.

Freud, Sigmund. *The Basic Writings of Sigmund Freud.* Translated and edited by A. A. Brill. New York: Modern Library, 1938.

Gallup, Donald. *T. S. Eliot: A Bibliography.* Rev. ed. New York: Harcourt Brace and World, 1969.

Goethe, J. W. von. *Wilhelm Meister.* Translated by Thomas Carlyle. London: Dent, 1912.

Gordon, Lyndall. *Eliot's Early Years.* New York: Oxford University Press, 1977.

Granville-Barker, Harley, and G. B. Harrison, eds. "Shakespearian Criticism I: From Dryden to Coleridge." In *A Companion to Shakespeare Studies.* Cambridge: Cambridge University Press, 1934.

Hesse, Eva. *T. S. Eliot und "Das wüste Land: Eine Analyse.* Frankfurt: Suhrkamp, 1973.

Hooker, Joan F. *T. S. Eliot's Poems in French Translation: Pierre Leyris and Others.* Ann Arbor: University Microfilms, 1983.

Hulpke, Erika. *Die Vielzahl der Übersetzungen und die Einheit des Werks: Bildmuster und Wortwiederholungen in T. S. Eliot, "Col-*

lected Poems/Gesammelte Gedichte." Neue Studien zur Anglistik und Amerikanistik, vol. 32. Frankfurt: Lang, 1985.

Johnson, Samuel. "Abraham Cowley." In *Lives of the English Poets.* Vol. 1. London: Dent, 1946.

Jones, Ernest. *Essays in Applied Psychoanalysis.* London: International Psycho-Analytical Press, 1923.

————. "The Oedipus-Complex as an Explanation of Hamlet's Mystery: A Study in Motive." *American Journal of Psychology* 21 (January 1910): 72–113.

Junkes-Kirchen, Klaus. *T. S. Eliot's "The Waste Land" Deutsch: Theorie und Praxis einer Gedichtübersetzung nach literatur- und übersetzungswissenschaftlichen Gesichtspunkten,* Trierer Studien zur Literatur, vol. 17. Frankfurt: Lang, 1988.

Kafka, Franz. *Dearest Fathers: Stories and Other Writings.* Translated by Ernst Kaiser. New York: Schocken, 1954.

Kearns, Cleo McNelly. *T. S. Eliot and Indic Traditions: A Study in Poetry and Belief.* New York: Cambridge University Press, 1987.

Laforgue, Jules. *Selected Writings of Jules Laforgue.* Translated and edited by William Jay Smith. Westport, Conn.: Greenwood, 1972.

Langer, Susanne K. *Feeling and Form.* New York: Scribner's, 1953.

Maurois, André. *Illusions.* New York: Columbia University Press, 1968.

Matthiessen, F. O. *The Achievement of T. S. Eliot: An Essay on the Nature of Poetry.* 3d ed. London: Oxford University Press, 1958.

Michaels, Walter Benn. "Philosophy in Kinkanja: Eliot's Pragmatism." *Glyph* 8 (1981): 170–202.

Miller, James E. *T. S. Eliot's Personal Waste Land: Exorcism of the Demons.* University Park: Pennsylvania State University Press, 1977.

Moody, A. D. "Eliot's Formal Invention." In *T. S. Eliot: Man and Poet.* Edited by Laura Cowan, 1:21–34. Orono, Me.: National Poetry Foundation, 1990.

Murray, Gilbert. *Hamlet and Orestes: A Study in Traditional Types.* New York: Oxford University Press, 1914.

Nunn, Trevor. "Memory." In *Cats: The Book of the Musical.* London: Faber, 1981.

Olney, James, ed. *T. S. Eliot.* Oxford: Oxford University Press, 1988.

Ortega y Gasset, José. *Man and Crisis.* Translated by Mildred Adams. New York: Norton, 1958.

Poirier, Richard. *The Renewal of Literature: Emersonian Reflections.* New York: Random House, 1987.

Pope, John C. "Prufrock and Raskolnikov." *American Literature* 17 (November 1945): 213–30.

———. "Prufrock and Raskolnikov Again." *American Literature* 18 (January 1947): 319–21.

Pound, Ezra. *The Letters of Ezra Pound.* Edited by D. D. Paige. New York: Harcourt Brace, 1950.

Pound, Ezra, and Wyndham Lewis. *Pound/Lewis: The Letters of Ezra Pound and Wyndham Lewis.* Edited by Timothy Materer. New York: New Directions, 1985.

Primm, James Neal. *Lion of the Valley: St. Louis, Missouri.* Western Urban History, no. 3. Boulder, Colo.: Pruett, 1981.

Read, Herbert. *The Innocent Eye.* New York: Henry Holt, 1947.

———. "T. S. E.: A Memoir." In *T. S. Eliot: The Man and His Work*, edited by Allen Tate. New York: Dell, 1966.

Richards, I. A. *Principles of Literary Criticism.* New York: Harcourt Brace, 1925.

Robertson, J. M. *The Problem of "Hamlet."* London: George Allen and Unwin, 1919.

Robinson, E. A. *Collected Poems.* New York: Macmillan, 1946.

Rosenthal, M. L., and Sally Gall. *The Modern Poetic Sequence: The Genius of Modern Poetry.* New York: Oxford University Press, 1983.

Ross, Ralph, John Berryman, and Allen Tate. *The Arts of Reading.* New York: Crowell, 1960.

Sandburg, Carl. *The Complete Poems of Carl Sandburg.* New York: Harcourt Brace and World, 1969.

Schuchard, Ronald. "T. S. Eliot as an Extension Lecturer, 1916–1919." *Review of English Studies* 25 (August 1974): 163–72, 292–304.

Schwartz, Sanford. *The Matrix of Modernism: Pound, Eliot, and Early Twentieth-Century Thought.* Princeton: Princeton University Press, 1985.

Seiler, Robert M. "Prufrock and Hamlet." *English* 21 (Summer 1972): 41–43.

Shakespeare, William. *The Complete Works of Shakespeare.* Edited by Hardin Craig. Chicago: Scott Foresman, 1961.

Shusterman, Richard. *T. S. Eliot and the Philosophy of Criticism.* New York: Columbia University Press, 1988.

Sidnell, Michael J. *Dances of Death: The Group Theatre of London in the Thirties.* London: Faber, 1984.

Simpson, Louis. *Three on the Tower: The Lives and Works of Ezra*

Pound, T. S. Eliot, and William Carlos Williams. New York: William Morrow, 1975.

Skaff, William. *The Philosophy of T. S. Eliot: From Skepticism to a Surrealist Poetic, 1909-1927.* Philadelphia: University of Pennsylvania Press, 1986.

Smith, Barbara Herrnstein. *On the Margins of Discourse: The Relation of Literature to Language.* Chicago: University of Chicago Press, 1978.

Smith, Carol H. *T. S. Eliot's Dramatic Theory and Practice: From "Sweeney Agonistes" to "The Elder Statesman."* Princeton: Princeton University Press, 1963.

Smith, D. Nichol, ed. *Shakespeare Criticism: A Selection.* London: Oxford University Press, 1946.

Smith, Grover. *The Waste Land.* London: George Allen and Unwin, 1983.

―――. "Yeats, Eliot, and the Use of Memory." *Yeats Eliot Review* 9 (1988): 131–39.

Solomon, Maynard. *Beethoven.* New York: Schirmer, 1977.

Southam, B. C. *A Student's Guide to the "Selected Poems of T. S. Eliot."* 4th rev. ed. London: Faber, 1981.

Spender, Stephen. "The Influence of Yeats on Later English Poets." *TriQuarterly* 4 (1965): 82–89.

―――. *T. S. Eliot.* New York: Viking, 1975.

Stead, William Force. "Mr. Stead Presents an Old Friend." *Alumnae Magazine of Trinity College* 38 (Winter 1965): 59–66.

Strand, Karin. *W. B. Yeats's American Lecture Tours* (Ann Arbor: University Microfilms International, 1978).

Strich, Fritz. *Goethe und die Weltliteratur.* 2d ed. Bern: Francke, 1957.

Tate, Allen, ed. *T. S. Eliot: The Man and His Work.* New York: Dell, 1966.

Tennyson, Alfred. *In Memoriam.* New York: Norton, 1973.

Unger, Leonard. "T. S. Eliot's Images of Awareness." *Sewanee Review* 74 (January–March, 1966): 197–224.

Vivas, Eliseo. *D. H. Lawrence: The Failure and the Triumph of Art.* Evanston: Northwestern University Press, 1960.

Voegelin, Eric. *From Enlightenment to Revolution.* Edited by John H. Hallowell. Durham: Duke University Press, 1975.

Whitman, Walt. *Leaves of Grass.* Edited by Harold W. Blodgett and Sculley Bradley. New York: New York University Press, 1965.

Woolf, Virginia. *The Diary of Virginia Woolf.* Vol. 2. Edited by Anne Olivier Bell. New York: Harcourt Brace Jovanovich, 1978.

Yeats, W. B. "An Introduction for My Plays." In *Essays and Introductions.* New York: Macmillan, 1961.

———. Letter to Lady Ottoline Morrell. 29 October 1934. Ransom Humanities Research Center, University of Texas at Austin.

———. *Letters of W. B. Yeats.* Edited by Allan Wade. London: Hart-Davis, 1954.

———. *Letters on Poetry from W. B. Yeats to Dorothy Wellesley.* London: Oxford University Press, 1940.

———. Letters to George Yeats. Private papers, Michael B. Yeats: 3 December 1922; n.d. (late October 1934); n.d. (1934); 17 December 1934; 3 January 1935; 5 April 1935; 10 April, 1935.

———. "Modern Poetry: A Broadcast." In *Essays and Introductions.* New York: Macmillan, 1961.

———. *The Poems.* Edited by Richard J. Finneran. Vol. 1, *The Collected Works of W. B. Yeats.* New York: Macmillan, 1989.

———. *Uncollected Prose of W.B. Yeats.* Edited by John P. Frayne. New York: Columbia University Press, 1970.

———. *Wheels and Butterflies.* New York: Macmillan, 1934.

———, ed. *The Oxford Book of Modern Verse: 1892–1935.* New York: Oxford University Press, 1936.

About the T. S. Eliot Society

The T. S. Eliot Society is an international community of individuals and institutions interested in the life and work of T. S. Eliot. The Society was founded in St. Louis in 1980 by Leslie L. Konnyu, a Hungarian-American man of letters. In September of each year, on the weekend closest to the poet's birthday (September 26th), the Society meets in St. Louis for a program which includes a keynote address and other intellectual and artistic events.

In 1988, on the occasion of the one-hundredth anniversary of the poet's birth in St. Louis, the Eliot Society sponsored a major international celebration which included over fifty participants from the United States, Canada, England, Ireland, Germany, Japan, and South Africa. The centennial program included lectures, panel discussions, performances of Eliot's plays, and musical compositions based on his poetry.

The T. S. Eliot Society is open to all persons interested in the life and work of this great twentieth-century poet. Inquiries on any matter related to the Society should be addressed to the Treasurer of the T. S. Eliot Society, 5007 Waterman Boulevard, St. Louis, Missouri 63108.

Honorary Members of the T.S. Eliot Society
Cleanth Brooks
Valerie Eliot
Donald Gallup
Robert Giroux
Russell Kirk
Andrew Osze

T.S. Eliot Memorial Lecturers
1980   Marcella Holloway, CSJ
1981   Robert C. Roach
1982   Charles Guenther

1983	Earl K. Holt III
1984	Jewel Spears Brooker
1985	Ronald Schuchard
1986	Grover Smith
1987	James Olney
1988	A. D. Moody
1989	Leonard Unger

Notes on Contributors

Jewel Spears Brooker, Professor of English, Eckerd College. President of the T. S. Eliot Society (1985–1988) and organizer of the Eliot Society Centennial Celebration. Coauthor with Joseph Bentley of *Reading The Waste Land* (1990) and editor of *Approaches to Teaching T. S. Eliot's Poetry and Plays* (1988). Author of numerous articles on Eliot and modernism.

Cleanth Brooks, Gray Professor of Rhetoric (Emeritus), Yale University. Honorary Member of the T. S. Eliot Society. Author of *Modern Poetry and the Tradition* (1939), *The Well Wrought Urn* (1947), *The Hidden God* (1963), and many other studies of modern literature, including four books on William Faulkner.

Armin Paul Frank, Professor of English Philology, Georg-August-Universität, Göttingen. Author of *Die Sehnsucht nach dem unteilbaren Sein: Motive und Motivation in der Literaturkritik T. S. Eliots* (1973), *T. S. Eliot Criticism and Scholarship in German 1922–1980*, and other books and articles. Founding Director, National Center for Study of Literary Translation, Göttingen.

Cleo McNelly Kearns, Visiting Lecturer, Princeton Theological Seminary. Author of *T. S. Eliot and Indic Traditions* (1987) and of articles on modernism.

Russell Kirk, President of the Educational Review Foundation and the Wilbur Foundation. Honorary Member of the T. S. Eliot Society. Author of *The Conservative Mind: From Burke to Eliot* (1960), *Eliot and His Age* (1971), and numerous other books and articles.

A. D. Moody, Professor of English and Related Literature, University of York (England). Author of *Thomas Stearns Eliot: Poet* (1979), *T. S. Eliot 1888–1965: Catalogue of an Exhibition of Manuscripts*

197

and Books (1972), and of numerous articles. Editor of *The Waste Land in Different Voices* (1974).

James Olney, Editor of *The Southern Review* and Voorhies Professor of English Literature at Louisiana State University. Author of *Metaphors of Self* (1972) and other books. Editor of *T. S. Eliot: Essays from The Southern Review* (1988).

Ronald Schuchard, Professor of English, Emory University. Editor of T. S. Eliot's Clark Lectures and author of many articles on Eliot and modernism. Coeditor of *The Collected Letters of W. B. Yeats*, vols. 3 and 4.

Carol H. Smith, Professor of English, Rutgers University. Author of *T. S. Eliot's Dramatic Theory and Practice* (1963) and of articles on Eliot and other modern writers.

Grover Smith, Professor of English, Duke University. President of the T. S. Eliot Society, 1989–1991. Author of *T. S. Eliot's Poetry and Plays: A Study in Sources and Meaning* (1956, 1974) and *The Waste Land* (1983). Editor of *Josiah Royce's Seminar 1913–1914* (1963) and the *Letters of Aldous Huxley* (1969).

Leonard Unger, Professor of English (Emeritus), University of Minnesota. Editor of *T. S. Eliot: A Selected Critique* (1948), and author of *T. S. Eliot: Moments and Patterns* (1966), *Eliot's Compound Ghost* (1981), and various articles on Eliot.

George T. Wright, Professor of English, University of Minnesota. Poet and translator. Author of *The Poet in the Poem: The Personae of Eliot, Yeats, and Pound* (1960), *W. H. Auden* (1969), *Shakespeare's Metrical Art* (1988), and various articles.

Linda Wyman, Professor of English, Lincoln University (Missouri). Author of articles on Eliot and modern drama. Editor of the *Missouri English Bulletin.*

Michael B. Yeats, Former Chairman of the Irish Senate and Former Vice-President of the European Parliament. Lecturer on political and cultural topics.

Index